Design for Community

The Art of Connecting Real People in Virtual Places

Derek M. Powazek

New
Riders

A Divison of Pearson Technology Group
201 West 103rd Street, Indianapolis, Indiana 46290

Design for Community

The Art of Connecting Real People in Virtual Places

Copyright © 2002 by Derek M. Powazek

International Standard Book Number: 0-7357-1075-9

Library of Congress Catalog Card Number: 00-1111153

Printed in the United States of America

First Printing: August 2001

05 04 03 02 01   7 6 5 4 3 2 1

Interpretation of the printing code: The rightmost double-digit number is the year of the book's printing; the rightmost single-digit number is the number of the book's printing. For example, the printing code 01-1 shows that the first printing of the book occurred in 2001.

Trademarks

Warning and Disclaimer

PUBLISHER
David Dwyer

ASSOCIATE PUBLISHE
Al Valvano

EXECUTIVE EDITOR
Karen Whitehouse

ACQUISITIONS EDITC
Michael Nolan

DEVELOPMENT EDIT
Victoria Elzey

**PRODUCT MARKETIN
MANAGER**
Kathy Malmloff

MANAGING EDITOR
Sarah Kearns

BOOK PACKAGER
Justak Literary Servic

COVER DESIGNER
Aren Howell

ILLUSTRATOR
Claire Robertson

INTERIOR DESIGNER
Suzanne Pettypiece

COMPOSITOR
Jay Hilgenberg

INDEXER
Sandi Schroeder

Contents at a Glance

Table of Contents

Chapter 3

Design Matters
…Architectural and Visual Design for Successful Communities

Chapter 4

Tools for Doing the Heavy Lifting
…How to Power Your Community

Chapter 5

Chapter 6

Chapter 9

Chapter 10

Chapter 11

Chapter 12

What's Next?

Postscript

Where Do We Go from Here?

About the Author

Derek M. Powazek is a writer, storyteller, web designer, community consultant, and professional troublemaker. Derek has worked on the web since there was one, cutting his teeth on ground-breaking sites such as HotWired and Electric Minds. As Powazek Productions (powazek.com), he created community-rich sites such as {fray} (fray.com), Kvetch! (kvetch.com), and San Francisco Stories (sfstories.com), as well as consulted on community features for clients such as Netscape, Lotus, and Sony. Derek believes in a passionate, personal web.

Acknowledgements

This book would not exist without the valuable contributions of some very talented folks.

On the professional side, I'd like to thank everyone at New Riders, especially my editors: Victoria Elzey, Karen Whitehouse, and Michael Nolan, as well as my fellow writers (and inspirations): Jeffrey Zeldman, Jeff Veen, and Nathan Shedroff. And huge, happy thanks to Claire Robertson for her fantastic cover illustrations.

I'd also like to thank all the people who took the time to lend me their expertise in interviews for this book: Lance Arthur, Phil Askey, Tom Burns, Steven Champeon, Caleb Clark, Joshua Davis, Rusty Foster, Noah Grey, Matt Haughey, Steven Johnson, Philip Kaplan, Rob Malda, Terrence Parr, Howard Rheingold, Adrian Roselli, John Halycono Styn, Emma Taylor, and Matt Williams.

And on the personal side, I'd like to thank my sweetheart Heather Champ, for putting up with me during the writing process, and my parents Morris and Lois Powazek, for their 28 years of unrelenting encouragement. I get my hope from you.

I'd also like to thank the Reverie Coffee Shop, where much of this book was written, and DJ Shadow, who unknowingly provided the soundtrack.

Finally, I'd like to thank all of the people who have ever shared their story in the {fray}, posted a complaint in Kvetch!, or participated with me in any virtual community. Without you, I'd never have learned the lessons in this book. Thank you.

A Message from New Riders

As the reader of this book, you are our most important critic and commentator. We value your opinion and want to know what we're doing right, what we could do better, in what areas you'd like to see us publish, and any other words of wisdom you're willing to pass our way.

As Executive Editor at New Riders, I welcome your comments. You can email or write me directly to let me know what you did or didn't like about this book—as well as what we can do to make our books better. When you write, please be sure to include this book's title, ISBN, and author, as well as your name and phone or fax number. I will carefully review your comments and share them with the authors and editors who worked on the book.

Please note that I cannot help you with technical problems related to the topic of this book, and that due to the high volume of email I receive, I might not be able to reply to every message. Thanks.

Email: karen.whitehouse@newriders.com

Mail: Karen Whitehouse
         Executive Editor
         New Riders Publishing
         201 West 103rd Street
         Indianapolis, IN 46290 USA

Visit Our Web Site: www.newriders.com

On our Web site, you'll find information about our other books, the authors we partner with, book updates and file downloads, promotions, discussion boards for online interaction with other users and with technology experts, and a calendar of trade shows and other professional events with which we'll be involved. We hope to see you around.

Call Us or Fax Us

You can reach us toll-free at 800-571-5840 + 0 (ask for New Riders). If outside the U.S., please call 1-317-581-3500 and ask for New Riders. If you prefer, you can fax us at 1-317-581-4663, Attention: New Riders

Everything I Needed to Know about Web Community I Learned in High School Algebra Class

It's a little-known fact that I failed algebra in high school. Twice. That second time was with Mr. Payne. He took great, well, *pains* in spelling his name to the class. P-A-Y-N-E. We all spelled it the other way, anyway.

Especially me. I can say without any embellishment that I sucked at algebra. I sucked the air out three classrooms over. Two years later when my sister took the same required algebra courses that I kamikazed through, the teachers all sighed, "Oh Lord, please, not another Powazek."

But Jenny was good at algebra. Not me. I was good at writing. I was good at design. I even survived a weightlifting class by hiding in the corner and pretending I was a coat rack. But algebra massacred me every time.

So there I was in algebra class, bored out of my mind, one hot Southern California day in the late eighties. Claremont High School wasn't going to let me go to college unless I got through this class, so I was trying desperately to concentrate. And failing.

In a moment of panic, I made a desperate graffiti plea to the universe. "Save me," I wrote on the fake wood veneer of the desk. "I am so bored."

And little did I know that it would work so well.

The next day, when I entered Mister Pain's class for another hour of torture, there was a message waiting for me, scrawled in pencil on the desk.

"Me, too," it said.

Contact.

Claremont High had six class periods. So there were five other bodies that sat bored in that seat besides mine on any given day. And one of those people had reached out to me. I had to know more.

"I hate algebra," I wrote in my trusty number two. "You, too?"

And I sat there, excited, waiting for tomorrow. I couldn't believe it, but for the first time in my life, I was actually looking forward to tomorrow's algebra class. My mother would have been so proud.

When the next day arrived, I had a new note. "Yeah," it said.

It went on like this for weeks. It wasn't deep, it wasn't witty, it was just there. A voice in the darkness. An unknown friend.

And then *they* came.

I never found out who *they* were, but they threatened to ruin everything. We had such a good thing going, the mystery person and I. We were two of the six people who used that desk each day, and we were happy. But there were four others who sat there, lurking, reading our conversation. And now they wanted in.

"You're stupid," said a new voice in unfamiliar handwriting. "Shut up!" wrote someone else. And thus our fragile communication was facing its first challenge.

When I came into class the next day, I was greeted by a totally blank desk. My heart sank. I sat down, looked up at Mister Pain's back at the blackboard, and sighed.

It was only later, as Mister Pain was handing me my pop quiz back, emblazoned with a bright red D+, that I noticed it. As the pop quiz drifted across my desk, it stopped right at the corner, where the faux wood met the metal bar that held the whole chair-desk contraption together. And there, where real metal met fake wood, was a tiny arrow written in pencil.

Ignoring the test much to Mr. Payne's chagrin, I fingered the arrow. What did it mean? I followed its direction with my eye and turned around. I wound up face-to-face with Eric Hashiguchi, all of 15 years old and raising the curve for everyone. His pop quiz had an A on it, naturally.

"What?" he said, looking annoyed.

I spun back around in my seat. But the arrow was still there, unexplained. I started to fondle the desk, reaching around, and still nothing. Finally, too frustrated to keep my cool, I just put my head in my lap and looked up at the underside of the desk.

And there it was. In between the bumps of abandoned gum and the occasional booger, there was a piece of paper, jammed between the metal bar and the desk. I ripped it out and sat upright just before Mr. Payne turned around to examine the class.

His eyes fell on me. I smiled. He went on with his lecture.

I opened my entirely unused algebra book, using it as a cover to unfold the note. It was my friend's handwriting. "Are you there?" it said.

"Joy!" I wrote.

We went on writing like this for the rest of the semester. The daily notes were my salvation. A friend in a cold, dark, mathematical universe I didn't understand. In hindsight, I probably should have used this discreet communication channel to glean answers to tests or help on homework, but all I was really interested in was this new person and our fragile conversation.

We talked for weeks, gradually revealing more of ourselves, growing our trust. We had agreements and disagreements. We faced the pressure from too many voices and devised a clever solution. We had a pseudo-public conversation as strangers, and gradually grew a friendship.

Sound familiar yet?

In our time together, we learned many of the lessons of virtual community. We learned that communities are formed out of necessity—some spark that unites far-flung people with a common need (in this case, camaraderie). We faced flamers and trolls and persevered. We learned that communities are sometimes better with fewer members, not more. We basically created an atom-based, user-filtering solution—anyone smart enough to find the arrow and see what it meant could have participated. And we learned that virtual intimacy takes time, and that strong bonds can be formed without a single real-life glance.

In the end I did end up meeting my pen pal. We even ended up at the same college, working on the same college newspaper. We never shared a desk again, though.

And I had to repeat algebra that summer.

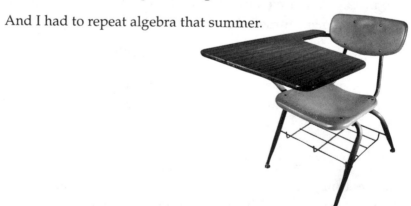

Introduction

Some time ago, I found myself at my father's house, telling a wise family friend about the book I'm writing. My dad's friend is a college professor, a real silver-bearded, elbow-patched kind of guy. And he was astounded at the notion of a web-based community.

"If it doesn't happen in real life," he said, "then it doesn't happen. It's just not real."

"But what about the Jewish community?" I asked. "We're not all in the same room, but it's a community, right?"

"Sure," he said. "But we have a shared history."

"Okay," I said. "So if I share history with a group of people I've never met, that makes it a community?"

He fidgeted.

"What if I talk with a group of people online for a few years?" I asked. "Is that a community?"

"Not if you never *meet*," he said.

"Okay. So what if I talk with a group of people on a website for a few years and then we all get together in real life? Are we a community after the meeting, but not before?"

He fidgeted again.

"Look," I said. "I'm not saying that web-based communities and real-life communities are exactly the same. Of course they're different. But one is no more valid than the other. They're both emotional, intimate, and real."

"Dinner's on!" my dad shouted from the kitchen.

When it comes to the "what-is-community" question, the answer is that there are no hard and fast answers, only personal ones. Community building is an intensely subjective experience that must be respected. Everyone will have a slightly different interpretation of what being a community means. It's up to each community to define what it is, and to constantly evaluate that definition on a personal basis.

And here's the first great lesson to be learned about community, whether in real life or on the web: Never expect everyone to agree.

The Web Is Different

With the advent of every new media come proclamations of how it is going to change the world. The creators of television thought it would bring the arts to the masses, sending opera and theatre to people in remote places. One glance at Friday night primetime proves that goal was never exactly reached.

The same pronouncements came with the web. It would spark a digital revolution that would change everything about everything. It would turn anyone with a rudimentary knowledge of HTML into a millionaire. It would change the face of business and the economy. It would get your coffee in the morning and find your keys under the couch.

And while the web really has changed mainstream media in some significant ways, the real revolution wasn't in the new economy. As we've watched the paper millionaires of 2000 become regular working stiffs in 2001, the dot-com collapse has left many wondering what all that web hype was about.

For all the false pronouncements and smoke and mirrors, a digital revolution has taken place, but it wasn't in the stock market or the boardroom. The revolution took place in the bedrooms and cubicles of the world, where parents pecked out email to their children, where people met in chat rooms and web boards, where lives were changed because of a new kind of personal connection.

The web was revolutionary (and still is) because it does one thing that no other media has been able to do, ever. The web grows communities, almost without trying, because the web is the only media that allows its users to communicate with each other directly, publicly, and instantly.

Other media have glimmers of that connection, but none so successful or meaningful. Newspapers publish letters to the editor. Radio has call-in shows. Television has, well, Jerry Springer. All of these contain a hint of what is possible when you let the users of your media communicate directly with each other. But the web makes direct user-to-user communication a reality. Because, on the web, the device you usually use to view it is the same device you need to create it. (You can't make a radio show with your car stereo.)

The web grows communities because it allows everyone to have a voice. Unlike the one-way communication of television transmission, or the static information of a dead tree newspaper page, the web makes dialogues real, immediate, and public. The medium this communication takes place in is virtual, but the connections themselves are real, intimate, and indeed revolutionary.

In the midst of all the hype of digital revolutions and e-everything, the web has been quietly doing what it does best, what no other media can do better: creating communities.

Defining the Terms

The word "community" is dangerous. It's the kind of word that shows up in taglines and quarterly reports to make stockholders feel warm and fuzzy. But when every corporate website brags about its community, the word begins to lose all meaning.

I believe the only relevant context to judge a community is a personal one. Community is immensely personal. Community membership can be a major part of an individual's internal self-image (the way a devout religious person identifies with a place of worship) or external professional life (professional organizations and guilds, for example).

Members of a community will identify themselves with the community when they feel strongly connected to it. But slapping a community label on an unwitting individual will usually be met with annoyance or worse.

When I want to sell my old camera or buy a new book, I'll visit sites such as eBay (ebay.com) or Amazon (amazon.com). In these cases, I'm just there for a transaction, not a conversation. Yet both these sites have generous community features, and both brag about their communities to their stockholders and the press.

And while it's true that some of eBay's users feel strongly connected to the site, simply going there to sell my old stuff doesn't really make me a community member, any more than using a can opener makes me a member of the exclusive can-opening community.

I advise clients to never call their sites "communities." Instead, provide adequate tools for your members to communicate with each other, plenty of relevant material to talk about, and an elegant structure that encourages conversation. If you're successful, your members will start calling it a community on their own.

But since community is a personal business, I'll give you my personal definition of the word. Here goes:

> Web communities happen when users are given **tools** to use their **voice** in a **public** and **immediate** way, forming **intimate relationships** over **time**.

Let's look at each of these pieces individually:

1. **Tools:** This is all about power. Giving your users tools to communicate is giving them the power. But we're not talking about all the tools they could possibly want. We're talking

about carefully crafted experiences, conservatively proportioned for maximum impact. Common tools are web boards, chat rooms, and discussion areas.

2. **Voice:** Giving your users the ability to use their voice and say what they think or feel is an incredibly powerful act. When users see their words on your site, it becomes their site, too.

3. **Public:** Private email exchanges and instant messages can help foster private communities. But for a community to succeed on the web, it has to be public, at least to some degree.

4. **Immediate:** The web is an instantaneous medium. If you're calling for user participation, you need to have systems in place to accept and reward that participation immediately.

5. **Intimate Relationships:** In the end, communities are all about relationships. And participating in a web community can be a powerfully intimate experience. If your users develop a strong emotional bond with each other and the site, you've done your job well.

6. **Time:** The last element is time. Whatever your goal, it's not going to happen all at once. Patience is not just a virtue here—it's a requirement.

What to Expect from This Book

In this book, I'm going to focus on building **community features** into websites, not building communities. There's a key difference. When I talk about building community features, I'm talking about giving the users of a website the tools they need to relate to each other in a productive way. If they use them, and keep coming back to use them, then maybe they'll start to call it a community.

But, in the end, that's up to them.

There are many different tools you can use to build communities online, including Internet Relay Chat, instant messaging programs, and Usenet. And while all these things will be mentioned, the primary focus of this book is the web, because the web is the most active, exciting area of virtual community, and it's the one where design matters the most. We'll also cover web-based chat and email lists, especially as they relate to cultivating virtual community.

I expect that this book will be of interest to people who have websites already, and are thinking of adding community features — a web store that's thinking of adding user-generated product reviews, a city newspaper that wants to add user-posted classifieds, a fan site that's going to add chat, a national society that just wants to let its users communicate directly, a personal project to collect stories on a certain theme — all of these are good examples of groups that might be interested in this book.

The focus is on the design issues that arise when working with these features. How do you present a discussion system that encourages friendly conversation? How does color influence the tone of conversation? Should there be fewer barriers to entry in a site with community features, or more? How can the community police itself?

This book deals with the practical problems when designing these sites, based on my experience designing and interacting with sites with community features. The issues raised cover everything from visual design to information architecture to mob dynamics.

But this is not a technology book. I do not review software or write code. And this is not a psychology paper or a business book, although I do touch on all of those things. This is a book about the issues around, conversations about, and stories from my experiences in designing community-based websites.

Each chapter focuses on one specific issue of community building on the web, from moderation to intimacy to using email. Each chapter culminates in an interview with an expert in that particular area of virtual community. These are the people in the trenches every day, all of them chosen for their leadership in, and experience with, a specific area of community building. I don't always agree with everything my interview subjects have to say, but they're all interesting people with smart ideas that bear some thought, especially when they challenge existing notions.

In addition, be sure to visit **designforcommunity.com**, where you can find unedited transcripts of the Q&As, more information and current events on web community, and special insider information.

Who I Am

This book is the culmination of more than six years of doing nothing but eating, drinking, and thinking about the web. I discovered the web in 1995, just before I graduated from college with a degree in photojournalism. Every newspaper I applied to said that they didn't hire photographers anymore. They advised me to look into the wire services such as the AP, or maybe even this new digital stuff.

When I found the web, it was like getting infected by a virus. I'd had an email account for years, but the web, as a graphical medium, changed everything. I soon found myself staying up nights making homepages and working for clients on the side.

Through my homepage (and a fair bit of good luck), I was hired by HotWired (hotwired.com), *Wired Magazine*'s sister publication, as Associate Production Editor. That meant it was my job to test out pages in the two major browsers at the time: Netscape 1.0 and Netscape 1.1 (which was a major difference, by the way, because Netscape 1.1 supported tables!).

It was a simpler time, back then. But HotWired had created a place called Threads, where the HotWired readers could respond to the stories. Threads was a fractured, dissonant, often hostile place. And most days it was far more interesting than what was going on at the main site. I learned many of my early lessons about web community from watching Threads.

After more than a year at HotWired, I went to work at Electric Minds, a company started by virtual community pioneer Howard Rheingold. There the goal was to further blur that line between content and community. The site was a cultural success, but a business failure. We were out of money in less than a year.

From there I went freelance. I worked for big names such as Nike (with vivid studios), where we created user feedback loops on topics such as heroes, and Netscape's Professional Connections (with Abbe Don Interactive), where we got tens of thousands of professionals talking to each other.

I also created my own sites under the moniker Powazek Productions (powazek.com), each of which enabled users to join the community in some way. In 1996, I created {fray} (fray.com), a site devoted to personal storytelling, where users could read true stories and respond with their own. Later I created Kvetch! (kvetch.com), where users could post complaints, and San Francisco Stories (sfstories.com), where I wrote my own personal tales of The City and invited everyone else to do the same.

Since then, {fray} has spawned the {fray} organization (fray.org) — a group of volunteers devoted to holding storytelling gatherings in real life. The community that started its life online has now evolved offline. For me, that was the moment that proved, without a doubt, that the virtual bonds formed online are as real as any made offline, and sometimes much more.

All of these projects, both professional and personal, have contributed to my understanding of the beautiful, ephemeral dance that is virtual community. I refer to the previously mentioned sites throughout the book. It's my hope that these examples will allow you to learn from my successes, and be warned away from my mistakes.

I hope you get as much out of this book as I've gotten putting it all together.

Thanks for reading.

Chapter 1

Is This Trip Really Necessary?

...*What to Know Before You Begin*

I have a terrible admission to make. As much as I believe in community on the web, and as much as I want to see more of it happening, in my years of work as a web designer and consultant, I have convinced about 80 percent of my clients not to add community features to their websites.

There are a lot of really good reasons to add community features to your site. A thriving community can be a boon for your enterprise. When people feel connected to your site and to each other, they'll maintain the kind of bond that marketers and CEOs dream about. They'll help code solutions to your technical problems, become advocates for your site, stick by you in times of trouble, educate each other so you don't have to, and so on. They'll spontaneously create content for your site and help their fellow users. I once even witnessed community members composing poetry for a product. It happens.

But, then, there are a lot of really bad reasons to pursue community, too. Here are two of the worst I've heard.

Bad Reason #1: "Because It's Cool!"

One CEO wanted a chat room because someone told him it was the cool thing to do. So I outlined the technology and staffing requirements for him.

"We'll need to add several new employees," I said. "Tech, help desk, moderators, that kind of thing."

He looked stunned.

"Well, if someone comes in and starts talking trash about the company, you'll want them kicked out, right?"

"Right!" he said.

"Good," I said. "Then it's settled. We'll have moderators in there 24/7. Who wants the night shift?"

Nobody in the meeting room spoke up.

"Then there are the technology requirements," I said. "That Pentium under Bob's desk is good for serving up the static pages, but a hot chat room would kill the thing. We'll have to buy some hardware and get someone in here to administer it."

Bob stared into his coffee.

"And there's one more thing," I said, meeting their eyes. "You sell insurance! Why on earth do you need a chat room?"

The CEO cleared his throat.

"Perhaps," he said, "we should think this out a little further."

As web designers, we should never underestimate the magnetic allure of "The Cool." We are, after all, in the cool business. It's the designer's job to make people look at a website and say, "Wow! Cool."

But "because it's cool" is a lousy reason to add community features to your site. Communities cost a lot of money to begin, take a lot of work to support, and require a constant vigilance to maintain over time. Being cool is just not enough.

Bad Reason #2: "Because We'll Get Free Content!"

In my freelance business, whenever people refer to community features as free content, my rates immediately double. It is clear they have no idea what is involved.

On the face of it, when your users contribute to your site, it is like getting free content. But like my mom always said, "There's no such thing as a free lunch in this world." The web is no different.

When users post to your site, it isn't a gift from them to you; it's the beginning of a very real relationship between you and the user. And relationships are two-way. You have to keep up your end of the conversation.

This doesn't mean that you have to respond to each user individually. Instead, it means being there when something goes wrong or someone has a question. Timely help is a lifesaver in a web community setting. Sometimes it's that personal touch that turns a faceless server with a few CGI scripts into a living, breathing community.

And when you reach that magical moment when your community really takes on a life of its own, you'll know it. And not just because a lot of people will be there, but because the community will begin to lead you, instead of the other way around.

Seeing your users' contributions as "free content" is missing the point entirely. It's not content—it's conversation, and that means you have to stay involved.

There are also pragmatic costs associated with a community site. You may have to pay more for server technology and administration, not to mention paying people to moderate and maintain the community. In the end, the money you spend on community features may be more than what you'd have to pay a bunch of writers to write stories. But the result will be so much richer.

Just remember mom's advice and don't expect a free lunch.

Questioning Assumptions

One of my clients was the Mississippi Partnership for Health, a non-profit organization that wanted to create a site at questionit.com to go with its national campaign against teen smoking. Because teens are quick to adopt new technologies, a web community seemed like a natural way to reach them. The organization behind the site had big plans for discussion boards, chat rooms, and more.

But the web is a big place, and you have to be aware of the kinds of people you may attract to your site. Starting a site that says "Welcome, teens!" and adding an unmoderated chat room is a recipe for disaster. Teens could gather to talk about how much they like smoking. Or worse, pedophiles could gather, looking for teenagers. I'm no lawyer, but that sounds like a bad idea to me.

I suggested abandoning plans for an unmoderated chat room in favor of an occasional moderated chat that would be announced to the membership via email. And instead of a free-for-all web discussion, I suggested using public feedback mechanisms in more subtle ways. For example, one feature solicited real-life stories from teenagers who'd quit smoking, and provided the capability for members to add their smoking stories to the mix. The response was amazing. Intimate, sincere, personal stories came flowing in—teenagers advising other teenagers to quit smoking.

The lesson is, sometimes you have to be selective in how you deploy community features. If you don't have the time or resources to support a fully featured community discussion area, there's no

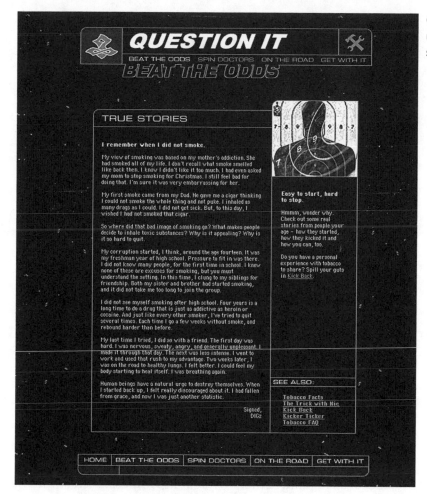

Questionit.com's user-contributed story section.

shame in giving your audience a very specific feedback mechanism. You should always examine your audience and consider how they'll use these features before you begin. Your users may surprise you.

The Good Reasons

There are some great reasons to add community features to your site, and some of them are very cool indeed. User-generated reviews of products in a web store can influence your users' buying decisions. Adding posting to the end of local news stories creates a real sense of community. Creating support forums for your product will enable your users to help each other out of common problems.

The one thing you can count on is surprise. Your users will engage in conversations that you never dreamed of.

Letting any group of people with like interests communicate directly with each other is an intense experience. When your users put their words on your site, it builds a powerful bond between you and the user. I've personally seen staggeringly intimate exchanges in public community areas, the kind that make you feel a little bit better about the world we live in.

Recently, my associate Jeffrey Zeldman's mother died. He wrote a touching note about it on his personal site, talking about his sadness. It caused an emotional ripple that spread out across the web. Fellow homepagers posted their condolences on their sites, too many to count.

Jeffrey is also a participant in an online community called Dreamless (dreamless.org). There, someone started a thread simply called "A moment of silence for Mr. Zeldman." The first post was blank. Within 24 hours there were 66 posts. Most were just blank—a small demonstration of empathy when a fellow community member was in pain. Others wrote long, impassioned stories of similar experiences to commiserate. The next day it was up to 130. After a few days it was over 200. After two weeks the page stood at 247 posts, all sincere and touching. What started as a simple moment of silence had become 367 kilobytes of raw text emotion.

All Systems Go: Adding Community Features

You know what it takes, you've got a good reason for adding community features, and my dire warnings haven't scared you off. Good for you! It's time to begin.

There are a lot of issues you should consider before embarking on this journey. Here are the Big Three.

Who is your audience?

The first step is to decide who exactly you are talking to, because this will be the foundation of everything you do from this point onward. You need to understand who your audience is and what they're likely to want at any given moment. Get in their heads as much as you can. Figure out what they want most when they visit your site.

It's a common mistake to avoid thinking about your audience by assuming that all audiences are the same. But when you're making a site for a community, it's imperative that you build the site around the community from the beginning. And every community is going to be different.

For example, a community site for teenagers is going to be fundamentally different than one for stockbrokers. Each audience brings a different set of goals and expectations to the equation. It's your job to make sure you structure your site around the community you want to attract and retain.

Begin by developing a core set of ideals for your site ("make pages that load fast and are easy to understand") and then apply them on a case-by-case basis, using your audience as a guide. After all, this is all for them. They're your customers, your fans, your bosses, your community.

After some examination, you may find that you have multiple audiences. That site for teenagers may also attract their parents, for example, who are looking to see what their kids are into or to meet other parents. That's fine, but you should prioritize them. Who are you really talking to, first and foremost?

One of my recent clients was a site for Lotus Notes developers called Notes.net. They had put up a simple web posting area for their users to trade tips and tricks, but it quickly became one of the busiest (and best) places for Lotus Notes developers to get in touch with each other.

But they were victims of their own success. Users began posting comments and questions so frequently that the comments only lasted on the homepage of the community area for a brief time. The more popular they became, the faster the posts scrolled away before getting responses.

Notes.net came to me for help in redesigning its community area. The company wanted to know if it should integrate multiple sections, add a rating system, or make other big changes to the system. But before we could talk about any of that, my question was then, as yours is now, who are your users and what are they trying to do?

Not sure who your users are? Ask them!

If you're already running a community site with feedback forums, try asking your members who they are and why they visit your site. You may be surprised by their answers. Web-based surveys can be enlightening as well, but remember to take any survey results with a grain of salt. Survey participants sometimes can embellish their answers in order to cast themselves in the best light possible. And surveys are self-selecting to begin with— only people who really love (or really hate) your site will be motivated to take a survey.

My advice in this case was that the primary audience of this site all had something in common: They were people with problems, specifically with Lotus Notes. They were frustrated developers. They needed help, and they needed it fast.

Therefore, Notes.net needed to do everything it could do to help them find the answers they were seeking as quickly and easily as possible. The solutions included improving search and browse features, cleaning up the interface, adding filtering options, and flattening the threaded conversations into a single page so the user could scan one page instead of clicking from link to link.

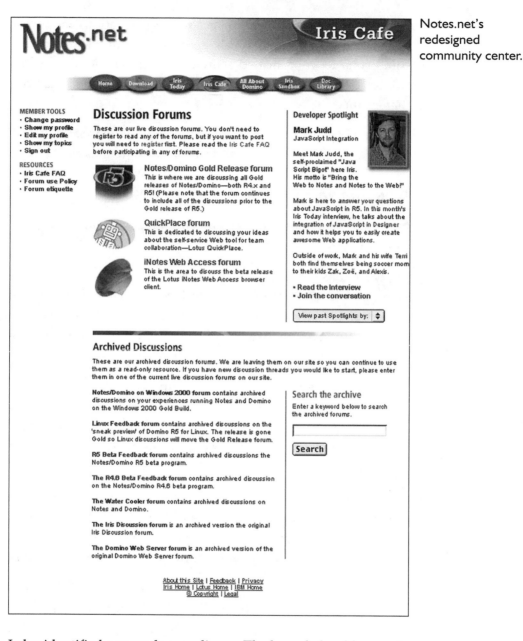

Notes.net's redesigned community center.

I also identified a secondary audience: The knowledgeable experts who spent their valuable time on the site answering questions. These people are worth their weight in gold, so I wanted to make their experience with the site as easy as possible. Solutions here included the creation of positive feedback loops, homepages where users could save bookmarks of conversations they were watching, and saved searches (so an expert in a specific area could conduct complicated searches for the kinds of topics he wanted to help with, perhaps even creating automated searches that emailed the results to the expert).

The main idea here is easy: Identifying your audience and understanding its goals make every decision easier to make.

Creating valuable content

Now that you know to whom you're talking, what are you going to say?

Every site has content. If your site is a web store, your product pages are the content. If your site is a webzine or newspaper, your articles are the content. Even if your site is a purely community-driven endeavor, there will be pages that are more like static content than dynamic community.

In today's web, where anyone can put up a chat room or a bulletin board in a few minutes, it's the content of your site that will differentiate it from all the others. And the quality of that content has a direct and unmistakable impact on the quality of the conversations on your site.

It's a very common mistake for community sites to spend all their time crafting the perfect backend system, completely forgetting, about the content of the site. This also relates to issue number one, because if you know your audience, you know what will attract them to come talk.

Phil Askey is the creator of Digital Photography Review (dpreview.com), a site for users of digital cameras. He got his start by posting well-written, impeccably detailed reviews of new digital cameras as they came out, as well as up-to-the-minute news. Over time, he grew a loyal readership of digital camera enthusiasts.

After three months of steady content, he introduced a home-brewed forum system to the site in January 1999. Divided into sections by camera manufacturer, the forum was an instant success—connecting passionate photographers all over the world to discuss the latest news and reviews, as well as their own camera questions.

Static cling

In this case, when I say "dynamic," I don't mean "management material." When you have a system in place that assembles pages on the fly (like many community software packages do), that's often referred to as "dynamic." On the flip side, simply making a page in HTML and uploading it to a server is called "static" content, because it is unchanging.

I'm certain that, had Askey not primed the pump with high quality content from the beginning, the quality (and quantity, for that matter) of the forums would not have been nearly as high.

The moral of the story is clear: Give your users something to talk about, and they will reward you with high-quality conversations.

Community

Now that you know who you're talking to, and you know what you're saying, you're going to have to decide how you want your users to respond.

There are many different kinds of user participation on the web, but you can separate them all into either synchronous or asynchronous communication. **Synchronous** communication is when all the users are at the same place, at the same time. This often means chat or instant messaging. **Asynchronous** communication allows for users to participate at different times. This often refers to posting to web boards or email lists. Don't confuse asynchronous with chronological—a posting forum can be both chronological (in the order occurred) and asynchronous (without the users being there at the same time).

Digital Photography Review's homepage. Each news story links to the news discussion forum.

First, decide which mode you want to employ, and for what purpose. An entertainment site, for example, may want to employ a synchronous online chat at a specific time with a big star. Or a book site may want to have a famous author take part in an asynchronous Q&A over a week in a posting forum. Each method has its own strengths and weaknesses. Asynchronous communication is often more convenient (scheduling events on the web is always a hassle with all those time zones to consider), but it lacks the visceral real-time impact that a live synchronous chat can have. And while a synchronous event has a strong emotional impact (all those users are here with you *right now*), they're often more like a slow phone conversation than a well-thought-out exchange of letters. Asynchronous communication gives the participants more time to craft elegant responses.

You may find that you want to employ a variety of synchronous and asynchronous communication methods for different tasks. Just make sure you weigh the pros and cons of each before proceeding.

There are a host of other factors to think about, too. If you choose an asynchronous web posting mechanism, should you require users to create memberships before posting or not? Do you need hosts and moderators, or can the users police themselves? We'll deal with all of these topics later in the book. For now, consider the audience and content you've identified, and think of the ways you'd like to let your users react.

Ready for Your Close-up?

At the end of each chapter in this book, I've included an interview with an expert in this space—someone with a unique perspective on the specific facet of community that the chapter discusses. Because this chapter is all about the work you do before beginning a community site, the expert in this case is you.

So grab a pencil! I'm going to interview you about your community project. Consider this an important exercise in creating a community. If you've already got a community project going, answer the questions with it in mind. If you're only in the planning stages, write down your answers now—they'll come in handy later. If you're not anywhere near beginning a community project, well, just read them over and consider them when you are ready.

Finally, don't feel bad if you don't have all the answers yet—this exercise is just intended to get the gears turning.

Please introduce yourself. Who are you and what's your background?

This is especially important if you're going to be the voice of the community as a host or a moderator. The more self-revealing you are, the more that your community will feel comfortable revealing themselves to you.

Please tell us about the community project. What is it about?

What is the intent behind your project? What do you hope to achieve?

Let's talk audience. Who is the site community project for, exactly?

Who are the people you want to attract to your site? What do they do with their lives and how will your site fit in? Try building a user profile. Write a little story about a person in your audience and how your site fits into his or her life. Feel free to identify several audiences and prioritize them.

Let's talk content. What is on this site for the community to talk about?

Communities form around a basic need or theme. What are you offering your users that they can't get anywhere else?

What kind of community features do you want to provide?

What kind of participation do you want your users to have? How much of a voice should they get? Will they have free range, or do you want to limit their participation to one area? Do you want to have synchronous communication or asynchronous communication?

Your answers to these questions will help you make the decisions ahead. Write them down and put them away someplace safe. They'll make interesting reading later.

Chapter 2

Content Comes First

...Give Your Community Something to Talk About

In the chicken-or-the-egg relationship of content and community, it's easy to get lost in wondering which came first. Community areas generate content, but it takes content to draw people to the community areas.

I'm here to settle the debate. When you're talking about community on the web, content always comes first. In fact, the definition of "content" could be "that which the user experiences before he communicates with other users."

No matter what kind of site you run, there's always content. If you run an editorially driven site, you know what content is already— it's your stories, articles, and features. If your site is a web store, think of the product pages as individual elements of content. If your site is geared for tech support, the FAQs and tech support documentation are your content.

Whenever users enter a site with community features, there has to be something that draws them there, something that sets the tone, something that provides a clear example of what the site is about.

That something is called content, and it's probably the most important thing you have to consider in your site.

This chapter reviews a little history, discusses how content influences community, and gives you my recipe for content that encourages positive communities. It ends with a conversation with Matt Haughey, the creator of MetaFilter, a community site that is interesting because it uses external content to power its internal community.

The Well Is Dry

In the beginning, there was the Well, and it was good. The Whole Earth 'Lectronic Link (WELL) was a groundbreaking virtual community. It started in the eighties, long before the web, using command line interfaces to connect a community of thinkers and writers all over the world.

Once logged in, participants could discuss anything under the sun, with areas divided up into different conferences, each with an ever-growing number of conversational threads, all contained in a simple command line interface.

When the web came along in the mid-nineties, the Well developed a web interface and continued on, even spinning off a community software company, Well Engaged. The Well seemed poised to be the leader in the web community business. After all, they'd been doing it the longest.

But the Well itself floundered, business-wise. It suffered through a series of sales and dramatic near-death experiences. It's currently owned by online magazine Salon, which is keeping it alive but unchanged. And Well Engaged stumbled along with a clunky technology, ultimately merging with Delphi Forums (itself a company straddled by clumsy legacy technology) to create Prospero Technologies in 2000. Both companies are still alive and kicking, as of this writing.

But all that is business talk, and this is not a business book. There's a fundamental reason the Well stumbled when it took its technology and ideology to the web, and it's simple: There can be only one Well.

When the Well existed in a pre-web, command line universe, there was no place like it. There were no competitors. There was also a limited way of displaying static content. In essence, the content *was* the community, and the technology supported that perfectly. Nothing can diminish the amazing spark of life that the Well brought to the notion of virtual community.

But the web is a very different beast. It's graphical, so it has dramatically changed the way information can be communicated. And by and large, the web is free. Where the Well was a closed community, web-based communities are usually open to all.

When community features started popping up on the web, all of a sudden everyone could have a message board. Or a chat room. Or a guest book. These tools are now so ubiquitous, they've nearly lost all meaning. Savvy web surfers have come to expect community tools like they expect search engines and banner ads.

In a sea of a million message boards that all cry out "join our community," how do weary web surfers find the ones that are worth their time?

Simple: content.

It's not enough anymore to just give your users the tools to talk to each other like the Well did. You must also give them something to talk about. And the quality of that content will have a direct, unmistakable impact on the kind of community you create.

You Get What You Give

If I've learned anything from my years of observing and creating online communities, it's that the tone of the content you give your users is replicated and amplified a thousand times in the responses it generates. It works almost like an echo: If you scream into a canyon, you'll hear three screams back.

If your content is pushy and opinionated, you can count on pushy and opinionated responses. If your content is personal and genuine, you'll get personal and genuine responses back. And as the responses grow, that tone is multiplied with each post. A gentle push in one direction can send a fledgling community up to the stars or straight into the gutter.

Take FuckedCompany (fuckedcompany.com) for example. This is a site devoted to watching, betting on, and mocking the collapse of dot-com ventures. In the beginning of 2000, when the site started, it functioned as a much-needed response to the avalanche of hype about the dot-com–addled new economy. After the market correction of early 2001, it's a little like shooting fish in a barrel.

As you could probably tell from the name, the site is full of snotty "told-you-so" attitude, which fits the mission of the site quite well. Take this recent news story on the front page of the site:

Pro iChoice
iChoose.com
You see, rumor has it iChoose ran out of money. Then Gator.com said "hey,
we'll rescue you with an acquisition." Then, at the last minute, Gator said "ha
ha... you honestly thought we were serious?" Apparently no severance or
vacation was given, although three of em were offered jobs at Gator...
When: 11/21/2000
Company: iChoose.com
Points: 199
Comment/view this fuck in the Happy Fun Slander Corner! (361)

A story from
Fucked-Company.

A site that takes this much glee in the demise of others is bound
to attract users with the same bloodlust. Here's a quick glimpse of
what you're treated to if you follow this thread to its posting
area:

Page down?   Nov 22 2000 04:27AM EST

Wow, ichoose.com is already down, that was quick...
View the 1 reply to this comment   Reply | Edit | Post a new comment

funny thing   Nov 22 2000 04:31AM EST

I sent an email to a friend just the other day because their site said they were
looking for Unix sysadmins, and I drive by their place every day.
View the 3 replies to this comment   Reply | Edit | Post a new comment

oops   Nov 22 2000 05:46AM EST

Last one out, please turn off the server......
View the 2 replies to this comment   Reply | Edit | Post a new comment

ichoose to pull the plug   Nov 22 2000 08:19AM EST

Its nice to see a steady stream of monkey see monkey do dot coms learning
the hard way, atleast it seperates the boys from the men. Lesson to be learnt
puberty in the dot com game is a painful learning experience...
View the 1 reply to this comment   Reply | Edit | Post a new comment

Some comments
posted to the story
above.

And it goes on that way for pages.

For FuckedCompany, this is a success. The site knows its audience,
and it's giving them what they want. The audience, in turn, is
responding in an appropriate manner according to the mission of
the site. The audience, content, and community are all in perfect
alignment here.

Of course, your site may not be designed to solicit these kinds of reactions. Even so, you can still learn a lot from a site like FuckedCompany. Note how the tone of the stories is amplified with each reply, and how the replies form a critical mass that informs the stories. The original tone of the site is echoed back over and over, each time getting louder.

Remember to pay close attention to the emotional tone your content strikes. It's your clearest example to your community of the way you want them to communicate with each other. Your content leads by example, and you can be sure that the audience will respond in kind.

The Power of Personal Stories

One way to draw people into intimate conversations is to engage them as people. Personal stories are a wonderful way to create a discussion that is at once inclusive, polite, and real.

That's the goal of my personal storytelling site {fray} (fray.com). For example, on the first day of the year 2000, I posted a simple story there about what I'd done to celebrate the new year.

I followed my brief personal story with a simple question: "Where were you when the clock struck midnight?"

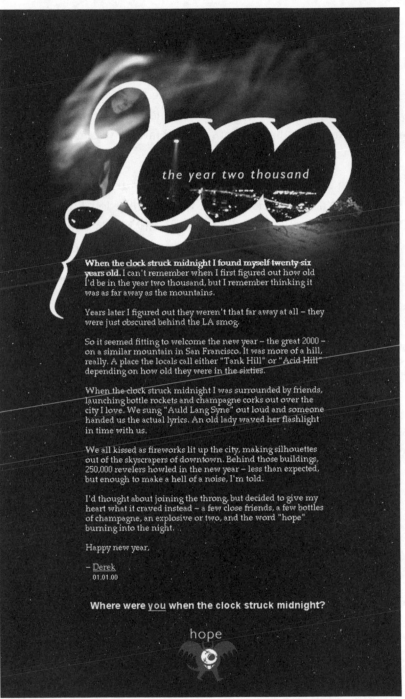

the year two thousand

When the clock struck midnight I found myself twenty-six years old. I can't remember when I first figured out how old I'd be in the year two thousand, but I remember thinking it was as far away as the mountains.

Years later I figured out they weren't that far away at all – they were just obscured behind the LA smog.

So it seemed fitting to welcome the new year – the great 2000 – on a similar mountain in San Francisco. It was more of a hill, really. A place the locals call either "Tank Hill" or "Acid Hill" depending on how old they were in the sixties.

When the clock struck midnight I was surrounded by friends, launching bottle rockets and champagne corks out over the city I love. We sung "Auld Lang Syne" out loud and someone handed us the actual lyrics. An old lady waved her flashlight in time with us.

We all kissed as fireworks lit up the city, making silhouettes out of the skyscrapers of downtown. Behind those buildings, 250,000 revelers howled in the new year – less than expected, but enough to make a hell of a noise, I'm told.

I'd thought about joining the throng, but decided to give my heart what it craved instead – a few close friends, a few bottles of champagne, an explosive or two, and the word "hope" burning into the night.

Happy new year,

– Derek
01.01.00

Where were you when the clock struck midnight?

hope

"The Year 2000," a personal story in {fray} (fray.com/hope/2000).

With all the talk about the Y2K bug and international excitement over the year 2000, it was safe to assume that all the readers would have a story about where they were when the new year began. And they did. At last count, the story had received more than 500 posts. The stories people posted came from all over the world (Amsterdam, England, Israel, and Sweden in the first two pages alone) and ranged from standard fare ("I was at a party with friends") to the sublime:

> With a small group of friends, quietly drinking champagne and conversing, and watching the local fireworks from the front lawn—with my hands wrapped around my wife's belly that contains our little child-to-be.
>
> – C. Ian Murphy

But the real wonder is that, of all of those posts, none were off target. There were no flames, no hassles, no bozos. Just good, honest people telling true stories.

This technique can be applied to any community site, not just literary collections. If you sell t-shirts online, tell a story about something interesting that happened to you when you were wearing one of the shirts and invite your customers to do the same. If you run a news discussion site like Matt Haughey's MetaFilter (interviewed in this chapter), adding a personal statement and a direct question can work wonders. As he said: "That's when it really started feeling like a place, and not just a site."

Caleb Clark (interviewed in Chapter 5) is a professional community builder with whom I worked on the Professional Connections community for Netscape. In his time as a host and moderator, he developed a core set of ideals on what makes a community grow. One of his techniques that I particularly admired was the creation of a standard "How was your week?" thread. This allowed people to tell the real stories of their real lives in an appropriate place.

Sometimes, simply asking someone how her week was can lead to an incredible conversation.

> **How was your week?**
>
> Community builder Caleb Clark on the "How was your week?" topic: "Everybody has an identity, but online it's tough to establish because we are separated from our bodies. One way I've found to get around this is to have a space where people can express how their weeks were. Seems trivial, but it's very powerful. As soon as someone writes 'this week was bad, my 10-year-old got sick just as I had a big presentation at work which I botched' they've made themselves unique and invested emotions in the community. When someone writes back, 'I hear you, I've got enough trouble juggling work and home life and I'm Single! More power to you' then you've got a community."
>
> – From "*How Was Your Week?*" A Handbook for Successfully Growing Web Based Online Communities by Caleb Clark (plocktau.com/writing/books).

The bottom line is that human beings are subjective, personal creatures by definition. And communities are about connections between people. Personal stories are the glue that holds any community together, online or off. So never underestimate the power of a personal story and a direct question.

Content That Works

Your task is to identify the goals of your community, select an appropriate editorial voice for your content, and then produce content with the same tone that you want to hear from your users. This tone should be carried through in everything on your site—from the headlines to the stories to the FAQs. This can be easier said than done, so here are some ingredients from my personal recipe for content that works.

Be personal

People are more likely to flame out when they forget that the words they see on their screen are being typed by a real flesh-and-blood person at the other end. One way to circumvent this tendency is to remind the community that their hosts and leaders are people, too. If you're the moderator of a community site, remember to introduce yourself and mention personal elements from your real life. You should also consider adding an area where people can introduce themselves, or perhaps biography pages where users can talk about their real lives. A site-wide "about us" area with personal biographies written in friendly, non-corporate voices can help personalize the site, too. If the community is constantly reminded that the leaders are all real people, everyone will stay a whole lot friendlier.

Be nice

It's incredibly hard sometimes, but community leaders must always be nice. Community leadership can be frustrating. There will always be members who test your patience with inappropriate comments, antisocial behavior, or outright insults. It's imperative that you remember that everything you type serves as an example of what is permissible in the forum. If you lose it and yell at someone, or use inappropriate language, you're inviting everyone to do the same. The high road may be difficult to take sometimes, but your community will thank you for taking it.

Be inclusive

Sometimes the best content for your website is the content that comes out of your community. You can create ways to feature exemplary community-generated content. Then link to it in prominent ways, or even invite members to author it themselves. It raises the bar another notch and offers a polite dare: If your work is this good, you could be featured, too. Many community sites have "members of the week," but I'm talking about taking it one step further. Find the proactive, positive members and get them involved in the production of your content. It sets a great standard and draws your community together.

Be honest

It's a common mistake to think of your community as children who need their hands held. They're not—they're adults and should be treated that way. So be honest with them. If your site is a business, and the business falls on hard times, be honest with your community. Tell them what's going on. They're bound to find out eventually, and they'll thank you for being up front about it (or be outraged if they catch you in a lie). Even if you're not facing a business calamity, being honest with your community will only help create a good atmosphere. If you talk to them as adults, from a place of honesty, they'll do the same for you.

Content with Content

The bottom line is, any community venture must begin with an examination of content. Next, we'll hear from Matt Haughey, proprietor of MetaFilter (metafilter.com), a community site that's interesting because its content is just a link to a story elsewhere. Yet even in that simple equation, the tone of that link becomes incredibly important. He and I spoke in email in early January 2001.

A Conversation with Matt Haughey

Matt Haughey

Matt, please give us a brief introduction of who you are and what you do.

My name is Matt Haughey, and I'm an Internet developer living in San Francisco. I started out in web design in 1995, after reading a lot of sites and wanting to create them myself. I remember being drawn initially to the artistic aspects of it. I had abandoned commercial art and design as a college major my second semester, and by the time I saw the web as a graduating senior, I was hooked. After a few years of goofing around in Photoshop and having small personal sites, I started playing with databases and various scripting languages. Once I started building database-backed websites, I realized that one person could create a whole lot more with very little work. MetaFilter.com was my first major database-backed project, and also my first foray into running my own community, though I had participated in several large community email lists prior to that.

Let's talk about MetaFilter. Why did you start it? What was the big idea behind it?

I originally set up MetaFilter as a site that would highlight interesting or newsworthy things on the web. I had seen a couple dozen sites that did this well, and they're generally called "weblogs." At the time, they consisted of a daily list of links to amazing websites or breaking news, and most would show 5–10 new links a day. Some were about a specific topic (Slashdot is a good example of an open-source news weblog), others varied between all topics, and some were more like personal journals. Overall, they were (and still are) good reflections of the authors' personalities.

I began building MetaFilter as an open-topic weblog, but I knew I couldn't produce a good one all by myself. I was new to it, and was constantly amazed with the quality of output from most popular weblog authors. So armed with my newfound scripting and database knowledge, I thought I could spread out the work of creating a top-notch weblog by allowing others to write on the site. I figured that there were probably others in the same position I was in, who only found one or two interesting sites each day, but together we could create something great.

As I built it, I figured a small group of authors and readers would probably like to comment on each other's work. They could create discussions around articles and sites in a small-scale way. It wasn't too much extra work to code the commenting capabilities, so I went ahead and added a built-in comment system that let authors and readers interact with one another. I never really intended the site to become a bustling community. I just wanted to make something useful that others could enjoy. Adding the commenting system was almost an afterthought.

After a few months of programming, learning, and testing, I put the site together, and by June of 1999 I launched the site. I thought it would attract a small number of people posting links to sites and articles, and that same small group would probably participate in discussions. It hummed along quietly for about six months, at the level I thought it would. There were four or five regular authors including me, and a small group of loyal readers. I tried to set a good tone, and went out of my way to comment on other people's work, asking questions to get discussions started, and kept a close watch to make sure nefarious threads or comments were dealt with quickly.

Then one day, I submitted it to Projectcool.com's Sightings (a prominent web awards site at the time), and a few days later, was awarded as the daily sighting. That day, a site that used to get about 100 page views a day by roughly 30–50 people exploded into 7,500 page views by 4,000 people. Many of them hung on after that day, and the site blossomed from that day forward.

One of the core ideas in my approach to design for community is the close connection between content and community features. But on MetaFilter, the content is just a link away from the site. So, in a way, the members of your site define themselves by what they find on the web, and what they have to say about it. Sometimes, the site even seems to serve as a surrogate discussion engine for other sites. What is MetaFilter really about: the link or the discussion? And has that changed over time?

Originally, the link was the most important part, as I wasn't sure discussion would even take place. Like most community endeavors, there needs to be a critical mass of sorts, before real interaction takes place. So, during the first six months of the site, there would usually be no discussion at all, so the links would have to be extremely interesting in order to get people to come back to the site. After the site got enough people talking about news or websites, the discussion became the focus of most readers' attention, and much of the "content" that was previously offsite became onsite. These days, the site gets 15 to 20 discussion threads started each day, and most threads have at least 5 to 10 comments in them. A couple note-worthy threads will have more. Frequently, I'll post a link to a news story or interesting site and ask readers to post additional information if they have expertise to offer. The best discussions seem to be exactly that—experts on a particular subject will see something mentioned on MetaFilter and then post informative comments that support or contradict the original thread. It makes for some really great discussions, and I think everyone benefits from the information sharing.

In a way, MetaFilter did start as simply a surrogate discussion engine for other sites, but I think now that there is a healthy community of vocal readers, when something of interest comes along, many people want to know what the "regulars" at MetaFilter think about a certain piece of news. There are a wide variety of characters that inhabit the site, so you never know how or where discussion threads will lead.

Any good stories from the site? Moments when the community surprised you?

I remember the day when the focus of the site changed, at least internally for me. I had looked at the {fray} for inspiration years before MetaFilter, and one day I wondered if I could transcend what was then mostly just pointing out wacky things on the web and having people talk about them. I noticed one thing at the {fray} that MetaFilter lacked, and it was a single character. A question mark.

So this one day, I decided to stop speaking at the community of readers and start speaking to them, engaging them. I can't remember what the first thing I tried this on was, but it was something like "here's a story of something embarrassing that happened to someone. What's the most embarrassing thing that's ever happened to you?"

Suddenly, instead of 2 or 3 comments following the post, there were 15. And they were funny, enlightening, and entertaining. Suddenly, I felt closer to the community.

After that day, I tried to do it as often as possible, and other people followed my lead, and that's when it really started feeling like a place, and not just a site.

Another moment of surprise happened recently, when I was commemorating World AIDS day (December first). The site has never had a strong central topic, but on that day (starting exactly at midnight), I simply asked that people post HIV/AIDS-specific links to news and information, and posted a couple as illustrated examples. To my amazement, when I woke up later that morning, the site was buzzing with information and discussion of health policies, touching stories, prevention ideas, and ways people could help those in need. For those 24 hours, everyone stopped thinking about the news of the day, focused on that one topic, and did it extremely well.

How has MetaFilter changed over time? As the community around the site grew, you've made some changes. What were they? Did they help?

The first few months were especially hard because the site was general topics, but low traffic. I tried copying the way others in the genre wrote, I tried writing personal things, I tried following a single topic for a day, but eventually I started spending more time writing for the site, trying to put the highest quality stuff out there for people to see and talk about. Later on, I made it as discussion-centric as I could. And as of late, most of the topics covered on the site have drifted almost exclusively to general interest news stories.

As the community grew, I kept a close eye on things and created guidelines to avoid unwanted shifts. At first, some people would figure out that anyone could post a link to the site, so they'd, of course, test it out by posting a link to their own site. I let it go for a while, not really enjoying it, but hey it was content. When the numbers really grew, it became the first thing people did when they discovered the site, so I made a rule saying you were forbidden from linking to your own site. I didn't want MetaFilter to become a self-promotional tool, so I did what I could to stop it.

The next major change was made after I noticed the way that many people posted to the site when they first discovered it. Now, for me, when I join a new community, like a mailing list, I sit back and lurk, figure out what the community's culture is like, and then slowly participate where I think I can add something. I noticed that on MetaFilter, not everyone did that, and many would barge in and break the rules, or set a tone that was disruptive. It was much like having your party invaded by people you didn't know, acting in a way that your friends normally wouldn't. So I instituted a couple controls on new members. First, anyone can sign up and comment moments later. But they can't post a new item to the main page until they've been a member for at least 24 hours, and they must have commented at least three times.

I felt this was a good way to keep spammers out (early on, there were a few people who saw MetaFilter as a place to broadcast their press releases or announce their new commercial site, so I found the 24-hour delay stopped that entirely). The requirement on comments before front page posting was so that people would get a feel for how people interacted on the site, and what kinds of topics started good threads, and how people acted in those threads. Essentially, the controls were a way to force people to sit back and watch the way the regulars act, and hopefully they'd follow suit when they were clear to do as they please.

In your view, what are MetaFilter's strengths and weaknesses as a community site?

I think its strengths are that it still feels small, even though there are over 2,000 members and about 8,000 page views a day. No one feels anonymous because there's a community and a code of ethics, guidelines, and unwritten rules that people follow. I think once people feel anonymous, all hell breaks loose.

So the small town feel of MetaFilter means that discussions are almost always civil and respectful. I'm amazed at the wonderful heated discussions that follow topics close to many people's hearts.

As for the site's weaknesses, it's a community site, so it's prone to the same pitfalls that other communities face. After a period of growth, will the original users stop reading and participating? How do you teach new users the ethics and guidelines the veterans of the site follow? How many people are too many?

I'd say that like any community, there are limits, and as you approach those limits, things fall apart. During this past presidential election, about 30 to 40 topics would show up each day, and it was so many in a short period of time that people wouldn't discuss threads, and they would fall off the front page quickly.

I wish the site were more easily moderated. I'm a busy person, and I only have a short amount of time in the morning and night to really check on things, weed out the bad posts, fix HTML errors, etc.

I hope the site can continue to grow, but I know eventually it has to meet some logical limits. Too many people posting too many things is going to become a reality one day. But as the site grows closer to that, I think it might find an equilibrium—when there are too many topics, people will be turned off by it, and the next day there will be fewer people.

So you're not afraid of turning people off? I think the political threads during election 2000 were a good example of a community finding its voice. On the one hand, it's good because it helps develop a community identity. But on the other hand, it annoyed a few folks, too.

I would hope that as many people as possible would read the site, and when people discover the site, I hope they come back, but with the large number of people the site currently supports, I'm not afraid of turning people off. On busy days, it takes quite a bit of effort to read everything and follow the discussions, and a key thing users like to do is revisit later to see how discussions progress, but that involves even more work on the part of visitors. Although I'd love it if more people visited the site, I totally understand why it may turn off visitors, and honestly, there are a lot of websites and a lot of web surfers, and everyone has to find a perfect place to hang out. I try to make MetaFilter a place worth hanging out at, but if people don't want to, that's fine with me.

This past election was kind of crazy, and new bits of information were coming out of CNN several times every hour. If it was interesting, someone would post something and start a discussion. But there was just so much political news that it drowned out the other topics, and many people turn to the web when they're tired of mainstream things like TV, and here was MetaFilter, looking like a complete reflection of the television news. Most of the people who were turned off by the political news just steered clear of MetaFilter for a few days, and it eventually died down.

What do you have planned for the future of the site?

I see some great things from time to time on MetaFilter, and I'd love to highlight them in some way, so I could show them to new users and say "this is what this site is capable of, isn't it amazing?"

I'm experimenting with several different things right now like an edited daily email, but I am always thinking of new things. I'd like to do community interviews of people, let the community say who they want to interview and what questions should be asked. I'd like to continue working on ways to keep the quality of discussions as high as possible. Perhaps I'll collect all the best bits and put them on another companion site.

I'd like to add more customization to the site, so people get exactly the experience they want from it. I've been playing with some rudimentary collaborative filtering, where topics that people like will come first, and topics or authors users don't care for will be hidden from view. I'm thinking of other implementations of the code behind it, perhaps localized news versions for different regions of the country, perhaps new sites focused on a single topic. I'm always tinkering with it, optimizing it, and adding new tweaks.

Any advice for other community site builders?

Don't underestimate the commitment required. Done right, a community site will take a lot of your time, and the payoffs, in whatever form you set for yourself as goals, may not come for a very long time. I put in hundreds of hours and nursed the site along for six months before anyone really noticed. Looking back at the start of MetaFilter, if I were as busy then as I am now in my personal life, I doubt I would have had time to properly launch, build, and maintain the project. If I knew how much personal free time I'd give up for the site going in, I probably would have had second thoughts about it.

Also, remember that once you get the site going, stopping it is almost out of the question. A very successful community creates a special place in a lot of people's hearts. People are what make a community great, not necessarily the administrator or moderators, so when someone on top says he might bring the whole thing down, people have something of theirs that they're in danger of losing. I remember the outcry that came when a few sites I frequented in the past closed. Members didn't want to lose their community, and at the very least, they wanted to be able to extract an archive of their postings. I've seen splinter communities spring up in the aftermath, and depending on the commitment and culture of the new proprietors, they sometimes succeed in recreating much of the former community, and in a very few cases may grow beyond the original bounds.

I've been a part of a few communities that had some success, and watched a lot of others, and I wouldn't discount the importance of honesty on the part of the creator or creators. Let's say you want to build a community site around a topic. Then you should let your passion for that topic come through in every way you can, and be completely honest with users when you're at your limits or when you might need help (your heaviest users will often be willing to help out, test things out, offer suggestions, or even offer their own free work to solve a problem). If you're hiding your feelings, or trying to keep news from folks, it seems like the astute users will figure it out and call you on it.

To sum up the good qualities of a community builder, pick something you're passionate about, devote the necessary time to building a site around it, stick with it for as long as it takes, keep it going as long as you can, and be open with your users. That's not too much to ask, now is it?

Chapter 3

Design Matters

...Architectural and Visual Design for Successful Communities

Web design is a complicated business. When you start to talk about what a site should look like, you invariably wind up in conversations about other things: audience, browsers, technologies, staffing, budgets, etc.

Further complicating the web design process is the fact that everyone seems to have an ironclad definition of what Good Web Design is. Web design do's and don'ts saturate the web, and for every one there's a web guru there to tell you the One True Way. DON'T use frames. DON'T use Flash. DON'T use forms. Actually, come to think of it, usually they're just lists of don'ts.

You won't find any of that here. Web design is complicated, and I have yet to find a single rule that's always true, with the exception of one: the "it depends" rule. It states that the only real answer to any web design question is "it depends." Should you use Flash? Maybe. Frames? Could be. It depends.

It's enough to make a guy not want to write about design at all. But talking about designing community sites means talking about designing websites in general. So here's a quick overview of some of the general design concepts I use. If you're new to designing websites, or if you'd simply like a refresher course, read on. If you're impatient, you can skip ahead to "Design for Community," where I talk about how these concepts apply to the design of community sites.

Design in General

When I was a teenager, I decided to learn how to play the guitar. I'd like to be able to attribute this to a noble need for self-expression, but it probably had more to do with impressing girls. I bought myself a guitar and took classes at the local music shop. There I learned old folk songs—combinations of chords and stories that traveled through history long enough for people to forget who originally wrote them. I was enraptured.

Before long I began to write my own songs and play in bands. It was the combination of people and instruments in the bands that was the most challenging and enjoyable aspect to write for. Each song needed to have its own beat, a single rhythm to hold the song together. But it also needed solos and improvisation to highlight each player's individual contribution. In the end, if it worked, the whole became more than the sum of its parts.

I've always felt that it was my years of songwriting that prepared me for web design—not my work in print or art. Because, in many ways, songwriting and web design are really the same thing. Each of them involves setting a beat and then improvising around it.

Web design as music

In web design, the best thing a designer can do is move beyond considering each page a piece of art. Instead, the designer should consider the user's entire experience as a work of art. When you do, you'll begin to see the same patterns you see in music.

The navigation of your site is the beat—the drums and bass—that anchor the design into a solid, predictable rhythm. It's crucial to establish that beat and be consistent with it. Just as you wouldn't change tempo in the middle of a song without a good reason, neither should you change your visual navigation in the middle of a website.

Your design flourishes are the lead guitar parts. They can be flashy in parts—solo guitarists are always spotlight hounds. But they should never be louder than the lead singer. And who's the singer? You guessed it: the content. The text of your site is like the lyrics of a song—it should never be upstaged.

Then there are breaks, bridges, and solos—things that improvise around the beat. These things have components in visual web design as well. Think about interstitial elements as breaks and recurring elements as choruses. Other design elements (photos, titles) will vary from the beat, but none of them should disrupt it.

The key is to think about your site, from beginning to end, as an experience. I'm a songwriter, so I can see the similarities in that. Maybe there's a concept that you know well that makes sense for you. The key concepts here are consistency, experience, and attention to detail. You'll see these concepts recurring in all of the following design guidelines.

The Nuts and Bolts

I promised you that I wouldn't give you a list of design rules, and I won't. Instead, here are a few design guidelines—things to think about in the design process.

1. Design for your audience

Since the only thing you can count on in web design is that "it depends," it helps to narrow the scope of whom you're designing for. Identify and profile your audience before you even start the visual design process. Who are these people? What do they like?

What kinds of objects surround them in their daily life? Drawing inspiration from these things will help you design a site that resonates with your audience.

For example, Firehouse (firehouse.com) is a site devoted to firemen, with an active community area. The site's design might not be a great design in general, but it fits its audience to a tee. The bold lines, red and black color choices, and strong font treatments all communicate directly to firefighters.

A post view in the Firehouse forums.

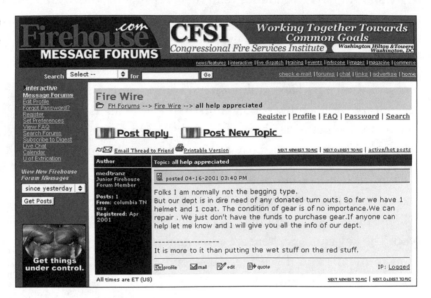

2. Design for flexibility

Remember that the web is made up of millions of different combinations of people, browsers, and computers—even within your targeted audience. Some of these people will have special needs like large text for the vision-impaired or avoiding color combinations (like red on black) for colorblind people.

And even aside from the special needs of users, the web is all about flexibility. What other medium asks designers to set type but can't tell them what font the user will see, or even how big the page will be? It can be frustrating, for sure. But successful web design uses this flexibility as an advantage instead of a limitation.

As a web designer, you can code your pages to allow people to change the font size in their browser and design the page to look good in an increased font size. You can also design liquid pages that expand to gracefully fill the browser window, no matter the size. Pages at Kvetch, for example, use frames to gracefully contain the community content, no matter what size the user makes them.

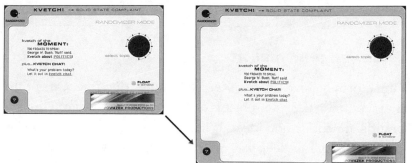

Same site, two sizes. Kvetch uses frames to adjust to any size.

3. Design for experience

Remember to look at your site the way the user does—as an experience, with a beginning, middle, and end. The first few pages the user encounters should be welcoming and explanatory. The middle of the experience should contain the main content and functionality. The end should provide closure.

It's the experience that's most important in web design—not the individual pages. So make sure that all the pages on your site follow the same rules. If an icon of a house means "take me to the homepage" on one page, make sure it means that on every page. If you're using blue links, make sure they're always blue, and that shade of blue isn't used in instances where it's not a link. This is the beat of your site, the baseline structure around which you can improvise.

Kaliber 10000 (k10k.net) is one of my favorite sites. Each of the different sections reveals a different take on its theme, and yet the common elements all remind you where you are. The site carries its gray grid pixelated theme across a diverse spectrum of pages and features absolutely flawlessly.

Three different pages within Kaliber 10000—consistent without being boring.

4. Design for simplicity

I am a firm believer in the "Keep It Simple" doctrine. One of the most common design problems on the web is an overcrowding of brands, functions, and ideas. When it comes to a community site, it's imperative to keep it simple. That means clear navigation and easy-to-understand sections and titles, but most of all it means staying focused on what the user's main task is at any given time, and not crowding the page with competing ideas.

This is especially important for a community-driven site, as community functionality is so often presented in a needlessly complex fashion. Part of the issue here is that, while new users may need a lot visual hand-holding, advanced users want more functional shortcuts. The result is often a visual cacophony of basic tools and a smattering of advanced tools in a visually dissonant fashion.

The folks at Prospero Technologies had a good solution for this problem. Prospero Technologies makes web community software for other websites. In this case, the site was for CBS News (forums.prospero.com/cbsbreakingnews). Prospero's solution was to create two different views on the same community space: "basic" and "advanced." Toggling these views hides and shows extra functionality—an elegant solution to a common problem.

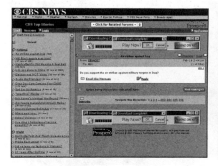 

The CBS News forms in basic and advanced view. Can you tell the difference?

Unfortunately, in this case, both views are way too complicated. Look at all those competing brands, interface widgets, and links. It is hard to distinguish which is which.

5. Design for readability

No matter what you've heard about the brilliant broadband future of the Internet, for now it's still a text-based medium. See that thing in front of the monitor? It's called a keyboard, and every computer has one. Every computer does not have a camera and a microphone, let alone the bandwidth to carry it. So until that fantasy future where we all talk to our computers and take hover-cars to work (if there even is work), we're stuck with text as the primary mode of communication online.

As long as we're stuck with text, we'd better make it readable. That means nice high contrast difference between the text color and the background. It also means a narrow column of text—newspapers have been doing it that way more that over a hundred years for a reason, and that reason is readability. It's simply easier to read 5–10 words per line, instead of 10–20. (It's amazing how many otherwise smart people make this mistake.) Finally, don't get sucked into the small, sexy type trap. Don't ask me why web designers like tiny type, we just do. But don't do it—at least, not for text you expect anybody to read.

Digital Web Magazine (digital-web.com) is a site for the design community that, refreshingly, does not look like a site for the design community. Notice how the text is given all the attention:

The gutters are nice and wide, the font is big, the leading is generous, and the other items are given a subordinate role. This is clearly a site for designers who like to read.

Digital Web Magazine (digital-web.com) is designed for readability.

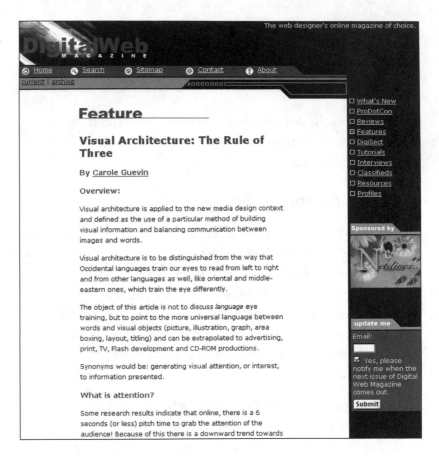

6. Design for beauty

In the end, you could do everything listed previously and still fail. Don't forget that every pixel counts. In addition to being readable and understandable, your site should also be beautiful. After all, that's what designers do, right?

Alt.sense, for example, is a community site that's primarily frequented by designers, so the design has to be good. In addition to the usual discussion boards, the site features nifty tools like photo galleries and birthday reminders, all of which flow together seamlessly with astonishing attention to detail. This one's a looker.

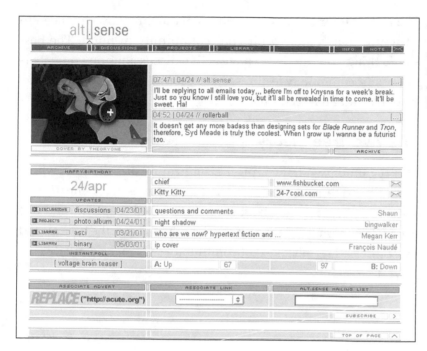

Alt.sense (altsense.net) is easily one of the most beautiful community sites I've seen.

These are my general guidelines to good web design. Now you need to examine how these can be applied to community sites.

Design for Community

Remember how I said I wouldn't give you any rules? I lied.

In my experience designing sites with community features, I've come up with three rules. I'm not usually a rule-making kind of guy, but these three have proven themselves again and again to be not only true, but also necessary to the success of a community-oriented site. If you want your site to have good, positive conversations, follow these three simple rules.

Rule #1: Tie Content Directly to Community

The last chapter discussed the idea of content—now you need to structure that content with your community in mind. The best single thing you can do to create active discussions on your site is to tie your community features to your content as much as possible, visually and architecturally.

The two-tree theory

You're familiar with the typical visualization of a sitemap, where the homepage is at the top and the subpages fall beneath like roots of a tree. Imagine planting one tree called "content" and one called "community" right next to each other. This is the typical, and most infuriating, mistake that community sites make. I call this the "two-tree theory."

The two-tree sitemap.

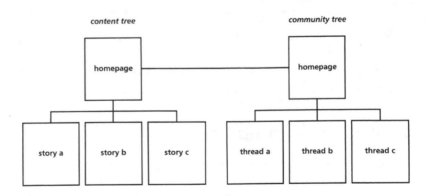

When you grow two trees that never connect, you get separate plants. The key to creating a vibrant online community is to inter-link the content and community at the most granular level possible. That way the content is always acting as an example and inspiration for the community. The community, in turn, becomes active in the content of the site, and can even sometimes help feed back ideas to the authors of the content. This forms a positive feedback loop that benefits both the community and the content.

But separate them and all you'll get is two trees, growing separately. In fact, they may even fight with each other for natural resources. A good (and incredibly frustrating) example of this problem is online magazine Salon (salon.com).

Salon.com cranks out insightful journalism on a daily basis. It's even scooped mainstream media outlets on occasion. It's content has inspired debate countless times.

The homepage of Salon.com.

Salon.com is also host to a community area called "Table Talk." It's a very active subsite with thousands of members, powered by Web Crossing, a community backend that also powers sites like the New York Times. There you can find spirited discussions on everything from art to politics.

And yet, in most cases, when you read a story in the news section of Salon, the only link to the community area is in the bottom of the page, obscured in the text navigation. And even then, that link just leads to the top of the Table Talk section, not a relevant discussion based on the news article you just read.

This is a missed opportunity of immense proportions. Here, on one site, you have some of the best journalism online, and a discussion system to discuss it, sitting next to each other with no connection. In some cases, you even have active conversations about the current news. And yet, there is no architectural connection from one to the other on a granular level. A shame.

The interlinked sitemap.

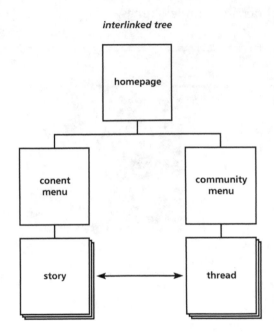

interlinked tree

Connecting the dots

This figure illustrates the most basic solution to the two-tree problem. That horizontal line from content to community and back is the single most important thing you can do to create active, informed conversations on your site, because that line carries with it a priceless stream of interested and informed potential community members.

This connection should not only be architectural (simply linking from the content to the community functionality), it should also be visual (carried through in the design itself). A common mistake is to design a community area that is unique unto itself, because this separates it from the rest of the site. Here the design change carries with it an implicit value judgment: The community area is foreign, outside the proper content of the site. Often, this is what sites do when they're afraid of what their community is going to say about them.

Remember the song metaphor of web design outlined at the beginning of this chapter? Here's where it comes into play. Changing the design, from the content to the community, is like changing the beat of a song halfway through. It breaks the flow, disrupts the user, and ruins the experience. If you're paying attention to the flow of your site as an overall experience, it's clear that the design of the community functionality should be totally integrated with the design of the rest of the site.

This makes an emotional statement as well. Whenever I'm reading a site with a beautiful design and then I link away to a bargain basement area for the discussion tools, I feel like I've just been sent to the kid's table. It's just next to the real table, but it's clearly not as important.

With an integrated design, the look and feel of the content areas and community functionality are the same. This puts the users on par with the content, which makes them feel important, and thus more likely to participate. It also creates a cohesive experience, from the beginning of the site to the end—a beautiful song.

And what's more, it creates better content. The community areas get a steady stream of people who have been informed by the content and, presumably, have something to say about it. And the creators of the content get an active discussion, spawned from their work, which can inform their future work. This forms a positive spiral that can benefit everyone.

Not bad for a single link, huh?

Enter the {fray}

{fray} is a good example of connecting content with community. Here, the content is multipage personal stories. Each is a true, first-person story, and each is individually designed. Every {fray} story ends with a question posed to the reader. That question forms the bridge from content to community.

For example, one recent {fray} story ("Big Brother"—fray.com/criminal/bigbro) was about the abuse a younger sister took from her older brother while growing up. Now, years later, both of them adults, she is trying to forgive him, but can't quite do it. The question at the end is "Who have you almost forgiven?"

The entrance to the community area points at you.

In this question, as with all the questions at {fray}, the word "you" is the active link. This is a personal reinforcement. When the user mouses-over that link, and the cursor turns into a finger, it is clear that the question is pointing at you.

Clicking this link takes you to the posting area. The design of this area matches the story, reinforcing the idea that you are still in the experience—the melody is unbroken.

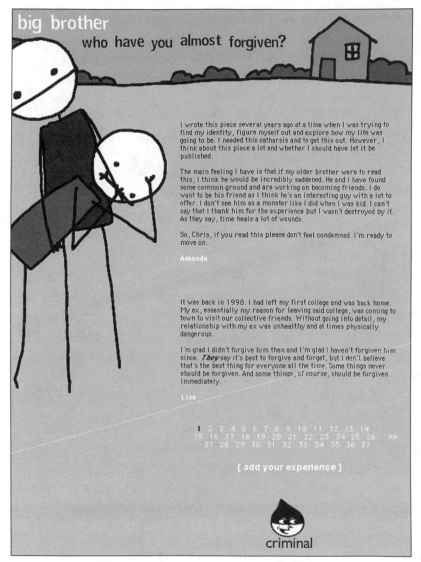

The posting area
for this {fray}
story.

In the community area, the first thing the user is greeted with is other people's answers to the question. Here are still more examples of the kind of conversation you're looking for. The first example, of course, was the content itself—the story. Now the user has pages of other people's posts to read, illuminating again what is expected.

The posts are divided into pages and linked linearly, like search engine results. At the bottom of each page of posts is the call to add your own. In {fray}, this is labeled "{ add your experience }." Clicking on this link brings you to the posting form.

Finally a chance to add your story.

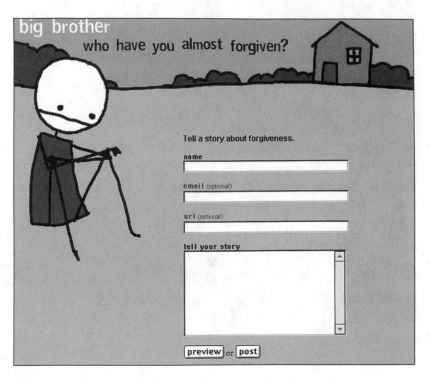

I call these pages "add pages" because that's what the user is there to do—add to the posting area. Again, the add page looks like the post pages, which look like the content that started it all. Here users can preview their posts and then commit them to the posting area. When they do, they're redirected to the page that contains the post—reinforcing their post and providing closure to the experience.

Whether your site is a collection of personal stories or a catalog of product reviews, the rules are the same. Creating a tight visual and architectural link between your content and community is the single most important thing you can do to create positive conversations, because it provides a vivid example of what is expected, and maintains a consistent visual experience.

Okay, so hopefully by now I've convinced you to link from the content to the community. But how? And where? That brings us to rule number two.

Rule #2: Bury the Post Button

When I say "bury the post button," I mean this: Go to the front door of your site and start clicking. Take the most direct path to the post button—the button that a user would click to commit his post to your site. Count the clicks it takes to get from start to finish. **The more clicks it takes, the better the posts will be.**

In my experience with community features, I have observed a proportional relationship to the distance that the post button is from the front door of the site and the quality of conversation on the site. The farther away it is, the better it gets.

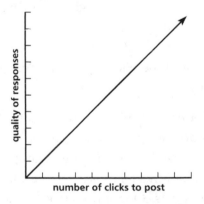

A non-scientific visualization of what happens when you bury the post button.

Why would this be? Because, in this case, the multiple clicks it takes to read the whole story are actually a great screening mechanism. Users who are looking for trouble or aren't really engaged in your content will be put off by the distance. They'll lose interest and drift away. But the users who are engaged by the content and interested in the results of the conversation will stick with it.

These are the people you want to retain, because they're much more likely to post great thoughts.

Real-life communities are informed by local customs and common knowledge. But on the web, because communities are so easy to enter, cultural misconceptions and arguments are common. The best way to raise a community is to make sure your members have something in common. By burying the post button, you're bringing your users together and letting the content act as a filter. When your users get to the posting area, they'll all have some degree of commonality. At the very least, they all will have read your site deep enough to get to the place where they can discuss it. For more on screening your users, be sure to read about barriers to entry in Chapter 8.

Kvetch.com vs. fray.com

Since I hold the administrative keys to both of these sites, I'm in a unique position to talk about the kinds of content each solicits.

Kvetch (kvetch.com) is a site I created to be an oracle of complaint. The site is set up like an old radio, with plenty of dials and buttons. All the user has to do is enter the site, click a topic, click the "add" button, and there's the post button. He can post to the site in three clicks.

{fray}, on the other hand, works quite differently. It takes only one click to get to a story. But {fray} stories can be anywhere from 1 to 20 pages. The story used in the previous example is 7 pages long. So if that was the month's featured story, it'd take 8 clicks to get through it to the posts. One more click to the add page, and you're at the post button: 9 clicks.

Can you guess what happens? Posts to {fray} are consistently on topic and honest. The site is known for the quality of its posts, and threads can go on for months, with hundreds of posts and no dip in quality.

Kvetch posts, on the other hand, can be very funny. Sometimes, they're even insightful. But mostly they're brief, off-the-cuff posts, with a few that are downright regrettable.

Admittedly, there are many reasons for this. The sites have different goals, different audiences, and different designs. But the fact that it's considerably easier to post in one than the other cannot be overlooked.

The moral is clear: Content acts like a filter. The more of it you put in between the front door of your site and the post button, the better your posts will be.

This can translate into different things when applied practically. For example, perhaps the best place for the call to action ("Post your thoughts!") is at the bottom of a page, instead of the top. That way, at least users will have had to skim through some content before they're given the chance to respond. If your content is multiple pages long, put the link to the community functionality at the bottom of the last page. You may get fewer posts, but the ones you get will be higher in quality.

Rule #3: Give Up Control (and Let Your Users Surprise You)

This rule isn't really about the structure of your site, it's about protecting your sanity.

Let's say you've identified your users and defined your site (as discussed in Chapter 1). Let's say you've produced sample content (as discussed in Chapter 2). And now you've tied content to community and buried the post button, as we discussed here. What's left to do? Give up.

Remember that inviting user participation is wonderful because it teaches you about your own site, and your own users. One of the main reasons for doing it is to learn things you didn't know already. So don't be annoyed when your users do something totally unpredictable. They're doing you a favor—they're teaching you about your site. It's your job to pay attention and fix the problems as they come up.

Internet history is littered with "gotchas." The L'eggs pantyhose people learned this lesson the hard way back in the early days of the web. They put up a discussion board with no moderation and not much guidance. They were happy to see that people started using it madly. They were less thrilled when they realized that those people were drag queens.

Another story: A Kvetch user once sent me an email sounding quite upset. She wanted to know if the Kvetch chat area was logged or spied on somehow. "No," I said. "Anything you say in a private chat is entirely private." But I couldn't help asking, "Why do you ask?"

"Well, I can't be sure," she said. "but last night I was talking with some guy ... and one thing led to another ... and I think we had cyber-sex."

Never in my wildest dreams did I think that somebody might use my humble site to score.

I assured her that the chat was totally private, and that cyber-sex was nothing to feel guilty about, so long as she used an anti-virus program in the morning.

Again with the kvetch.com?

When your users surprise you, it can be very frustrating. You've worked very hard on your site, only to have users come along and misunderstand it. The nerve!

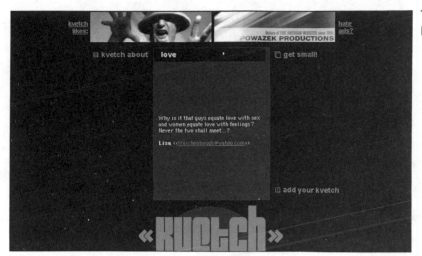

The original
Kvetch design.

When I first launched Kvetch in 1997, the colors were dark
burgundy, orange, and black. It was very hacker. Very dark. This
tended to inspire dark, bitter posts.

The Kvetch
redesign.

When I redesigned it in 1998, I changed the palette entirely. This
time I used light yellows and khaki. The tone of the posts lightened
to match. People still posted complaints, of course. That's what the
site is for. But the posts took on a more light-hearted tone that I
attribute to the change in color.

The way posts are presented on Kvetch is a little different than other places. In order for the site to be a safe haven for complaining, the posts are presented randomly. When you choose an area to kvetch in, the individual posts are presented randomly in a frameset that reloads itself automatically. The result is an area of the screen that is continuously presenting you with new, randomly selected Kvetch posts.

This had a side effect I hadn't expected. To some users, seeing individual posts come and go so quickly looked like web-based chat. They mistook the random posts as a real-time chat conversation, and wanted to join in the fun. As a result, the site saw a lot of posts that said things like:

> "Hi!"
> "I'm Joe!"
> "Hello?"
> "Is anyone there?"
> "Helloooooo!"
> "Why won't you people talk to me?"
> "Fine. I'm leaving!"

At first, I was just annoyed. It was such a simple interface. How could anyone misunderstand it? But the mistake kept happening, and eventually I had to admit that this was not my users' problem, it was mine. So when I redesigned from version one to version two, I included another change, besides the change in color. I did something I said I'd never do—I added chat. I added a web-based chat system to the site, with a clearly labeled toggle from "live chat mode" to "randomizer mode." I also added a help section that reiterated that the randomizer was not chat. If you want to chat, just click the button at the top of the page.

After the redesign, I sat back and waited. After a week, I checked: no mistaken posts.

In this case, not only was there a flaw in my design that I hadn't considered, but there was another set of functionality that my users craved that I hadn't been able to predict.

The lesson is to sit back and let your users surprise you. So long as you remain calm and flexible, your users will help you build a better site.

Design Matters

So what does all this look like, exactly? As always, it depends. But in my experience with the visual design of community spaces, I've seen some common threads. And though it's hard to quantify exactly how much the visual design of a community space contributes to quality of the contributions, it's impossible to deny that one directly influences the other.

Here are three areas to consider in the design of community spaces.

Consideration 1: Color choice

The most interesting thing about the Kvetch redesign story is how the tone of the posts changed when I altered the design of the site. This experience has always fascinated me.

Part of the problem in judging this logically is the difficulty in codifying what actually goes on in a community. Labeling posts "good" or "positive" or even "funny" is a subjective judgment. So you'll just have to believe me when I say that the posts seemed more light-hearted after the redesign. More funny, less bitter. It's subjective, but it's true.

Consideration 2: Shapes and patterns

When you are creating a community space, it's important to create a space that is warm, welcoming, and inclusive. When translated into pixels, these things often mean soft warm colors, curved elements, and photos of friendly faces. Are these things cliché by now? Probably, but only because they really work.

Think about real-world objects—things that feel good in your hand. The curve of a stone that's been polished by the ocean, the feel of an old baseball that's worn soft from use, the feel of a warm blanket on a sunny couch.

You can't replicate the sensual feel of these things on the web, but you can create visual reminders of them. These things have elements in common: smoothness, curves, and warmth.

That's why so many community areas used curved elements with warm colors. They're designed to make you feel more comfortable. The idea is for them to feel organic (which they are, since they grow with people) instead of cold and technological (which they are, being websites on computers and all).

Consideration 3: Photos and illustrations

Another common element is photos or illustrations of people. This is designed to humanize a site and remind you of the real people on the other end of the usernames. This can be a great way to make a site feel personal, but be careful with it, because it can just as easily backfire. Once you've seen one fake clipart smile, you've seen a million. And if your users sense that they're being manipulated, they'll resent you for it. So if you're going to use humanistic imagery, my advice is to use real photos of real people connected to your site. An amateur photo that's real will do more to accomplish humanizing your site than a legion of fake smiles from Photodisc.

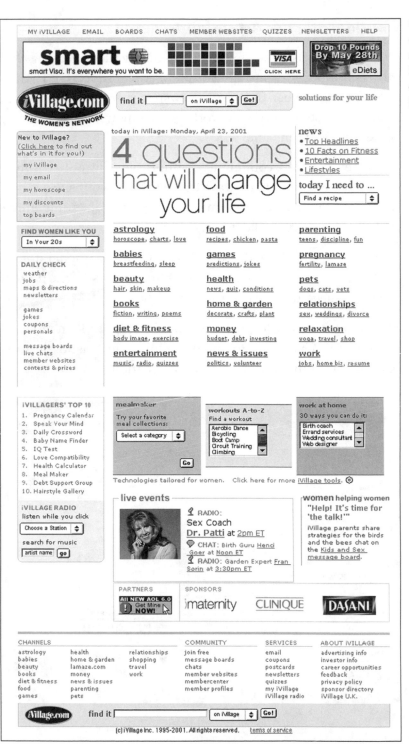

Curves, soft warm colors, and a smiling photo— iVillage.com covered all the bases.

Consideration 4: Attention to detail

One of the most common issues in community sites is making clear who is speaking at any given time. People understand who's talking to them when they read a newspaper. A newspaper writer, who is a trusted voice that works for the newspaper, is saying something you can believe.

But when you add community features, you introduce a third voice, and one that's not always trustworthy. If your site has both official editorial and community contributions, it's imperative that you differentiate the two visually.

It gets more complicated, too. If you have official moderators or hosts, they speak with more authority than the rest of the posters. They, too, need to be visually distinguished.

Design can answer each of these issues in delightfully non-verbal ways. Simply changing a font color slightly to increase or decrease contrast can communicate a lot of information.

Color cues in Kvetch Chat (kvetch.com/chat) help communicate who's talking.

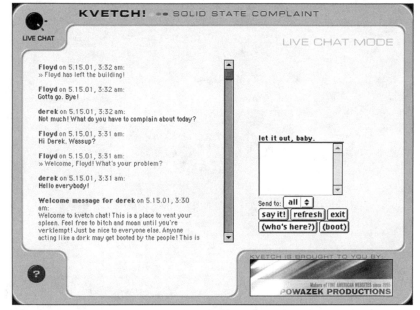

For example, in Kvetch Chat, the system automatically welcomes you as you enter and announces the arrivals and departures of people in the chat room. Since this is an automated message, it was important to differentiate it from the text that was coming from other real people. So I changed the font color just slightly to decrease the amount of contrast between the text and the background. This calls attention to the chat participants, because they are higher contrast, and lets the less important system messages recede into the background a bit.

Everything Is Design

After reading all this, you may be ready to throw your hands up and say, "Forget it—I won't design it at all!" If only it were that easy.

There is design to everything in the world. The key is giving it a push in the right direction.

Don't let all the advice in this chapter scare you away. This is all simply to get you headed in the right direction, perhaps with a little more to think about. In the end, as with all things, design is a subjective, personal business, for the designer and the users. The most important thing is to create a design that speaks to your audience. The rest is icing.

Steven Johnson

A Conversation with Steven Johnson

Steven Johnson has been designing sites with a strong interplay between magazine-style content and rich community functionality for as long as the web's been around. As co-founder of the experimental webzine FEED (feedmag.com) and its associated community area the Loop, he's learned a lot about the way interface design influences community. As one of the founding partners of Automatic Media, he's now working on Plastic.com—a site built on the same engine as Slashdot.org, but with a different audience in mind. I spoke with him over email during April 2001.

Steven, please give us a brief introduction to who you are and what you do, specifically your work in community and the web.

Over the last six or seven years, I've tried to play a dual role with respect to online communities—I've tried to be an advocate and critic with my writing, particularly in my books *Interface Culture* and my new book *Emergence*, and I've had a hand in building a few influential communities on the web, at FEED and at our new site Plastic. If there's a theme that connects both roles, it's the idea of seeing the web as a potentially urban form, capable of the open-ended, self-regulating, serendipitous interaction between strangers that characterizes the best urban environments. Cities are great examples of how collective intelligence can be harnessed to create higher-level organization—it's my hope that the web could be capable of the same thing.

Let's talk about FEED and the Loop. I've always been a fan of the way you mix content and community—bringing a quality post up and running it alongside the article text. What lessons have you learned about the structure of community features in your years in the Loop?

When I look back at our early experiments with FEED, I'm amazed we managed to do as much as we did, given the resources we had at the time. We programmed the Loop in-house at a time when FEED was only five people, and Irwin Chen and I collaborated on the design and functionality, while Irwin wrote all the code. There were actually two key ideas for our Loop design that we were very excited about at the time. The first is what you mention: We wanted the site to automatically pull out recent comments and put them in the margins of the "official" articles, giving our community members a place on the main stage of FEED. That worked out fine, and, in fact, we still use that basic functionality now, even though we've switched over to the Plastic community tools for our discussions.

But the other idea we had was that we wanted the Loop to be designed so that you could respond to specific sections of articles. You'd read a particularly incendiary middle section of an essay, and you'd want to respond directly to that section, not to the entire piece. So, in our original design, there were four or five Loops per article, which made the system work more like an annotation system than a traditional message board. (This was modeled after our FEED Documents, where we'd invite a panel of commentators to hypertextually annotate a book excerpt or speech, etc.)

It was an interesting feature, but it fundamentally failed, because it made the original article too important, and it splintered off all the potential responses into different subsections. When our community members posted in the loop, they were usually not posting in response to specific passages; they were posting because they wanted to get into a conversation on the general topic of the original piece. By breaking the conversation into separate annotations, we dampened the outbreak of big 50–100 post threads, which are what really drive the community environment at a site like FEED.

At FEED, you've been through several major redesigns over the years. How has visual design influenced the quality of discussion in the Loop? Did different designs inspire different flavors of community?

Well, let me answer the question in a slightly different way. The different designs invariably inspired a very specific response from the community, which was an intensely passionate—and sometimes intensely critical—

meta-thread about the design changes. After our first design change, we made it very clear that every new look was a public beta, and we expected to change things in response to what the Loopies had to say. Those are some of my favorite threads in FEED's history, actually—despite the fact that folks were often quite critical.

It can be hard to take critical feedback on a new redesign. It seems like everybody has a passionate opinion. How do you sort out the valuable feedback from the angry noise?

Well, here's my own home-brewed technique: If you assume that critics are twice as likely to write in as fans are, then any feature that is doing 50/50 pros versus cons is probably a hit with the great majority of the audience. But you also have to pay attention to the details of the critiques—if there's a sizable group that keeps weighing in with the same justifications for a complaint, then you start to pay more attention, even if they're in the minority. You don't want to make the process turn into a pure popularity contest.

Let's talk about your newest project, Plastic.com. What's the Big Idea here?

The big idea is that communities online have moved beyond message boards, and the post-a-response-to-published-article format. On FEED, the community always played a secondary role, albeit a more prominent one than at many content sites. At Plastic, the community does just about everything. They submit stories—in the form of links and short commentary—which are posted on the front door; they discuss stories in a relatively traditional message board format; and they rate other contributions from users, separating out signal from noise. So the community is authoring the content, commenting on it, and filtering/editing the content. It's a great system—the community really feels like the site belongs to them, because it does. We have two people running the site because we wanted to make sure that the front door write-ups had a distinctive flavor to them, and because communities need leaders. But it could theoretically run without any supervision.

Plastic was built on top of the same engine as Slashdot, but you've made some changes. What did you change and why?

We made the site much more user-friendly throughout, and changed quite a bit of the default language. We added a number of new features, like an internal Plastic Notes email service, and the ability to see overviews of all the stories posted about a given topic. We've also done quite a bit to promote the Karma system, which was what both Plastic and Slashdot call the reputation-management tools built into the code. Users who contribute highly rated stories and posts to Plastic accumulate Karma points—we started rewarding each week's highest Karma accumulators through a little contest. (There's literally a scoreboard on the front door of the site, with winners announced each week.) It's a nice mix, I think: It encourages good community behavior, and at the same time, it doesn't take itself too seriously. Of course, we had an epic meta-thread about the Karma contest and what it would do for the community when we announced it. But if that thread didn't break out, I'd be really worried.

Plastic has been online for about three months now. How has the response been? Any surprises?

I think the most striking surprise has been how political the site has become—thanks almost entirely to the responses of the users. When Joey and Tom first started, I think they had no idea really what the most popular topics would be—popular being defined as "most likely to generate 100+ post threads." Very quickly it was clear that political threads—whether about George W.'s environmental policies, racial profiling, or the Nader Left—were tremendous discussion generators on Plastic. And so the site quickly became a political and pop culture site, rather than a pop culture site with some occasional political threads. It was the right decision to make, of course, but it wasn't as though we were really in control of the decision.

With FEED and now Plastic, you've been designing community spaces for a good long time. Based on that experience, when it comes to the visual design of community spaces, what do you think works and what doesn't?

Well, I know a lot of people will disagree with this, including a few at Automatic Media, but I think the overall lesson I've learned is that text is far, far more important in community space design than any kind of visual metaphor. People want information fast when they come to a site like Plastic and FEED, and they want as much detail as possible about changes in that information since they were last there. Swapping out a lead graphic can be helpful in that respect, but for the most part, text is still the most efficient delivery vehicle for that kind of information. I'd much rather have a dozen sidebars on Plastic showcasing text accounts of user activity on the site (most popular user, most highly rated post, most active thread, etc.) than a giant Flash-based map of the community space. But maybe that's just me.

Chapter 4

Tools for Doing the Heavy Lifting

...How to Power Your Community

The problem with writing about tools is that they change too fast. I can promise you that as soon as the ink hits this page, right when this book is rolling off the presses and into a box, headed for a store near you, at that very moment, one of the companies I mention in this chapter will go out of business, one of the products I criticize will put out a new version that nullifies everything I had to say about it, and one of the programmers I profile will get fed up with the web biz altogether and take up underwater basket weaving.

It's a bet.

Still, no practical discussion of virtual communities would be complete without a glance behind the curtain at the gritty backend, where all the heavy lifting takes place. So let's talk about tools. Just remember that this is not going to be an all-inclusive list of every community software package out there, nor will it be software reviews to make *Consumer Reports* proud.

Instead, this is going to be an exercise in how to go about deciding on a tool to power your community, an overview of the different genres of tools out there, and a selection of a few noteworthy examples. Then we'll end with a conversation with the gurus behind jGuru (jguru.com), a site for the Java developers' community that's had experience with both adapting to someone else's tools and coding its own.

To Buy or Not to Buy?

Let's start with the fundamental question. If you're going to have community features on your site, you're going to need some server-side software to accomplish the task. There are two ways to get that software: You can buy it, or you can build it. Each comes with its own set of advantages and disadvantages.

Buy it

There are some amazingly powerful community packages out there, if you can afford them. Buying software is nice, because it often comes with someone who will take care of installing and configuring it on your server, leaving you to do all the fun stuff.

But buying has its downside, too. It can be expensive—some packages come with charges that get more and more expensive the more successful you are. Do you really want to be paying for your software by the user, message, or month? And, of course, sometimes companies go out of business, in which case that expensive software you bought just became worthless, because there's no one left to support it.

If you are going to buy, be sure you get everything in writing, and ask all the tough questions right up front. Does this come with technical support? Who do I call if it stops working? Who will help me integrate this with my current site? How much is it going to cost?

Build it

Nine times out of ten, you'll be better off building something yourself that's custom fit to your needs. The advantages of this are that you're not at the mercy of another company when something goes wrong, and there are no hidden charges.

Of course, that doesn't mean that it's going to be any less expensive. If you're like me, you know Photoshop like the back of your hand, but databases and programming languages? It's time to call in a friend.

To build your own, you either need to be a programmer, have a talented programmer friend, or an employee. Still, this takes work, too. If you're going to start talking to a programmer, you're going to need a very clear vision of what you want built, how it looks, and how it works. Programmers tend to get grumpy when you change your mind a lot.

It is possible to do this on the cheap, though. There are a number of free scripts floating around on the web (more on that later), and sometimes all it takes is a programmer to sit down with one and hack it to do your bidding.

But, in the end, it all depends on what you want out of your site and your community. So before you can really decide to buy or build, you have to decide what you want to create.

Getting the Vision

Every backend, whether bought or built, comes with design limitations. Some packages have a standard set of buttons that you can't change. Sometimes, you can change the look of the buttons, but not their placement. Some systems always look a little boxy, some always look a little plain.

Every package comes with its own quirks and peculiarities. The trick is to find the one that matches your own the closest.

I suggest you begin by writing a document that outlines your community area in the broadest sense. Summarize what you want users to be able to do and what the goals of the project are.

Then take that one step further and get specific. Write a user scenario—a first-person story about a user of your site and how the user interacts with it. Describe the steps the user goes through to view and participate in your community area.

If you don't know what those steps would be, that's an important discovery. I'd advise you to go out and participate in some community forums. Pay attention to the steps you have to take to participate. Try to think of ways to do it better.

Once you've got a specific, step-by-step guide for how you want your users to interact with the site and each other, it's time to build a prototype. Forget about the backend for now—just build static pages that show how things look. This is an important exercise, because it's not until you start putting pixels to screen that you realize just how many controls and interface widgets you're going to need.

You may feel tempted at this point to cheat—to go look at how other community sites have solved these problems and just adopt their solutions. I urge you to forge ahead on your own path. There are many horrible design elements and interface mistakes that get passed on from site to site this way. And besides, just because another site does it a certain way doesn't mean that would be a good solution for your site. Forge ahead, and design tools that match and complement your site.

Once you have the prototype done to your satisfaction, then it's time to start looking at backend tools. If you're considering buying, look around at the sites that are powered by the tool you're considering. Pay attention to their design similarities. If they all have certain things in common (placement of interface widgets, certain icons, etc.), it's a fair bet that the tool is not customizable in that area. If your design doesn't match the examples, look around for another tool. Of, if you do move forward with buying a tool, having your prototype done will help you in your negotiations. You can show the salesman your documents and the prototype and ask good, specific questions. "I see in the demo that the next post button is there, but as you can see in my prototype, I want to have that button here. Is that going to be possible?"

If you're going to build, having ample documentation and a well-thought-out prototype will make your programmer's day. Expect the programmer to happily disappear into a dark room, only to emerge a week later with six empty pizza boxes, countless cans of flat Jolt cola, and the perfect backend software.

The bottom line is, it's up to you to have a clearly articulated vision for your community functionality before you begin the process of finding the backend software to power it. The last thing you ever want to do is just get the software and build the community around it, because you'll wind up with a half-baked, disconnected site that looks like everybody else's.

Let's Go Shopping

So, you say you've got a clear vision of what you want, and you're ready to find the perfect backend? Okay. Buckle up. Let's go shopping.

There are hundreds of different tools out there for hundreds of different sites. But in my experience in the web community biz, I've categorized four different genres of community tools. Here they are, cheapskates first.

Web-based: Just add people!

There are some really powerful web-based tools out there to jumpstart a community. On the positive side, these sites enable you to sign up and have some powerful community features at your fingertips in minutes. And usually, they're absolutely free.

Take a look at CommunityZero (communityzero.com), for example. There you can set up a community area in five minutes flat. You can choose from a wide assortment of features (polls, message board, chat, file uploads), set user privileges individually or as a group, and even set the access level for your community (open to the public, invitation only, or closed).

CommunityZero does a good job of interlinking content and community, too. For example, you can upload a document and associate a specific discussion with it. And when you retire a poll, you can automatically start a thread to discuss the findings. Very smart.

And, best of all, it's free. There's a limit to how much server space you can take up, and if you exceed it, you've got to start paying. But it's possible to run a small community there for months and come nowhere near the limit.

But, like any web-based tool, there are limitations. The biggest of which is that, essentially, you're creating a site out of a cookie-cutter mold. CommunityZero is very good at making a certain kind of site that looks and works a certain way. The tool allows for very little deviation from that norm.

So, while you can change the color of the bar on the left and upload a custom photo to the top of it, that bar will always be there. The navigation will always be in the same spot. And you have almost no control over the presentation of the content itself.

Finally, if your goal is to have a community feature that integrates with an existing site, the closest you'll come to that here is linking from one to the other. CommunityZero sites exist only on the CommunityZero server, so it will always be separate from the rest of your site.

I used CommunityZero while writing this book to create an interim community site and had mixed results. While the tools were powerful, I was frustrated by the lack of customizability. And since the sites were set up to host many conversations on many subjects, each thread was several clicks away from the home page—nested in a folder that you couldn't get rid of. There was also no way to view more than one post on a page, so it became laborious to click though a whole conversation. Finally, since the

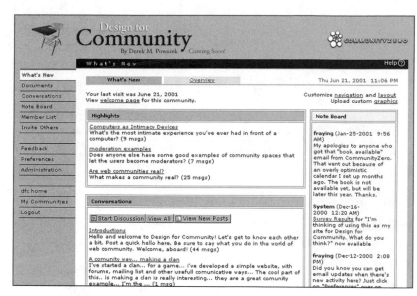

The CommunityZero-powered Design for Community community (communityzero.com/dfc).

site is frames-based, and uses obfuscated URLs for the pages, it was impossible to link from a page on my site to a specific thread in the community. That meant I had to break one of my own cardinal rules—I couldn't interlink content and community.

As a result of all these things, I found that conversations tended to die out quickly or continue on without focus. So, while the tools were powerful, the implementation and lack of customizability were a turnoff. I recommend sites like this and Yahoo Groups (groups.yahoo.com) as training-wheel community sites. They're great to experiment with and learn what works and what doesn't, without having to install any software or spend any money. But for long-term community building, I suggest looking elsewhere.

A free lunch (and other bedtime stories)

Another genre of community tools to consider is the open source, shareware, or freeware that's all over the web. Some of these programs are truly works of genius, hacked on and perfected by programmers all over the world, using the Net to work in concert. And some are aborted first-attempts or worse.

This genre is alluring because the software itself is free. You can download it, tweak it, put it on your server, and use it absolutely free (some open source projects have conditions, though). What is not included, however, is installation, customization, support, or maintenance.

So, while you may save some money in purchasing the software, don't think that these free options are without cost. The costs are just different.

That aside, there are some incredibly powerful programs out there. Slashdot (a great community site, described in more detail in Chapter 6) has open sourced its engine, called Slash. It's free to download and use.

What that means is that, if you want a site that looks and acts like Slashdot, that's easy to make with Slash. But, again, if you want your site to depart from that model, you'll either have to hire a programmer to hack the program to make it do what you want, or keep shopping for another tool.

The Net is littered with other free software tools, so I suggest taking a spin on your favorite search engine looking for "free discussion tools"—you never know what you might find.

Cheap and cheerful

If the web-based options weren't for you, and the free lunch options looked too spicy for your taste, maybe it's time to consider going with a member of the next genre: low-cost tools. These are programs that cost a few hundred bucks to set up and use, and have pretty good functionality. And since the companies are actually making a little money on them, chances are, they'll continue to be developed.

The leader in this space is Infopop (infopop.com), the creators of one of the bellwethers of community tools, the Ultimate Bulletin Board (or UBB for short). UBB-driven sites are everywhere, from personal homepages to professional sites. Infopop also makes

UBB's younger, more expensive cousin, OpenTopic. Pricing and specifics run the gamut between the two of them, from hosted versions to installed ones, from a couple hundred bucks for a lifetime license, to thousands a year, depending on the features you want and the size of your organization.

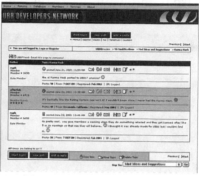

Two UBB-powered sites. See the structural similarities?

UBB is the leader in the cheap and cheerful category, because it's all over the web. In fact, it's so common, its interface has become a kind of de facto standard. The only problem is that the look and feel of UBB is so distinctive and so hard to change. The standard UBB look is boxes upon boxes. So, if you had a boxy design in mind from the beginning, you're in luck. But if you had something else in mind, too bad.

Personally, I find UBB extremely hard to use. The standard navigation elements are hard to find, and when a conversation thread reaches the point where it splits into multiple pages, the secondary pages are a pain to get to. Worse, the administration features are placed in plain view of everyone in the forum. (Why crowd the interface for everyone when only administrators are able to use the feature?) Finally, the design variations are very limited, so every UBB-powered site looks remarkably like every other one, which is bad if you're trying to differentiate yourself from a crowded market. Though I know people who swear by the system, many of whom are even mentioned as great examples in this book, to me, as a designer, it just feels clunky.

In the end, if you want a system you can really customize, you're going to have to pay for the privilege.

Swimming with the pros

Ready to get in with the likes of the New York Times? Got some cash to throw around? Welcome to the world of the big fish.

Two Prospero-powered sites. They have distinct colors, but the differences end there.

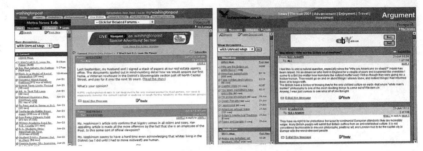

Companies such as Prospero Technologies and Web Crossing power some of the biggest community sites online. Prospero Technologies (prospero.com), itself the combination of old-school community software makers Delphi Forums and Well Engaged, can claim many newspaper sites, several record companies, as well as CBS and FOX broadcasters. Web Crossing (webcrossing.com) has been around for years and can take the blame for Salon, CNN, and the New York Times' discussion areas.

Packages like this run into the thousands and can do almost everything you could ask for, although sophisticated web-based discussion is still their bread and butter.

Yet the same rule still applies to the big fish—each technology begets a site that looks and acts like every other site with that backend. A thread at the New York Times looks very similar to a thread at Salon, because they're both powered by Web Crossing. Sites powered by Prospero have strikingly similar looks to them. So if your goal is to really integrate your community functionality with the content of your site (which is what I strongly recommend), even the big fish aren't completely up to the task.

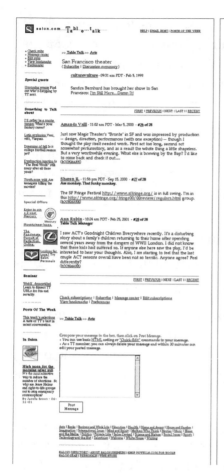

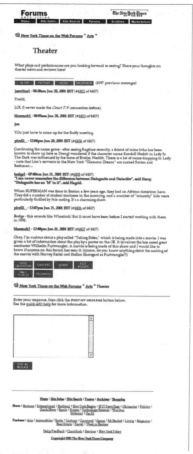

Salon's "Table Talk" (tabletalk.salon.com) and the New York Times' Forums (forums.nytimes.com) are both powered by Web Crossing. Again, note the similarities in the structure of these thread pages.

Deciding What's Right for You

Of course, there's nothing necessarily wrong with any of the sites mentioned above. If one of the examples above is the perfect match for your site, by all means go for it. But if you want your community areas to look different from the rest of the crowd, you may want to consider hiring someone to make something custom. It means a little more development time in the beginning of your project, but it's worth it if you get the community site of your dreams.

If you're still undecided, here are some considerations to ponder when making the decision.

Hosted or integrated? Do you want someone to host your site for you, or do you want to keep all the functionality on your site? Different tools have different hosting requirements, so know what you want starting out. (I recommend keeping it all in your site, if for no other reason than it begets member trust to not have to leave your site to discuss your content.)

Uptime? If you're looking at a hosted or web-based tool, inquire about server uptime. The worst feeling in the world is going to your forums and finding they've gone AWOL, thanks to someone else's server.

Features? Know what you want to enable your users to do, both today and tomorrow. Then look for a tool that accomplishes this (not the other way around).

Expandability? If you settle on a tool, can you add features tomorrow? Is the system closed to outside innovation? If you have programmer friends, and expandability is important to you, consider going with an open source project like Slash, so that you can work on it, too.

Design customization? This is perhaps the most important question for designers. Ask the people selling the tool: Can I move that button? Can I lose the frames? Can I format the posts to match the site? Most of the tools out there fall very short of the mark in this category.

Design First

Picking a backend system is one of the most important decisions you have to make. Unfortunately, it's also one of the hardest, because you'll have to make it in the beginning before you have much input from your future community members. Community sites are, by nature, evolutionary, so your site could take off faster than expected, requiring more robust tools. Or, on the other hand, you could start out with more features than you need, which could backfire and turn people away.

If you're just dipping your toe into the community space for the first time, try starting out with a free web-based tool. There are the obvious shortcomings (lack of design control, offsite hosting, poor interlinking), but it's free and will allow you to begin a conversation with your community and gather feedback from your users on what they want. Doing this for a while can teach you some valuable lessons and help prepare you for designing a tool of your own.

In the end, just remember that every tool comes with its own set of design constraints. So design first, then decide on a tool. And when in doubt, build.

A Conversation with the jGurus

jGuru (jguru.com) is a great example of a niche community site with a specific problem to solve. In the beginning, it used a commercial backend product to help power the site. But as it grew, it needed a much more powerful tool, so Chief Scientist Terence Parr and CEO Thomas Burns wrote their own backend.

While their story isn't universal (how many startups are lucky enough to have a Chief Scientist who studied linguistics and pattern recognition in college?), it tells a common tale of outgrowing a backend system. In their case, the jGurus wound up building something entirely customized, unavailable anywhere else, and perfectly suited to their needs. And it's no wonder. When Parr talks about the system, he starts to confuse his pronouns. Several times in our interview, he said "I" to describe the actions of the system. With people this passionate at the helm, it's little wonder jGuru's community is thriving.

I spoke with the jGurus over email and phone in mid-2001.

Please introduce yourself and jGuru.

Burns: I'm Tom Burns, the CEO of jGuru, which is the largest independent site for Java developers. It features over 5,000 answered Java questions, 40+ Java forums, 14 Java training courses, articles from the major Java sites, and news. I co-founded jGuru because I was frustrated at how bad companies were at marketing to and supporting developers (I have 13 years experience writing software). I also decided that the absence of a good/cost-effective means of reaching developers greatly slowed down the progress of software. If it takes a huge amount of money to get developers to look at a new technology, there will not be many successful new technologies. The goal of jGuru is to improve the situation—make it less expensive for companies to provide developers with the information they want and less

Tom Burns

Terence Parr

Photos by Heather Champ

expensive to reach them (hopefully putting developers in reach of smaller companies).

Parr: I'm Terence Parr, the Chief Scientist at jGuru, responsible for the implementation of the software that generates the jGuru website, and an all-around nice guy. jGuru is a portal for Java developers that provides all the tools they need to do their job. Basically, I call it "your view of the Java universe."

In the beginning, you used a commercial backend product to help power the site. What were the pros and cons of this?

Burns: The biggest advantage was eliminating choices! I know that sounds strange. We were in a big hurry, and I (correctly, it turned out) assumed that everything we thought was important would be wrong. So I didn't want us to worry too much about the detail—just get something up that was worth criticizing. The product that we used (Epicentric) had a definite bias with regard to site design, and it forced us to use its approach. I think it would have taken much longer to get the site done if we had started with a blank slate. Ultimately, we ended up completely changing our site design, and Epicentric was no longer appropriate.

Parr: In general, I've found that, as a fairly experienced hardcore technoid, the things that other people want tend to annoy me. So 90 percent of their effort goes into making the software soft and fluffy, with a great web interface, which is really irritating for me.

How do I install that on a machine by just unzipping something? I can't—I've gotta go *click click click*, delete this guy, *click click click*, add that guy. It was annoying as a programmer, because, in general, the things that people will provide are for people unlike me.

Even if you do like fluffy interfaces, in general, you're gonna be able to beat it, if you have the time and expertise, you're gonna be able to do a much better job yourself.

Ultimately, you decided to code your own backend. Why did you make this decision? How was the transition?

Burns: The transition was fairly easy for us. Epicentric was really in the middle—we did the back and the very front. The new design of the site was fairly easy to implement in the sense that it has just a couple of concepts (basically, view lists sorted and filtered in various ways).

You've put a great deal of thought into creating your current custom backend. Tell us a little about it.

Burns: From a performance perspective, the biggest change we made to the backend is that we put everything except "person records" in memory at startup (there are too many registered users to load them all). This makes a *huge* difference in both complexity (it is much simpler) and performance. I would recommend it to anyone who inherently has a manageable amount of data (our machines have a gig of RAM). Other big features are that we made the look templatized—we can change the look by just changing a few files.

Parr: Our goal is to build a great set of FAQs. We have managers who used to answer questions. People would submit questions, and if they were good enough, we'd add them to the FAQ. So we had a human who was the direct interface to the outside world.

So there was a choke point there, right? It had to be the expert who answered your question, and they had to have the time to get to it. So we came up with a highly structured forum that was really just a series of questions, and then everybody could answer them. That way you don't have to wait to get your question answered by the expert at the choke point. Anybody can do it.

Then the expert, who's now a manager, could come in and say, "Hey, that was a great answer!" and promote it, pull it out of the forums, edit it, and stick it into the FAQ.

So you've got the jGuru community answering each other's questions. But how do you keep the forums from discussing the same questions that are already answered in the FAQ?

Parr: What we do is, when you submit a question, we search for an appropriate answer and provide you with a list of potentials, in an effort to say, "Here's the answer." That way the system automatically tries to reduce the amount of noise in the forums.

Further, it tries to guess when you're in the wrong forum. You don't want someone in the database forum asking a question about building a GUI (Graphical User Interface). So, if someone does that, the system says, "There's an above average chance that you're in the wrong forum. I suggest one of these topics." Then the user can just click on it and switch to the right forum.

The system also tries to detect when you haven't said anything about Java. So if somebody just says, "Hey, what's this site about?" or posts a thigh cream commercial, the system says, "You know, there's not a single word in there that I recognize as part of the Java lexicon. So click here to re-edit and add something that has to do with Java."

How do you know what is and isn't Java talk?

Parr: We have a fuzzy logic search engine that tries to strip out everything but the important keywords in your question. Then I do a fuzzy comparison against all of the other FAQ entries in our system. I do this not by which FAQs have these keywords, but by how important these keywords are in that particular FAQ. In other words, how often they're used, and the frequency of the use of that word, and how important this document is compared with the rest, so I can bubble the most important one to the top.

The way we started this system was to spider the New York Times website. I got, I dunno, 250,000 words. And I said, okay, that's English. And then I spidered our own website, and I said, that's Java. And then, to distinguish the Java lexicon from the English, I did some complicated fuzzy logic stuff that revealed a set of keywords that are specific to Java.

Because those words don't appear in the New York Times?

Parr: Well, they may appear in the New York Times, but it's a difference in their usage. For example, the word "compile" is probably at the New York Times website. However, when you're talking about Java, it's used *way* more. So, if a word is overused in the Java lexicon, and underused, relatively speaking, in English, I say, "Aha! That's Java."

So once I get a definition of what Java looks like, I can take any question you ask me, strip out all the English words, and then do pattern matching to figure out what you're talking about.

So in the "buy vs. build" debate, you're on the build side?

Burns: I am actually generally for buying when you can, but Ter prefers to build (and he is the one actually doing all the work, so his vote trumps mine). One thing to watch out for when "buying" is that integration can be a nightmare—if you can't buy something that does almost everything you need, you will probably be better off building.

The biggest advantage to our approach—a fully custom site—is that it is all very integrated and easy to maintain. We can build a new jGuru box and get a site up with just a few commands.

Parr: If you don't have the expertise, buy. It's as simple as that.

One of the things I would recommend is: Keep your setup as simple as possible. For example, Oracle (databases) have to have several partitions on the disk, you gotta have a full-time administrator, it's just a mess. We had a very simple database problem, so we bought a very simple database (from Solid Technology) that runs on a small amount of memory. It installs by unzipping the thing. You back it up by copying a file! That solves a huge amount of trouble.

Also, use stuff where you have the source. Like we use Apache (web server). Use free tools if you know that they are good and you get the source. Just make it as simple as possible.

Chapter 5

Policies and Policing

...Setting, Communicating, and Enforcing the Rules

He liked cheese.

That's all I knew about "Dangerman" when he posted to my personal site (powazek.com). He liked cheese.

Unfortunately, he posted that comment to a long, emotional story I'd told about growing up. My twenty-eighth birthday was on its way, and I'd grown nostalgic for my college days. I wrote: "So I'm sitting here on this rainy Friday, in an apartment in San Francisco, almost 10 years later, looking out over the rooftops of the city. I'm wondering if 10 years really is a long time or not. I'm wondering if this is the kind of melancholic nostalgia that old people feel."

"I like cheese," he posted.

Cheese.

So I deleted the post. It was easy enough to do. And it seemed so clear—everyone else was posting appropriate comments to my stories. He must have been confused, or perhaps he had a screw loose. In any case, it was my site, and the post was inappropriate, so I deleted it.

And, in doing so, I walked into a trap I should have seen coming.

The post reappeared a few minutes later. "I like cheese." I deleted it again. The poster wasn't leaving an email address, so I had no way of contacting him to explain the problem. Instead, I banned his IP address from the system, so he would be unable to post again. Then I went to sleep.

That night, Dangerman's friends started showing up. And they, too, liked cheese.

"I dreamt of cheese."

"Cheese is in!"

"I like cheese too. Cheese rules."

This was war.

I deleted all the posts, banned all their IPs, and closed off the thread. Eventually, I got to Dangerman's site to find my site, and my person, being burned in effigy. Bravely (or perhaps stupidly), I posted there, myself. I politely explained why I had deleted the posts and was resoundingly booed off the stage.

Lesson Learned

In the wake of what has become lovingly known as The Great Cheese-Off of 2001, I began to reevaluate the cues my site was giving to users. It's true that most people had been able to figure out what was appropriate and what wasn't without much guidance from me. The only verbal cues I'd provided were a disclaimer right above the posting button. It said:

> This is my personal site. It's like my living room. I don't let anyone come into my living room and say whatever they want. Posting to my site is a privilege, not a right. If

you post inappropriate things, they will be deleted, and you will lose the ability to do so in the future. In other words, be nice. Thanks.

While this seemed pretty clear to me, it was obvious that it wasn't doing the job. So after some reflection, I made two changes to the user experience of my site.

Change 1: Change the disclaimer

First, I changed the disclaimer above. Even though I felt it was perfectly clear before ("If you post inappropriate things, they will be deleted"), that statement was getting lost in the text. Also, it never defined what "inappropriate things" were.

The new version was:

> This is my personal site. It's like my living room. I hope you'll come in, have a seat, and be cool. But if you're not and you post something off-topic, mean, or just plain stupid, I will delete it and kick you out. **I reserve the right to delete any post for any reason.** I also reserve the right to believe that people are essentially good, in spite of overwhelming evidence to the contrary. Thank you.

In addition to defining what the verboten behavior was ("off-topic, mean, or just plain stupid"), the line in bold was the most important touch. The new phrasing was much more direct, and the bold made sure it was hard to overlook. And the whole disclaimer was placed below the posting form and above the button that users would click to commit to their post. Its placement was designed to make it hard to ignore.

The placement of the rules should make it hard to ignore.

Change 2: Get an email address

Next, I made the email address field required. Before, leaving an email address was optional. That meant when Dangerman posted his inappropriate post, I had no way to communicate with him outside the forum. If I had, I might have been able to avoid the whole scenario by emailing him privately. Making this change also meant introducing some new error messages and explanatory text that clarified that the email address was only required for our records, and would not be posted publicly.

Would someone be able to spoof the email address requirement? Of course. There's nothing stopping anyone from posting to the site as "billgates@microsoft.com" or "foo@bar.com." But, interestingly, since making this change, no one has.

The idea here is to give me a way to contact people who are posting inappropriately *by mistake*. If someone with good intentions accidentally violates the rules of the site, he'll be happy to hear it from me personally, instead of just returning to find his post missing.

Of course, if someone is looking for trouble, he'll always find a way to make it, and requiring an email address will only slow him down for a moment. But I'm not worried about offending troublemakers by removing their posts. I'm only worried about contacting those who make an honest mistake.

And I'm happy to report that, since making these changes, the comment forms on my site have been completely free of cheese.

Unseen Rules Aren't Rules at All

Like it or not, every community site comes with a set of rules. There is behavior that is welcome, and behavior that is not. And no matter how elegantly designed your site is, when push comes to shove, you still need to have rules.

The challenge, then, is to set the rules wisely, communicate them clearly, and enforce them fairly.

Step 1: Set rules wisely

Nobody likes following the rules, least of all the average Joe on the Net. The Internet, even now in 2001, is still rich with the ethos of the hacker. The web is the place where everything is free, and you can do whatever you want, remember?

So it's up to you to set the rules for your site. If you don't, your users may set them for you. And you may not like the ones they come up with.

Thinking up some rules for your site can be a worthwhile exercise, because it forces you to think critically about what kind of material you want from your users. No matter what kind of site you're going to have, take this opportunity to ask yourself some tough questions: What is it you want your users to contribute? What do you want them *not* to do? Would a post like "I like cheese" be acceptable on your site? Can you think of a post that would be unacceptable?

Aside from the personal considerations, there are also some legal issues to consider. **The Digital Millennium Copyright Act (DMCA)** was signed into law in 1998, but its effects are still being sorted out.

Among other things, the DMCA stipulates that site owners are responsible for their site's content, even if it's a community site where members can post whatever they want. That means if one of your users posts, say, the lyrics to an entire song to your community site, you'll be held liable when the lawyers come calling. (Don't confuse this with Fair Use, which would be the case if your user posted one verse from a song in a discussion about great songs. Using a portion of a copyrighted work for comment and critique is still fair game—just like all the screenshots in this book!)

But don't worry, compliance is easy. The DMCA spells out, in excruciating legal detail, the process by which a complaint must be filed with you, and what you must do to make it right. Here's the Cliff's Notes version: Put up a notice on your site that specifies where copyright complaints should go (this is your Designated Agent, in legalese). If someone submits a copyright complaint, investigate it right away, and if there is indeed a copyright violation (someone has posted something that he does not own the copyright to, without the permission of the owner, in an instance that is not Fair Use), remove the material right away.

If you want to be ultra-secure, you can post a DMCA compliance page on your site that goes into greater detail about what a copyright infringement is and how to report one. For a great example of a compliance page, take a look at Bianca's, a long-standing web-based chat community that has a very specific compliance page (bianca.com/misc/dmca.html).

The bottom line is clear: Site owners are responsible for the content of their community areas. As a result, many sites state up front that reposting of copyrighted material in the community area is strictly prohibited. So long as you remove any disputed material in a timely manner, you won't have any legal worries.

In general, my advice to clients is to use that magic line from above: "I reserve the right to remove any post for any reason." This covers you, no matter what. And while users may not like it, if you prove that anything within the bounds of acceptable behavior will stay on the site, they'll still participate. In the end, the "any post for any reason" is just a great last-ditch insurance policy.

Once you have a roadmap of what you do and don't want from your users, it's time to figure out how to break the news to your users.

Step 2: Communicate rules clearly

Rules are all well and good, but if they're not communicated to the user in a clear way, they might as well not exist. So the question becomes how to best communicate the rules in a community space?

First of all, there are several traditional documents that communicate the rules of a site. Depending on the depth of your community features, you should consider including some, if not all, of these documents on your site:

About—This page introduces the people and ideas behind the site.

Help—This is the user's first stop when she feels lost.

FAQ—The Frequently Asked Questions list can be a great way to help users do what they're trying to do. But be warned: If you keep getting the same questions, you may want to look for ways to insert help text where users need it, before they go looking for the FAQ.

Privacy Statement—This document outlines the user's rights in your community space. Here is where you should outline exactly what personal data, if any, you collect on each user and what you will and won't do with it.

Terms of Service—This is where you want to be as clear with your users as possible about the service you're offering and the terms it comes with.

Posting Guidelines—Sometimes, this is part of the Terms of Service; this is where you should outline what is and isn't allowed in the community areas.

These documents provide a wonderful opportunity for you to communicate with your users. I encourage you to use them to do more than simply tell your community what isn't acceptable, but to also explain a little more about who you are. How you communicate in these documents sometimes says more about you than your About page.

Ben and Jerry's, a company that makes some of the tastiest ice cream on the planet, has a site that does this quite well. Its Privacy Statement (benjerry.com/privacy.html) states very clearly what information it collects, and what it does with it. But a personal voice comes through to make you feel comfortable.

We keep everything we find out through our Web site to ourselves. Usually, we (the WebHeads) don't even share it with the marketing folks. We do not send spam, we do not solicit personal information from children, etc. We do accept voluntary subscriptions to e-mail and/or snail mail newsletters. If you want to hear from us, you have to ask.

Since Ben and Jerry's is a company that makes ice cream, it has to be clear about its relationship with children. So their Privacy Statement addresses them (and their parents) directly:

Hey KIDS! If you are under 16, please get your parents' permission before contacting us. We'd love to hear from you and your parents.

Hey PARENTS! Ben & Jerry's encourages children to ask their parents before submitting any information to us. There is software available that can keep children from giving out personal information online without parental permission. Of course, there is nothing better than personal supervision of your children while surfing the Net. For more information about parental control tools, please consult the "Privacy Action" page of the Direct Marketing Association home page (www.the-dma.org).

There's no reason you can't have fun with these documents, too. CitizenX.com, a community site that includes webcams and chat rooms, has a very entertaining Terms of Service document (citizenx.com/reg/terms.asp). It includes gems like: "If you're being a jerk, we have the right to de-activate your account and put gum in your hair." And: "In this lawsuit-happy day and age, we should probably add something here about liability. Basically, we're not responsible. Got it? If you see someone on their cam, you fall in love, then they turn out to be a deadbeat—it's not our fault."

Step 3: Communicate rules visually

Not long ago I got to watch the mother of a one-year-old baby in action. It was inspiring. Every time the child did something wrong, like pick up a sharp stick, the mom did not scream, "NO!" and whack it out of the infant's hands (which, admittedly, would have been my first reaction).

Instead, she simply offered him something more interesting. "Hey! Look at this!" she said, waving a red plastic lid in front of his face. "Woooo!"

And every time, the baby dropped the sharp thing and latched on to the toy like magic.

In the same way, it's always easier to guide users along the path than it is to bully them into behaving. Instead of being heavy-handed about it, a simple visual cue, at just the right time, can work wonders. (And, yes, I realize I just reduced all users to a metaphorical one-year-old. Sorry about that.)

Take, for example, the Blogger Discussion area (blogger.com/discuss). Blogger is a web application that I worked for in late 2000. Since the tool was web-based, it made sense to also have a web-based discussion area for peer-to-peer support. I oversaw the creation of what ultimately became Blogger Discuss.

The team and I used non-verbal cues in several places to guide the user at different stages. Icons turned orange to indicate activity, while inactive conversations turned gray, for example.

I also decided that we needed to communicate the rules of the site directly in a posting guidelines page. I wrote it to be short and to the point, with the most important ideas in bold for easy scanning:

> Thanks for taking part in Blogger Discuss. Please keep in mind a few simple rules for posting.
>
> 1. **Stay on topic.** If it's about the thread starter topic, everyone is happy. And please remember that this is a discussion area for Blogger. If it's not related to Blogger, it's probably off topic.
>
> 2. **Be nice.** Flames, insults and put-downs will be deleted.
>
> 3. **HTML will not be rendered.** That means you can include code examples, and they'll be visible. If you want to include a link, just start it with http:// and end with a space, and it will become a link.
>
> 4. **Replies are limited to 5,000 characters** (about a thousand words). If you submit a reply that is over the limit, you'll be asked to make it shorter.
>
> 5. **Blogger retains the right to delete any post for any reason.**

Now that we had the rules all spelled out in a document, I just had to figure out where to put it. If we put it in the About section, it would be completely out of sight. If we linked to it from the Discussion homepage, it would be more prominent, but still easily forgotten, since it was possible to navigate from section to section without ever going back to the homepage.

Then there was an additional problem: context. I wanted to place the posting guidelines as close to the actual posting mechanism as possible. But if we linked away to it, it would actually harm the users. Because, if the users had a half-composed post in the form and clicked away to a new page, they'd lose what they'd typed so far. And we couldn't just run the guidelines in the margin of all the

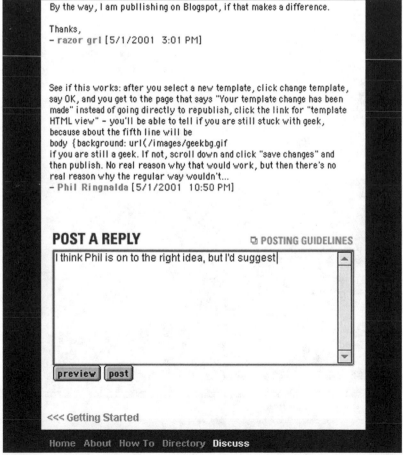

Note the "POSTING GUIDELINES" link above the post entry form.

threads—that would be a waste of space, not to mention visually annoying.

After a lot of thinking, I decided to insert the guidelines into the process where users were likely to need them: as they're posting. And instead of just putting the text on every page to the point of annoyance, or linking away to a new page, I placed it in a pop-up window, linked prominently from every posting form.

So, as users are posting, they're given a visual cue that there are posting guidelines. In fact, that link serves as a reminder, adjacent to every posting form. And the link's placement over the posting form reinforces its importance. The near-universal "new window"

The posting guidelines' pop-up window.

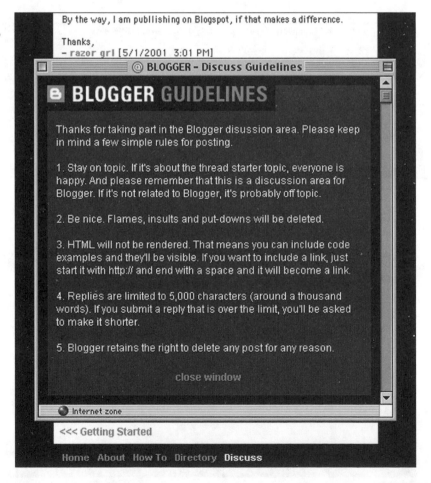

By the way, I am publishing on Blogspot, if that makes a difference.

Thanks,
– razor grl [5/1/2001 3:01 PM]

@ BLOGGER – Discuss Guidelines

BLOGGER GUIDELINES

Thanks for taking part in the Blogger disussion area. Please keep in mind a few simple rules for posting.

1. Stay on topic. If it's about the thread starter topic, everyone is happy. And please remember that this is a discussion area for Blogger. If it's not related to Blogger, it's probably off topic.

2. Be nice. Flames, insults and put-downs will be deleted.

3. HTML will not be rendered. That means you can include code examples and they'll be visible. If you want to include a link, just start it with http:// and end with a space and it will become a link.

4. Replies are limited to 5,000 characters (around a thousand words). If you submit a reply that is over the limit, you'll be asked to make it shorter.

5. Blogger retains the right to delete any post for any reason.

close window

Internet zone

<<< Getting Started

Home   About   How To   Directory   **Discuss**

icon to the left of the text tells users that this click will create a pop-up window (and won't take them away from their post).

If users click the link, they're presented with the posting guidelines in a pop-up window.

The guidelines are designed to be a quick read. Then, with the click of a mouse, the window is gone, and users are right back where they were, in context, with their half-composed post undisturbed.

Enforce the Rules

If you've done a good job of setting rules wisely and communicating them clearly, this last job should be something you don't have to do with a heavy hand. Or, at least, hopefully you won't have to do it too often. You never know when a cheese-lover is going to show up.

Unfortunately, no matter how elegant the design of a community space is, at some point you may have to step in and lay down the law. When that happens, it's time to call on your host.

The host of a web community is akin to the host at a party. In addition to enforcing the rules, the host speaks with authority, sets the tone, and makes sure all the guests are getting along. The importance of the role of the host depends on the depth of the community area and the complexity of the tools. But make no mistake, every community site has a host. And if you can't name who that person is, it's probably you.

Job description of a host

This is not a job for the faint of heart. The host acts as an enforcer of the rules, guardian of the gate, helper to those in need, and example to the community of how to behave. The host is the human face of the community, setting the rules and then sticking around to examine their impact. This is the person who people come to if they've got a beef or a question.

Clearly, this is a big job. In my experience, I've found that good hosts are harder to find than good designers. There's a certain Zen about hosting a web community. You need to be active enough to lead the way, but know when to fall silent and let the community lead itself. You need to know when to rise to the challenge of an angry user, and when to leave the flame bait alone. You need to be friendly in the face of trolls looking for trouble, to always act as an example of how you'd like the community to behave.

In other words, it shouldn't be you.

Let me explain. This book is primarily for designers, so when I say "you," I'm talking to the designer of the community space. All too often, the designer winds up acting as a host as well, a practice I've been a victim of on more than one occasion. Unfortunately, in my experience, the people who are very good at designing websites are usually not the same kind of people who are good at hosting and moderating them.

There are other reasons besides the personality dynamics. As the site designer, everything about the site is going to be obvious to you. But the host should be more attached to the community than the site. When the users cry out for a change (a new thread, a new feature, whatever they're passionate about), it's good for the host to be on their side. It's always easier to manage the community when you're with them than against them. But a site designer may be too attached to the site to hear the criticisms with an open mind.

So my advice is always to find someone to be a host besides the person (or people) who built the site. You can have multiple hosts, if your site is big enough, and you can even cull them out of the community itself. Just don't underestimate the importance of the role. Your hosts will create many users' first impression of the site. You want to make sure it's a good one.

How important is the host?

That depends on whom you ask.

Traditionally, "hostliness" has been next to godliness in the virtual community world. And many virtual community theories center on the idea of an all-knowing, all-powerful host to guide the community out of the darkness and into the light.

But, like most things on the web, it depends.

In some ways, the role of the host was overplayed in the past. When a system is poorly designed, or too large in scope, or just plain new to everyone, the role of the host is, of course, going to become hugely important.

On the other hand, if you're using the kind of small, elegantly designed, tightly focused community features advocated in this book, the role of the host is diminished. There is always a host—make no mistake. But the importance of the role depends on the complexity of the community space.

For example, ZDNet News (zdnet.com/zdnn) is a technology-related news site. There, each story is followed by a discussion

The call to action at the bottom of a ZDNet story.

thread on the same page as the story itself. The interaction here is bare-bones simple. A user reads the story and is presented with a call to "Talk back!" Clicking this presents the user with a form with just a few fields, only two of which are required: a name and a comment. There's not too much to explain here. (Not that the addition of a host would be unwelcome here—harsh words between posters are not uncommon.)

The ZDNet posting interface.

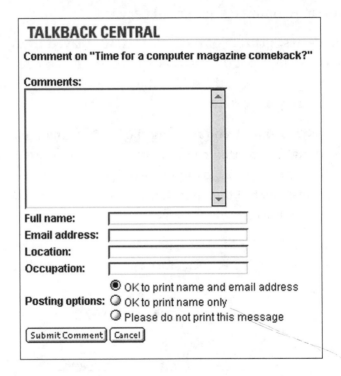

TALKBACK CENTRAL

Comment on "Time for a computer magazine comeback?"

Comments:

Full name:
Email address:
Location:
Occupation:

Posting options:
- ◉ OK to print name and email address
- ○ OK to print name only
- ○ Please do not print this message

[Submit Comment] [Cancel]

On the other hand, there are complicated sites like Table Talk (tabletalk.salon.com) and the discussion boards at CNN (community.cnn.com), where the user is presented with a barrage of options and a less than perfect set of visual cues. What to choose? Where to go? How does this thing work?

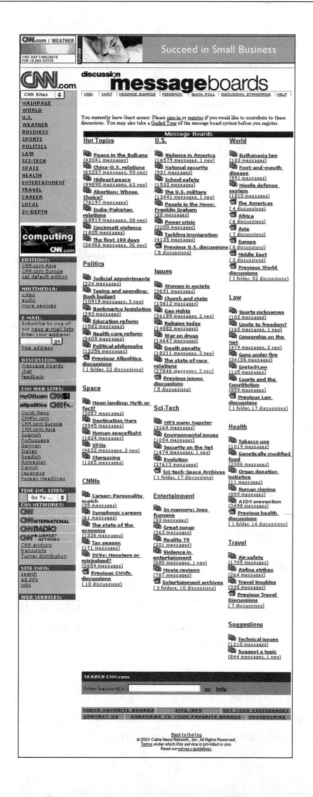

The river of blue links on CNN's community homepage. Where to go?

It's obvious that some sites will come to rely on hosts more than others. In general, the more tools you give your users, the more important the role of the host becomes. Good site design and clear navigation can minimize—but not eliminate—the role of the host.

If you're trying to decide how important the role of the host is to your site, try this test. Ask a friend or a relative to come participate in your community. This person should be a novice web user—a person with some experience in the web, but not an advanced user. Ask your volunteer to visit your site and participate in some way (more than just reading). If your volunteer has questions or comments, they should be written down in an email and sent to you.

If you get one or two questions, you're doing okay. Three or four? A host is pretty important. More than that and a host is downright critical (and you may have other problems in the design and interaction of the site, too).

Looking the part

No matter how important you determine the role of the host is in your site, having one user post with more authority than the others creates a design issue. It is crucial to communicate the host's authority visually; otherwise, any user could say, "Hey! I'm in charge! Listen to me!"

Sound fanciful? Tell that to whoever took the moniker "KVETCH CONTROL" in Kvetch.com. That person, whoever it was, told the visitors to Kvetch that they would all be evicted if they did not behave appropriately. He said that the site would be shut down if people didn't spell correctly

Of course, he wasn't the host—I was. But that didn't stop users from taking the posts seriously. When KVETCH CONTROL posted that the website had been infected with a virus, I got some very concerned emails from community members.

Aside from deleting the posts and fantasizing about smacking KVETCH CONTROL upside the head, there were only a couple of things I could do about the situation. Since Kvetch didn't require a registration, I couldn't ban the user. But I could block the user out by his IP address (which was available in the server logs). I also instituted a design change: From then on, whenever I posted something official, it was prefaced by "MODERATOR:" and the color was changed slightly so that the community would know that it was official. There was no way for anyone else to format his posts in the same way.

The main issue is that when someone with authority posts in the common space, his post has more weight. So his words should be differentiated visually as well.

Another good example of this is a site I designed for business guru and author Tom Peters in 1998. It was his first foray into the web, but he took to it with enthusiasm. At the top of his list of things he wanted out of the experience was the ability to converse with his readers—an ability his books lacked.

So when I designed his site, it came with a full complement of community tools. But Peters soon found that when he jumped into the community space, his words got lost in the cacophony.

The solution was a simple design change. When Peters posted to the community area, his comments were called out visually with a different background color. This subtle design change under-scored that this was his site, he was the authority here, and everyone took notice.

If you have hosts actively participating in your community space, you should consider a similar design solution. The change should be subtle, but different enough to be noticed. And it should be something that the community members are incapable of mimicking, lest you wind up with a KVETCH CONTROL of your own.

Barriers and Hosts

The egalitarian, inclusive, idealistic web is not dead. Far from it—the joy of the Internet is that everyone can have a voice, and there's always someone out there who wants to hear it. There really is a community out there for everyone.

But communities will implode without some structure, rules, and guidance. The rules you set also define your community, setting the tone for all the members. And the hosts maintain that tone, and nurture the members along the way.

When these elements work in concert, it benefits the entire community. The right people, with the right tools and just the right amount of guidance, can work wonders.

A Conversation with Caleb Clark

For the inside scoop on the Zen of hosting, I went to someone with more experience in the field than almost anyone I know.

Caleb Clark has been a host to countless communities over the last five years. From big sites like Netscape's Professional Connections, to smaller ones like Y-Ride, a community site for teenagers. Clark has the unique ability to be both supportive yet administrative, encouraging yet authoritative.

Caleb Clark

I spoke with Clark via email in early 2001 about what he's learned hosting communities in virtual places. His interview demonstrates all the things that make him a good host—he's exuberant and engaged, creative and attentive. Notice how he even compliments me on my questions. Clearly, this is a man who knows how to have a conversation.

I hope you find him as insightful and entertaining as I did.

Caleb, please give us a brief introduction to who you are and what you do, specifically your work in community and the web.

I'm a techno geek born and raised in the crossfire hurricane of the late 1960s, a flower child, not to be confused with a hippie like my mother. See man, my revolution is technology, power to the geeks. Grab your ray gun, Annie, we're going sci-fi story hunting!

OK … that was strange. Anyway, along the path of growing up, I was steeped in consensus-run groups, both successful and unsuccessful. There was a commune in the redwoods of Mendocino, California, the Haight in San Francisco, and three small free schools in New England that I attended up to sophomore year in high school.

This all resulted in a fairly flaky resume, elusive purpose at the hands of tremendous freedom, and 7 years/4 schools for a BA from ASU. My first formal flirtation with media and groups came with being a production assistant on several Hollywood feature location shoots. This was my first taste of a small group totally focused on one clear goal (screenplay), whose success depended a large part on good communication.

When the first *Wired Magazine* came out, I found myself working as a carpenter in Santa Fe, NM, while I freelanced for a local newspaper. After learning HTML and getting online, I followed *Wired* by moving to San Francisco and the web revolution in the mid-1990s, where I freelanced and wrote shorts for *Wired*. In January 1996, I was a lonely, small corporate webmaster so I started NoEnd, a group of web heads and artists hell bent on Humanizing Technology. My idea being that there must be other lonely webmasters out there doing a job they could not share, nor explain to hardly anyone.

We met upstairs in a North Beach cafe/bar and asked each other how our weeks were. Each week more and more people started showing up by word of mouth. Then a freelance web worker friend of mine, named Paul Vachier, who was thinking along the same lines groupwise came to a meeting with a bunch of folks he worked with. Paul and I then partnered up to grow this new entity called *NoEnd*. Since few people in the world had had weeks like ours, let alone understood our acronyms, the sharing became very popular, and we started using a warehouse for meetings. Big companies lined up to present to us. When they did, we insisted they sit on futons in the circle just like us, and cut short their presentations for ruthless Q&A. And they still came. We very quickly started a listserv that runs to this day. A hallmark of the NoEnd list is poetry, travel essays, family news, and personal sharing sprinkled in with a very high signal to noise ratio. I say without hesitation that the success of my professional and personal life is due in a large part to the people of NoEnd. NoEnd's success was definitely partly the luck of good timing and location, and it expanded quickly to what it is today, a quiet but vibrant and respected group of very experienced professionals who strive to humanize technology.

In 1997, I moved to San Diego to get a Masters Degree in Educational Technology at San Diego State University. I studied online community, usability, and stories. During this time, I was fortunate to work for

Netscape Inc. (Pre-AOL) as a host in their "Professional Connections" online community from Beta to launch and for a year of heavy participation, due to Netscape.com being a very high traffic site. After my MA, I taught graduate web development courses (both in person and online) at SDSU for a year with each class having its own online community. This gave me the interesting opportunity to host the birth to death cycle of six communities. I recently completed a year of doing the dot-com dance as director of online community and project management at an irrational, exuberant start-up. At the time of this writing, I am the Director of the BAT_LAB (Ballpark Advanced Technology) for the San Diego Padres' baseball team. We're working on evaluating integrated advanced technologies for the new ballpark and surrounding 26-block re-development zone in downtown San Diego.

You've been a host at many web-based communities. Why are hosts important?

Groups need leaders to achieve goals. Hosts are leaders. Let's take a cocktail party, for example. A good party usually has a good host. The host of a party provides structure, information, and a single point of communication. At a good house party, people don't pee in the bushes because they know who to ask where the bathroom is—OK, that's a weird example. How about: The partygoers don't drink warm drinks when the ice runs out because the host gets more ice, or if there's a fight, the host calls the cops and talks to them when they get there.

But online it's even more important to have a good host, and here's why. Imagine a cocktail party with 200 people under a tent. You're talking to two or three people in a din of other unintelligible conversations. You move from group to group and keep talking, and you can't hear what everybody else is saying.

Now compare this with an online community of 200 where, because of the way the technology is structured, you can read what every single person is saying. It's a lot more information and takes a lot more leadership (hosting). It's as if someone at a real life party quieted down the room and said, "Ok, we're all going to be quiet while one person talks and the rest listen." And then tried to keep it going with all 200 people while the party chemicals of choice kicked in. Hosts provide communication, macro-structure, information, and the law of the land—some fundamental basics of any community.

What makes a good host? Any helpful do's and don'ts to share?

A good host is the person most in touch with the community, the one who holds the group's goal safe and communicates it so the group will recognize its own success. Good hosts are more concerned with the community as a whole than with their own issues or any one person's issues. This does not mean they spend as much time actually in the community as some of the regulars, however. It just means they are the most tapped into the group as a whole entity than anyone else.

Specifically, they are good at posting short question posts that spur posts from others. They are good at giving more than getting and fostering gift economies. They know when not to post and let things take their own course. They are known by the community as the host and respected as a leader. They welcome new members and explain the "rules" of that particular community. They also respect the members of the community and know when to communicate one-on-one with them. They are strong enough to deal with trouble quickly so it does not destroy the community. Also, good hosts understand that they are not really in control of the community's future. They get that it's more like being a farmer than a construction worker. While you can build a community space, you can't force a community to use it and grow. It's more like a garden with the host making sure the soil is good: There's fresh water, the right amount of sun, and then planting seeds and helping them grow. It's all about environmental control. Good hosts should also have fun and obviously love their job.

What role does the host play in guarding the community? Can a host sometimes act as, or work to create, a barrier to entry?

Barriers to entry, good question. In my experience, the forces that govern the community set up barriers to entry. For example, the university that controls the number of students in an online class, the corporation that decides to run a normal web community where you can read for nothing, but have to register to post. The professional organization that decides to start an email list, or the moderated community that decides to approve each post. Rarely is it just one person/host.

So, a host usually plays the role of enforcing rules set down by a group. What I think is really important is that there are filters. A listserv can only handle a few hundred folks, a web community can handle as many as can register, but without rules of content, decency, and thread and subject control, can easily become a ghost town to half-started subjects and empty threads.

I believe exclusivity is not inherently bad, and that having to work to get into a community is often empowering. Perhaps barriers to entry are a result of the equation of the goal of the community balanced with its resources. I think of it like communities in real life. There are small towns whose barrier to entry is geographical. There are cities whose size means they have more good and more bad. Reminds me of Groucho Marx saying, "I don't want to belong to any club that will accept me as a member."

In your time with virtual communities, you've come up with a great standard set of topics to spur conversation. What are they, why are they important, and how did you come up with them?

Over the years I've invented and tested three topics.

1. How was your week? If I could have only one topic in a community, it would be this one. It is the single most powerful tool for community growing that I've come up with.

This topic was born during the NoEnd Group's early days when a bunch of webmasters would meet in a bar and go from person to person asking that question. I moved the group along by timing about 10 minutes per person (an example of why hosts are needed). The answers were always different, personal, entertaining, and started mini-discussions of sharing experiences. Two hours later, we'd have gone around the circle, and everybody had a strange feeling of comfort and release. Very different from being a spectator at some boring talking-head meeting.

Later in graduate school, I learned that this had a lot to do with identity and stories. From Judith Donath's work at MIT's Media Lab, I learned that everybody has an identity, but online it's tough to establish because we are separated from our bodies that help anchor our "real life" identities.

I found that a successful way to get around this is to always have a space where people can express how their weeks were. Seems trivial, but it's very powerful. As soon as someone writes, "This week was bad, my 10-year-old got sick just as I had a big presentation at work, which I botched," they've made themselves unique from everybody else by sharing personal details with the community—a mini story. When someone writes back, "I hear you, I've got enough trouble juggling work and home life, and I'm single! More power to you"—then you've got a community.

I started a permanent "How was your week?" in my Netscape forum, and it was successful enough for several other hosts to make it a permanent topic in their forums.

2. Outside. I came up with "Outside" after a WWII veteran told me a story about bar fights in New York city right after the war. He said there was a lot of tension and anger among the GIs coming back, so there was a lot of drinking and fighting, and the bars he went to adapted a system to handle it.

When two guys started getting in each other's face, the bartender or bouncer would grab some chalk and take them outside where he'd draw a circle on the pavement. Then he would make sure they had no weapons, and let them go at it. When one gave up for whatever reason, he'd make them go back into the bar and have the winner buy the loser a drink.

This is about the fact that fighting in a community is inevitable. But fighting is not the problem: It's where and how the fights take place that makes for problems. Most often fights, or flames as they're called, happen in the middle of the forum and make everybody angry. This is not appropriate, but stopping fighting is not realistic either.

Well, I thought why not have an "Outside" in an online community? A place to go when what you are doing is bothering other people, but you still need to do it. Most people hate to be told what they can't do. But they don't seem to mind so much a little structure on what they can do. So it's worked great whenever I've tried it. When I encounter flames sparking up, I send an email saying, "Take it outside." It's a great re-director of bad energy in a community. Interestingly, it seems to take the gas out of flames very fast, since there are not bunches of people "watching" the flame.

I've also found that people will go use an "Outside" topic to just pretend fight, thus limiting real flames. Very interesting...

3. Random Babble. We can't categorize everything people want to talk about, so I always have a Random Babble area. It's like a steam valve for a community, a rule-less place to play where you don't have to talk about anything that makes sense. As a host, your job is often to keep people on topic. If you're discussing politics and people start going off on entertainment, you need to either create an entertainment topic if there's enough need, or gently refocus the group on politics. But what about when you have something to say that doesn't fit into a topic and yet isn't fitting for starting a new one? Thus, random babble.

Surprisingly, the discussions can be amazing in such a topic, from silly to heartfelt. It's a place to blow off steam and be crazy, which makes it easier to stay on topic on the other forum because you have one that has no topic at all.

Has a virtual community ever surprised you?

Constantly.

I've seen people from the farthest corners of the globe connect with each other. For example, small business people from New Zealand connecting with ones deep in Mexico and sharing information that helped save both businesses.

Once a virtual snowball fight broke out in an "Outside" forum I was hosting. For two weeks we just wrote back and forth things like "Caleb falls to the ground from Sharon's ice/mud ball, but his force field protected him enough to stay conscious. Reeling, he calls in his secret alien ship and creates a storm of snowballs!"

Last question: If you could give one piece of advice to new hosts, one guiding principle, what would it be?

Grow, don't build.

Chapter 6

Moderation, Karma, and Flame Bait

...How to Survive Your Own Users

Imagine your worst nightmare of a dinner party.

Let's say you got invited by Ed from Middle Management, so you couldn't say no. You know Ed. He's the guy from across the hall who tells bad jokes constantly. Your ex-girlfriend is there, along with Billy Bratworst, the kid who beat you up in the sixth grade. The wine is vinegar, the music is horrible, and everyone is as fake as a bad toupee.

Now imagine that you had the freedom to do whatever you wanted. Let's say some magic force came to you and said that, as of this moment, you could say or do anything, to anyone, and no one would be able to stop you. In fact, no one would even realize who you were. There would be no repercussions, no matter what.

What would you do? Would you tell Ed his jokes stink? Dump the punchbowl on Billy Bratworst? Tell your ex-girlfriend that you really always liked her sister better? Leave the party in disarray, laughing maniacally?

Or would you be good, and just sip wine and try to maintain a conversation?

A Dimension Not Only of Sight and Sound but of Mind

It sounds like the kind of moral dilemma that only appears in a *Twilight Zone* episode, but it's actually the reality of many online community spaces.

The problem with virtual community spaces, like the moral dilemma, is that there can be few, if any, real-world consequences for bad behavior. A user can ruin a good conversation by posting nonsense all night and then simply turn off the computer and go to bed. In the real world, there would be consequences for acting like a jerk. Go ahead and scream at your boss and see what happens. But online, more often than not, there are none.

As a community site creator, you have to understand that no matter what you do, no matter how hard you try, there is always some bozo who wants to turn your immaculate community area into his own private circus. Some people take to the Internet to play out roles they can't act in their real lives (not that there's anything wrong with role-playing, *if* that's the intent of your community). Other people just like to cause trouble. Some, I fear, may actually be quite disturbed.

Concerned site owners have tools they can use, of course. Many discussion systems can automatically filter out certain words and even block troublesome users. Network administrators can sift through server logs and trace individual users by their IP numbers. I have personally blocked entire domains from accessing a partic- ular site because of the behavior of one troubled user.

But every solution creates new problems. Disallowing dirty words only creates a new lexicon ("f*ck censorship, a55h0le!"). Booting users from a free account doesn't stop them from simply creating a new one. And network administrators usually don't have time

IP freely

Whenever you visit a website, you leave a trail. Your web browser reports certain information to the server, including the name of the browser you're using, your computer operating system, and your IP address. Every device on the Net must have an IP address in order to talk to each other. IP addresses can be static or dynamic. In most cases, if you use a modem to dial up to an Internet service provider, you have a dynamic IP address, which is hard to trace back to a certain user. But if you're in an office, or you have an always-on connection (like cable or DSL), you probably have a static IP address, which is easier to trace.

to comb through logs just to find one user, and even then, IP addresses can be inconclusive. Long log searches can end in a publicly accessible computer in a library or an Internet café. Even then, IP addresses can be spoofed.

The clever hacker has an arsenal of weapons at his disposal, but don't fret. It's not as hopeless as it seems. This chapter tackles the issues around moderation. There are plenty of ways you can prepare, both technically and emotionally, for the inevitable problem users. Surviving these challenges with grace and humor is one of the most important things you can do to foster a healthy community.

You'll also hear from Rob Malda, creator and editor of Slashdot (slashdot.org), one of the hottest community sites out there. And I don't just mean "hot" as in popular. Slashdot has a reputation for heated arguments between brilliant nerds. As a result, Rob and company have come up with some very smart ways of turning the tide.

It's Going to Be Okay

But first, a note of caution. It's important to remember that, your users are not your enemy. There may be a few problem cases, and it's important to handle them well. But you must never lose faith in your users. Don't let the words of caution in this chapter scare you off—I truly believe that most people want to be good, productive members of their communities.

In fact, I believe that trust is the operating principle behind most successful community websites. Online auction site eBay (ebay.com), for example, features many ways for users to communicate with each other. Web boards and chat rooms fill the site, and users reputations there can make or break their auctions. The potential for troublemaking is great—one bored teenager with a borrowed credit card could ruin auctions all over the site in an evening.

Yet eBay's community values are all very optimistic. It has five basic values that are outlined in their community section (pages.ebay.com/help/community/values.html). They are:

> We believe people are basically good.

> We believe everyone has something to contribute.

> We believe that an honest, open environment can bring out the best in people.

> We recognize and respect everyone as a unique individual.

> We encourage you to treat others the way that you want to be treated.

These values help set the tone of all of eBay's community features, inform the site's community design process, and tell its members what is expected in a non-threatening way. I think this is the way to go. You should consider formalizing your own community values and posting them publicly.

But most importantly, it's essential that you remain as people-positive as you can. After all, if you don't like people, you probably shouldn't be running a community site.

Still, after all the hard work it takes to create and maintain a community-oriented website, it's hard to keep your cool when someone turns your quiet dinner party into his own personal battleground. Although you should assume a people-positive attitude in general, you must also put in place a system to manage the troublemakers. Here are some techniques I've learned over the years to minimize problem users.

Tie the Virtual to the Real as Much as Possible

Like the *Twilight Zone* example previously mentioned, the core problem with most virtual communities is their separation from real-world consequences. When users feel that they can get away with murder in a virtual space, they may try to do just that.

The solution is to tie your community to the real world as much as possible. One way to do this is to require users to create a membership before posting to your site. Make some information mandatory in the sign-up process. Community members will think twice about making trouble if they know that the site administrator has their name and email address on file. And though names can be faked and email addresses can be had on the web for free at any number of sites, requiring that information helps create a more stable, responsible atmosphere.

In my experience, allowing users to be anonymous can be very dangerous. It depends on the nature of the site, of course. Sometimes, anonymity can be a gateway to frank and open communication. I was once on a mailing list where all the emails went through an anonymous server. When they were delivered to the list, they came with no names attached. This was appropriate here, because the goal of the list was to encourage us to be honest with coworkers and bosses without fear of personal reprisal or professional retribution.

But in most cases, letting users remain anonymous while taking part in a web-based community is a recipe for disaster. Some people will take advantage of their nameless-ness and disrupt the space for everyone. Simply getting real names and email addresses is a good preventative measure that most people will have no problem with, so long as you also include a privacy statement.

> **The importance of privacy statements**
>
> Whenever you ask your users for personal information, you should also provide a clear privacy statement. Since mutual goodwill is critical in community spaces, tell your users what you will and will not be doing with their personal information. If creating a membership with your site results in the user receiving email of any kind, be sure to warn the user first. Hell hath no fury like a user spammed.

There are other ways to tie the virtual to the real. At eBay, users who default on delivering a payment after they win an auction, or people who never deliver the goods to the winner, have their ratings lowered. A low rating on the site makes it very hard for them to buy or sell on the site in the future. And since eBay requires a valid credit card to open an account, it becomes very hard for a user to simply start a new account after getting a low rating. eBay makes it clear that screwing someone over in a virtual auction has repercussions on your real-world wallet.

John Styn (interviewed in Chapter 7) has been involved in leading two community sites, both of which primarily use chat and webcams to connect their members. One of these sites, CitizenX (citizenx.com), is free to all. The other, The Real House (thereal house.com), costs $15 a month for a membership. Styn reports that, while one site sometimes has a problem with obnoxious members, the other has no troublemakers whatsoever. Can you guess which is which?

The bottom line is, if you're going to bring out the fine china, make sure your dinner guests understand that virtual transgressions have real-world consequences.

Community, police thyself

Many successful virtual communities have thousands of members. Sometimes, it is just impossible to rely on human-powered moderation. Even in a small community, there are not enough hours in the day to police every post in every thread. Even if there were, you probably wouldn't want the job.

The key, then, is to build systems that let the community police itself.

When I first added a chat room to Kvetch (kvetch.com/chat), I kept a web browser window open there to observe the patterns. What I saw intrigued me.

There was a pattern I saw play out over and over. A few folks would gather and start the ball rolling. Their conversation would gain steam slowly. As more people entered the chat room, the conversation got faster and faster. And then, as if on cue, some bozo would show up and post something inappropriate.

The chatters would then respond like a swarm of bees. Insults might fly back and forth a bit, until people started getting uncomfortable. Then people would start to leave, one by one. Since this was the only chat room on the site, when they left, they left for good. Eventually, the bozo would get bored, having managed to scare everyone away, and leave, too. A fantastic recipe for a dead chat room.

It presented an interesting challenge. I couldn't simply filter the room for bad language, because that wasn't the issue. As an administrator, I had the ability to boot the offending user out of the room, but I wasn't planning on policing the site all day, every day.

For a while I had an understanding with some of the Kvetch chat regulars that if a troublemaker came on, they could email me, and I'd come boot the problem guest out. I can't tell you how bad an idea this is. Trust me when I say that you should never, ever be at the beck and call of a website.

I could have selected a few frequent users and given them the ability to boot problem users, but I was reluctant to deputize certain users over others. I was afraid of the possibility that the power could go to someone's head. And besides, then I'd have to spend my time policing the moderators. That wouldn't fly either.

The real issue was that, while the community of participants in Kvetch Chat was constantly changing, there was always a critical mass of people who could judge what belonged there and what didn't. What I really needed was a way to let the community take care of itself. And that's when it hit me: What I needed was a way for the community to collectively boot out a troublemaker. And with the help of a talented programmer named Greg Knauss, that's just what I did.

I added a new button that said "boot" next to all the other functional buttons in the chat room. Clicking this produces a pop-up window that explains the rules. Every member of the chat room gets one boot vote. If more than half of the participants in the room vote for you to be booted, you get shown the door with a special message.

Congratulations! You've been booted.

The system notes the troublemaker's IP address, so that person can't get back in under another name. In one hour, the boot is lifted, and the user can come back in.

Now the community itself could decide what was acceptable or not. When a new chatter that spoke out of turn appeared, the community could decide to boot that person. And even better, I didn't have to be there all day, every day.

Once, as a test, I entered the chat room and started bossing people around. "This is my site!" I said. "You all better be nice or else!"

They booted me. I was so proud.

Moderation, Meta-moderation, and Karmic Justice

But the real poster child of user-controlled moderation is a site called Slashdot (slashdot.org). Started by Rob Malda in 1997, Slashdot's slogan, "news for nerds, stuff that matters," has become a rallying cry for the open source geek community. Slashdot has gone from being a pet project to a full-fledged business, and turned Malda into a minor celebrity. The site is so active (it serves more than a million pages a day), that it's given rise to a new term. When a Slashdot story links to your site, you have been "slash-dotted." Congratulations! But enjoy it while you can, because

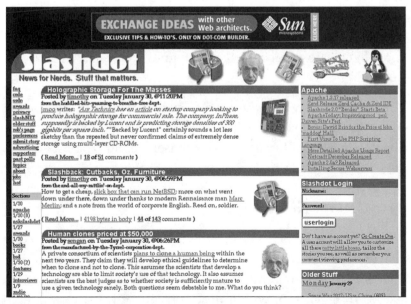

Slashdot's homepage.

slashdotted sites usually choke on all the traffic, sometimes going offline altogether.

One of the many things Slashdot is doing right is moderation. With a site this active, you learn a few things about how to manage your users. Slashdot's history of adding and tweaking moderation features serves as an interesting lesson in managing a growing community.

At first it was just Malda. He posted stories of interest to the geek community, namely himself and his friends. As the site grew, he started taking story submissions from the readers, and added discussion forums for them to discuss the stories.

Immediately, there was a debate about whether or not to require users to create accounts. Some said that anonymity would result in antisocial behavior. Others worried that there might be good reasons for users to post anonymously (if someone wanted to speak out against the company he worked for, for example).

The solution they came up with is pure geek brilliance. At Slashdot, you do not need to create a membership account to post to the site. You can read and post, just like everyone else. But if you choose to create an account—in addition to some nice personalization features—your name is automatically added to all your posts. If you don't create an account, the site names you itself: Anonymous Coward.

This is a great way to let casual web surfers take part, but quietly encourage them to take the next step and actually join the community as a member. Plus, it preserves a user's ability to post anonymously if he needs to. Personally, I love this solution. But like everything else at Slashdot, the Anonymous Coward issue continues to be hotly debated.

When the material being posted to the site became too much to be manageable by only one person, Malda deputized some of his friends to be moderators and gave them the ability to rate posts on a scale from –1 to 5, with a descriptive word. For example, a

Fun with jargon!

One of the fun things about moderating a web community is that it comes with all sorts of cool lingo! Here's a quick cheat sheet:

Flame—A harsh attack. Also: "getting flamed."

Flame bait—A comment designed to start an argument.

Flame war—A nasty fight.

Troll—Someone who's being disruptive or looking for a fight.

witty post could be rated "2, Funny." An inappropriate post could be rated "–1, Troll."

Logged-in users could then filter their responses to a thread. For a site where 600 post threads are not unusual, this is a life-saver. If a thread is 600 posts, and I set my filter to show only responses with a rating of 2 and higher, suddenly there are only 400 posts to read. If I set my filter even higher, even fewer comments remain. As a user, I can choose the level of comments I want to see. And best yet, no one is really being censored—everything that is posted to the site stays on the site. Filtering just puts the comments outside your threshold a click away.

It's a great idea, but it resulted in all hell breaking loose. Because human beings are subjective creatures, the moderators were subjective in their ratings. Users who were moderated down were livid, while users who were moderated up were pleased. It produced a rift in the community, and the moderators became the bad guys. Malda needed a new solution fast, and the one he came up with was a doozy.

Malda decided to let the users do the moderating. The Slashdot system is constantly selecting members to act as moderators. Which users are selected depends on a complicated set of factors, but any users can be chosen to be moderators if they act responsibly over time. Submitting stories that are accepted and posting comments that are moderated up increases your chances.

If you are selected to become a moderator, you are given five points to spend. Suddenly, every comment on the site is followed by a drop-down menu where you can add or subtract one point with an associated word. You only have three days to spend your points, so they can't accrue. And you can't moderate a thread that you're taking part in as a poster. The idea is that you're working for the site for a few moments, helping to make it a

A Slashdot thread in moderation mode.

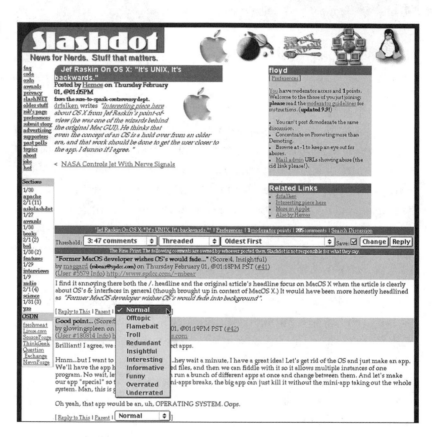

better place for your fellow users. As the Slashdot FAQ says: "The goal here is to share ideas. To sift through the haystack and find needles."

All you have to do is read the posts like you always do. But now, if you see one you think is great, you can up its rating by a point. If you think it's bad, you can knock a point off. Click the "moderate" button at the bottom of the page, and you're done.

Instant Karma

After you've spent your five points, your view of the threads goes back to normal, and you can go on with your life. But things get even more interesting when you also take karma into account.

Slashdot has taken the idea of karma, the theory of inevitable consequences, and made it digital. All users of Slashdot have a karma level that they can view (but not change) on their member pages. Their karma level is a byproduct of their behavior on the site.

Remember a minute ago when you moderated five comments? The users whose comments were moderated up all received more karma points. The ones who were moderated down lost some karma points. You can also get karma points for submitting stories that are chosen to be posted to Slashdot's homepage.

Here's the kicker: Users with more karma are more likely to get picked to become moderators. Users with fewer karma points are less likely. In this way, the site is in a never-ending sifting process of users rating content and helping select new moderators.

Karma points help out in other ways, too. While most users' posts initially appear with a score of 0, if you have an extremely high karma level, your post may start out up a point, at 1. It also helps the administrators of the site see, at a glance, who's been naughty and who's been nice.

But Wait, There's Meta!

After the user-controlled moderation system had been in place for a while, Malda and the Slashdot team of programmers took it a step further: meta moderation.

The meta-moderation system is designed to keep tabs on the moderators. To become a meta moderator, you must be one of the oldest 90 percent of the users on the system. If you are, you're invited to meta moderate on the homepage with the friendly greeting: "Have you Meta Moderated today?" Users can meta moderate once a day.

If you choose to meta moderate, you're presented with 10 random comments that have been moderated by the moderators. You're shown the comment, told how the moderator rated it, and asked if the moderation was fair or unfair. The comments are also presented without names, to try to keep personal bias out of the process.

On a recent visit, I decided to meta moderate and was presented with this:

A Slashdot post in meta moderation mode.

ff dnumero
by - on Friday January 19, @12:04AM PST (#1)
foo one bar one baz one efdhgdfh ljhfd dflf fdg
[Reply to This | Parent]
Story:Building VR Hardware Using A PSC1000a JavaChip?
Rating: 'Troll'.
This rating is **Unfair** ○ ◉ ○ **Fair**

I think this one was rated fairly, don't you?

When a meta moderator rates a moderation as unfair, the moderation remains, but the system remembers who the original moderator was. If a certain member's moderations are consistently meta moderated as unfair, that user loses karma and is less likely to be selected as a moderator again.

Meta moderation began as an experiment to see if the user-controlled moderation system was working. Now it remains as a constant balance to help weed out bad moderators. And it works.

Catch Me When I Fall

The common themes in all of Slashdot's complicated systems are trust and balance. The system trusts the community members to behave themselves. When they don't, the system trusts other users to point that out. And if those members stray, the system trusts others to correct that. Over time, the system is constantly correcting its balance, striving for perfection.

And yet, no one is ever banned, and no comment is ever deleted. You can always say what you want to say, and it's up to the community to applaud or decry your contributions.

These specific tools may be overkill for your community site, but the ideas are good to remember. If your community site is just a collection of friends keeping in touch, it would be unnecessary (or even offensive) to rate each other's contributions. But when your site is overflowing with more content than anyone could read in a day, you should consider the kinds of self-policing ideas presented here. In the end, your users *want* to help you manage the content in your site. Invested community members will jump at the chance to help police their virtual neighborhood—it's up to you to put a system in place to support it.

If you think the Slashdot system sounds perfect for your project, you're in luck. What kind of open source community would Slashdot be if it didn't open-source its source code? The entire Slash engine is available for download at slashcode.com. But be warned: It's not for the faint of heart or the technically challenged. If you don't know how to code in Perl, you'll need to hire someone who does.

Rob Malda

A Conversation with Rob Malda

I got to talk with the notoriously busy Malda in email in January 2001, about Slashdot's evolution, design, and moderation system. Here's what he had to say.

Rob, please give us a brief introduction to who you are and what you do.

I am Rob "CmdrTaco" Malda, creator and editor of Slashdot.org.

What I do is determine direction and post a large portion of the content on Slashdot.org.

Let's talk about Slashdot. Please describe it in a nutshell for anyone who is unfamiliar with it. How did it begin?

Slashdot is a news/discussion on "News for Nerds. Stuff that Matters." We talk about things ranging from Linux and Open Source software to astronomy, toys, anime, or really anything else we think is interesting. It began over three years ago when I was in college. The intent was just to create a place to kinda hang out and post things I thought were interesting for my friends to read.

Now we serve over a million pages every day, and the site is over three years old. We have a quarter of a million registered users, but most users aren't registered.

Whenever I see a green box that's rounded on the left I think of Slashdot. How did the visual design of the site come about? Who did the work? What changes were made along the way?

The design hasn't changed significantly since it first came up. A large part of Slashdot's design was a knockoff of my former employer's business card.

I moved the corner from the right to the left and gave it a more cartoony look. Fortune was always displayed on the bottom. The Slashboxes worked a little differently, and the top two stories originally consumed the full width of the browser. But the vast majority of the layout and design hasn't changed in over three years.

Ever think about redesigning?

We've talked about it quite a bit, and I'd be very interested in doing it. Readers occasionally submit HTML and images for a new layout, but so far they either haven't caught my eye, or the design didn't lend itself to the task at hand (people like to forget things like second-level menus, for example). If someone submitted an awesome design, yeah, I'd probably be willing to change it, but so far, the best design was actually used on slashcode.com, and included with the v1.0 version of Slashcode. It was a nice design, but it wasn't right for Slashdot. I'm horribly picky about such things. My guess is that even if someone submitted a great design, I'd still have to twiddle it around just to feel comfortable with it.

From the beginning, you've hosted a debate on whether or not to allow people to post without registering, and I'm particularly enamored with the solutions you've come up with. Could you talk about how you feel about this debate, and how you came up with this solution?

I've always felt that people should have a right to say things anonymously: There are certain things that you just wouldn't want your friends (or boss!) to read.

Originally, Slashdot didn't require any user accounts—all posts were anonymous. As time progressed, we created the user system to cut out imposters. Anonymous users are muffled, but not silenced. I'd like to keep it that way forever, but that will, in the end, be determined by the people who post anonymously. Many of them don't post anonymously for any reason except to be a pest. It's a very sad state when a small group of very childish people can wreak havoc for thousands of intelligent people wanting to engage in legitimate discussion.

Totally. So how do you moderate the posts?

We went through many iterations of the moderation system. Originally, only a few friends and I moderated. This group grew to 20 or so people, but since we were getting 500–1,000 comments a day, it was tough to keep on top of it all.

Of course, trolling was only a fraction of the problem it is today, but it still was problematic. At that point, we gave moderator access to about 500 users based on their karma (of course, nobody knew what karma was then since nobody knew it existed). That group moderated for a few more months, and we used the information we gained by watching a larger group moderate to design the framework for our current system where moderators are randomly selected from all eligible users.

Karma? How does that work?

Karma is essentially a sum of all moderation done to you, and by you. It's not that simple, though. Really all that matters is that if you have low karma, your comments post at a lower score.

If you have higher karma, your comments post at a higher score. And if you have negative karma, you can't moderate. People worry about karma far too much, though.

So how does the system work now? Are you satisfied, or is there more to come?

The system essentially selects users who have contributed positively to the discussions, and gives them moderator points that they can use to assign a value to other comments. It's sort of like jury duty: It only takes a few minutes every few weeks, and you only moderate a handful of comments.

The system works reasonably well. No other system that I've seen has scaled up to a million-page-a-day site. It's far from perfect, and we're constantly tweaking this and fine-tuning that: I'm satisfied, but there's always room for improvement. Most of the changes are very subtle, and users don't even notice.

Has the Slashdot community ever surprised you?

I can't think offhand of a specific event, but the thing that surprised me (but in hindsight, it shouldn't surprise me at all) is the passion they feel for anything.

No matter what I post, no matter how I say it, someone always is mad at me, and someone else is always happy. It's a very diverse group considering the niche that Slashdot serves. It's taught me that I can't do anything perfect ever, and the best I can hope for is to trust my instincts and hope it works. So far it has.

How do you deal with it when someone attacks you person-ally? You have the tools to delete the post—hell, you could delete the user!—do you?

I wish I could, believe me.

I've come to accept that if you ever make it to a level where your work actually affects someone, you will get both fans and enemies. I have both in abundance. It hurts me a lot when they use my system to attack me, but frankly someone attacking me is no more hurtful than simply posting a bunch of troll comments or ASCII art in an otherwise inter-esting discussion.

It's strange, though, [Slashdot columnist Jon] Katz and I have discussed the difference in public and private flames (we both get a fair amount of both). Public flames can usually just be ignored because it's being done purely for the benefit and ego of the flamer.

Private flames are usually much more evil because they typically really just want to get under the flamee's skin. And sometimes they succeed.

I mean, there are websites dedicated to hating me. But on the other hand, I need to remember that to many people, Slashdot is a website dedicated to hating Bill Gates. It's not. Although a lot of my readers have simplified all global problems to hating a single person, that certainly isn't my agenda, or the agenda that I've created for Slashdot. Other people suggest that I sue for slander, but that's just wrong.

Slashdot fights for people to have a voice on the Internet. I can't turn around and say "except when you want to bad mouth me."

I won't lie, sometimes it hurts. But I've been doing this for 3.5 years now, and I've been flamed for my work on Slashdot for about 3.49 years now, so at some point, you learn to let it roll off. Usually. Sometimes, I snap. ;)

Slashdot started as a labor of love for you, and now it's a business. How has that changed things? What would you say to other people who are considering starting a community site with commercial aspirations?

The major thing that has changed is that I'm kinda management now. I don't wear a beeper and fix the servers when they crash. I don't write all the stories.

And I don't write all the code. Instead I do bits and pieces of each of these jobs, and coordinate everyone else. Instead of working 80 hours a week, I work 40 or so. Slashdot used to be almost entirely me, but now I can do just the parts I enjoy doing.

As for advice, do what you know. Don't just try to take someone else's ideas, and don't try to do something unless you believe in it. Slashdot got successful largely because I was my target audience. I wasn't trying to make a site for someone else, I was creating the site that *I* wanted to read. I don't think you can fake that, and I think that even if you do, people can smell it.

Chapter 7

Chat, Cams, and Virtual Intimacy

...Seeing Computers as Intimacy Devices

Intimacy is one of the fundamental building blocks of any community, online or off. It's the spark of life that changes a primordial soup of HTML and CGI scripts into a living, breathing community.

Intimacy is the reason I'm writing this book. When I was in college at UC Santa Cruz in the early nineties, I got my first command line window into the Internet. Back then we had something called fnet (short for forum network) that connected Santa Cruz students into a citywide chat. It was my first experience with real-time chat, and it left a lasting impression.

It was one sleepless night in fnet that I met Mac. He seemed like just another student at first. As the hours crept by, and the other chatters logged off, we passed from the pleasantries to talking about things that matter.

Eventually, Mac admitted that he wasn't a student at UCSC as I'd assumed—he was a high school sophomore, desperate to escape from his teenage doldrums. He was a geek without a lot of friends, so he logged into fnet to be around college students and pretend he was one of them.

So I told Mac about when I was in high school. I took a job at the local college's dining hall. It was okay money for the time, but the real perk was that I got to meet and become friends with many college students. I looked up to them as examples of what I wanted to become. And, eventually, I did.

And you will, too, Mac.

And then there was this moment where we both knew that we'd found something special. This random, disembodied, virtual exchange had changed from a splash of ASCII across a telnet window into something personal, sincere … intimate.

That exchange left an indelible mark on my conception of the Internet. And I've found that when you start talking to people who are active in virtual communities, everyone has a story like this. It's the moment when you realize that computers aren't just for homework and business—they can actually be intimacy devices.

Intimacy Doesn't Mean Sex (Usually)

First of all, let me define the terms. When I talk about intimacy, I'm not talking about sex. Nor do I mean revealing personal trivia in a diary or smiling coyly into a webcam. Though all of these things can be *elements* of creating an intimate community space, none of them are intimate by default.

By intimacy, I mean that feeling you get when you realize that someone is speaking directly to you, telling you something personal that resonates deeply. I'm talking about spaces where that kind of intimate exchange can take place safely and without fear, like my exchange with Mac in college.

There are different examples of intimacy online. Here are a few.

Communities of support

Perhaps the clearest example of the benefits of intimate community spaces can be found in the support communities that flourish online. No matter what your ailment is, you can find support online.

Health sites litter the web, and it's easy to see why. Using the web to make contact with people who are experiencing the same thing as you are can be immensely powerful.

I have a personal story about that, but it doesn't belong to me. It belongs to my mom, Lois Powazek.

The discussion area of HealthAtoZ.com has everything from ADD to Y2K.

Four years ago, my mom's scoliosis became too painful to live with. She'd had a nasty curve in her back for years, but it was just getting worse. Her doctor wanted to do a major operation. She said she'd have to think about it.

That night, with the procedure on her mind, she typed "scoliosis.com" into her web browser. That led to a site with all sorts of scoliosis information, which linked to another, and another.

Eventually, she found herself at a site called Scoliosis RX (scoliosisrx.com) where she found a section called "In Touch" that contained posts from other people, all over the world, with the same condition. On a whim, she introduced herself, said she was considering the surgery, and left her email address.

First, she received email from the site's administrator, a doctor, who prepared her with questions to ask her own doctor. Then she heard from a handful of other women who had recently completed the same surgical procedure she was considering.

They gave her advice and told her stories. "Put your clothes in the top drawers—you won't be able to bend much after the surgery. And make sure you bring socks to the hospital—your feet will get cold."

One of them told her that two weeks after her surgery, she went out and bought a bikini. After years of having a crooked back, she was finally able to wear one. When I ask my mom about her experience in this support community years later, it's the bikini story she tells first.

These supportive conversations helped convince my mom to have the surgery. It was a complete success, and the first thing she did when it was over was send my sister Jenny home from the hospital to email her support group friends and tell them she was okay. The next day, one of them called to wish her well ... from England.

Had she been too scared to leave her email address or talk about a terribly invasive surgery procedure online, my mom would never have gotten the help and support she so needed. And when her recovery was over, she was able to post again to tell her tale, and help others who needed it. It surprised her a little to be giving support in the same forum she had first come to for support herself.

Visiting the site today, it's changed very little over the last four years. The community tools are bare-bones, and the design hasn't changed since the age of the 2.0 browsers. But you can still find posts from people introducing themselves, taking a risk, and reaching out for support.

Communities of shared stories

These are the kinds of spaces I try to create on the web. {fray} and San Francisco Stories both reach out to people with personal stories. I've always imagined the stories in {fray} to be like a quiet voice, whispering in the corner of a dark café somewhere. And the best part is, in an intimate community space, you can whisper right back.

Sometimes, I'm amazed by the intimate things people post in {fray}. Stories there have dealt with taboos like drugs and sex, and solicited amazingly personal posts from the audience. After five years of running the site, I'm still stunned by the pure emotional frankness of some of the stories.

One such story was called "In Lanes" (fray.com/hope/inlanes). Written by Greg Knauss, it tells the story of a suicide he witnessed on an LA freeway. The experience forced him to confront his fear of death, an experience that left him shaken. The story concludes with the question: "Have you ever considered suicide?"

The story is followed by almost 200 personal accounts of suicide, death, and loss. It's so heavy, I couldn't imagine reading it all in one sitting. The most recent post as of this writing is by someone named Robin who talks about her struggle with depression.

*two of my best friends killed themselves in less than a two week period a little over a year ago. they were brothers, Mykahl was 19 and Doug who was 17. Doug killed himself first, then Mykahl went two weeks later. **i tried**. i did. i'd talked both of them down several times over the years i'd known them. And then i was out of town and when i came back, Doug was dead. it almost killed me. i didn't get a chance to tell him i loved him or to hug him or any of that. i just got really drunk and stayed that way. i moved in with mykahl to make sure he'd be alright. we stayed unsober, in our own realities. i got alcohol poisoning, was put in the hospital. mykahl stayed with me for a few hours, then went home and hanged himself.*

when i found out, i ripped the iv out of my arm and used it to slash the other one open. i'd lost three pints when the nurse found me.

*i got trapped by the whole self-mutilation thing, i cut the living hell out of myself on my arms, my legs, even my stomach. i have a lot of scars. **the pain helped me find my way back to reality**. made me realize that i'm still here. and if i can get around physical pain, then i should be able to climb out of my depression too.*

*i should be strong. so here i am. alive and scarred. living a life that's fairly good, but one that i don't want. i have friends, i smile, i do well in my homeschooling. but i still cut, sometimes. **and i will always live life dangerously. i don't want the people who care about me now being stuck with the pain i have.***

but I don't want to live in all this pain.

The truly stunning thing about this post is that it ends with her name and email address. That allows members of the community to reach out to each other in support and camaraderie. It's also incredibly brave.

Communities of commerce

Even if you're not creating personal art projects, intimacy is still a crucial ingredient in the virtual community recipe. The same considerations necessary to create an intimate community space can be applied to any community site—even a corporate site.

When Nike wanted to extend its brand online, I worked with them (alongside Nathan Shedroff and the other talented folks at vivid studios) on a section called "Pulse." There, visitors were treated to a major sports star, talking about a subject, such as who *his* hero was. That led to a form, where visitors could talk back to the athlete. When we asked users "Who's your hero?" the responses were amazing.

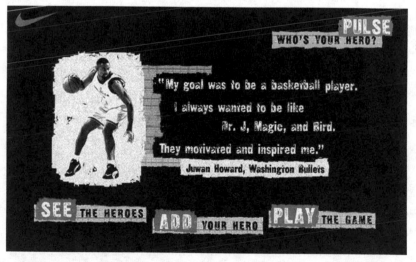

My treatment for Nike's Pulse section, circa 1997.

This is a great example of a corporation using a small, tightly focused community feature to cultivate a little intimacy on its site. The users not only got to interact (albeit in a limited way) with a famous athlete, but also with each other. By asking users to talk about their own heroes, Nike took the space beyond a simple athlete interview, and turned the users into the stars. Intimacy isn't a given in this situation, but Nike did everything it could to create an environment where intimacy between users could flourish.

The glue that holds all this together, from the smallest personal site to the biggest corporate site, is intimacy. Without it, a community space is just a bunch of web pages and HTML.

Intimacy Computes

Back when I met Mac, I, like most people, had assumed that computers were serious devices for serious matters. Computers were work machines, used for business and homework and other important stuff. The idea of having an intimate experience in front of one seemed weird. And, honestly, sometimes it still does.

But intimacy is a necessary component to creating community spaces online. So it becomes the web designer's challenge to create a space where the users feel comfortable enough to rise above their preconceptions of computers as solitary, emotionless machines and do something impressive: *feel*.

There is a barrier there, and community site creators need to understand it and come up with creative ways to overcome it. It takes extra attention to detail to make users feel comfortable and protected, to gently coax them into trusting you (and the site) enough to relax and open up.

I'm here to tell you that it is possible. It's a challenge, sure, but it is possible. And it's a necessary part of a vital community. This chapter describes some of the issues around virtual intimacy and discusses some methods to create sites that are truly intimate spaces. It also talks about real-time chat and webcams as tools for intimacy. Finally, we'll hear from John Styn, the ironically self-professed Cocky Bastard, who has created some very intimate spaces (and done some very intimate things) online.

Elements of Intimacy

The things that create intimate spaces online are the same things that create intimate spaces in the real world: trust, respect, and honesty. The difference in virtual spaces is that the participants in the community don't have the same control they do in real places, and they don't always feel the same investment.

So the challenge is to create a safe environment where users feel comfortable engaging each other on an emotional level. That takes a lot of work, because there are obstacles to overcome. Here are some of the biggest ones, each with some possible solutions based on my experience creating intimate virtual spaces.

Obstacle 1: Paranoia

Even users who are comfortable with computers can be hesitant to engage them in a personal way, and for good reason. Revealing personal data online can be risky.

Search engines (altavista.com or google.com, for example) routinely crawl the web and index everything they come across. So anything you post to a public website is available to anyone who knows how to perform a keyword search. That means friends, family, bosses, and anyone else online may be able to eventually find what you post. Some savvy bosses now routinely perform web and Usenet searches on job applicants.

There are caveats, of course. Site owners can use meta tags and robots.txt files to keep their sites from being indexed by search engines. And any site you need a password to access won't be crawled by a search engine. But don't feel too secure—not all search engines respect those methods. Besides, search engines aren't the only ones crawling web pages. Posting your email address on a public website is a great way to wind up getting unsolicited commercial email (called spam).

The bottom line is, users are wise to be wary of posting personal material in public spaces, so it's our jobs to protect them. As a site designer, remember to communicate clearly just who will read the user-contributed material, and what will become of it after it's posted. You should also use meta tags and robots.txt files to keep the search engines out of your community area. It's your job to woo users into an intimate space, in spite of their own well-founded paranoia, and then protect them when they do.

Ego-surfing USA

It's amazing what you can find out about someone after a few web searches. If you're curious, try doing a search on your own name. You may be surprised. Don't believe me? Try searching for "Derek Powazek" and you may find out more than you wanted to know about the author of this book!

Fighting paranoia

So what do we do for people who are not as brave as Robin? There are a few ways to fight the paranoia problem.

An elegant community space can reassure paranoid users by allowing them to be anonymous. Slashdot.org, for example, provides an option for users to post anonymously, even if they're logged in. That way, if users want to post something without fear of it coming back to haunt them, they can do so.

You could also consider making the contact information optional. In {fray}, it's up to the user if she wants to provide a name, URL, or email address along with her post. If you want to sign your story "Sleepless in San Francisco," you're free to do so.

Interestingly, the vast majority of posters in {fray} choose to leave their email address. This is the case with almost every community site I've been involved with. Are these people very brave, or are they simply unaware of the risks? I don't think either is completely true. Instead, I think they're hungry for connection with like minds, in need of a community, and they're relaxed enough to feel like they're among friends. That is the mark of a successful community site.

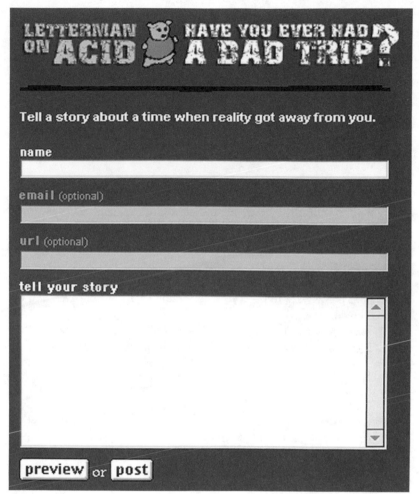

When posting to a story in {fray}, only the name and story fields are required.

Another thing that helps fight paranoia is a clear and honest communication about what will become of a user's contributions to your site. I encourage clients to provide a privacy statement that outlines the user's right to privacy in clear, non-legalese terms. If you're going to claim ownership of any content added to the site, say so. If you're going to compile what the users are talking about and sell it to advertisers, you'd better say so. (And then make sure you're giving the users enough to make it worth their while.) If you're not going to do any of those things, say that clearly and proudly. Treat your users with respect and honesty, and they'll do the same for you. It can sometimes take a lot of hand-holding just

The "Post Anonymously" check box at Slashdot.org allows you to post without revealing your identity.

Post Comment

Name <u>floyd</u> [<u>Log Out</u>]
URL <u>http://www.powazek.com</u>
Subject [Re:I wonder..]
Comment [ ]

(Use the Preview Button! Check those URLs! Don't forget the http://!)
☐ Post Anonymously
[Submit] [Preview] [HTML Formatted   ⬍]

Keeping the search engines out

There are a few ways to keep your community area out of reach of the search engines:

Meta tags. Some (but not all) search engines honor the "noindex" meta tag. All you have to do is place the following tag in the <head> of a document:

```
<meta name="robots" content="noindex">
```

A robots.txt file. Most search engines will respect a robots.txt file. This is a simple file (called "robots.txt," naturally) that you place in the top-most directory of your web server. The content of the file looks something like this:

```
User-agent:                                    *
Disallow: /
```

This would tell a search engine not to index anything on your entire site. If, however, you just wanted to protect the community area (and that community area was located at "http://yoursite.com/participate/"), the robots.txt file would look like this:

```
User-agent:                                    *
Disallow: /participate/
```

Password protection. If you require users to log in before viewing the community area, a search engine will not be able to index it.

For more on the robots exclusion protocols, visit the Web Robots Pages (www.rebotstxt.org).

to make someone feel secure creating a membership to a site, let alone revealing something personal. But if you're honest with them and provide avenues for them to protect their privacy, they'll be more likely to make the leap.

Beware the grifters!

In April 2001, Randall van der Woning met a girl named Kaycee in a chat room and struck up a conversation. There, and in subsequent conversations, they developed a strong friendship—even talking on the phone. When Kaycee told Randall that she was battling cancer, he cared. He even organized a site for her on his server, where she posted her daily struggles. In time, Randall also met her mom, Debbie, and set up a site for her, too.

The sites developed strong followings all over the web. When Kaycee posted that she was losing her hair from the chemotherapy, people sent her hats in the mail. More than a year later, Debbie called Randall. Kaycee had died. He posted the sad news to his site and, for a week, people all over the world mourned their loss and prayed for Debbie.

There was just one problem. There was no Kaycee.

After a weekend of speculating on message boards, websites, and email lists, Debbie came forward and admitted that she had no daughter. "Kaycee" had been a construct of several different people she'd known. She used the site to tell their stories. In her final post, apologizing for her actions, she said: "I alone bear the shame for what I have done, but it was not done for any reason other than sharing the love for life they gave to those they loved."

Of course, the community of people who had followed Kaycee's site erupted with betrayal. Some questioned if there ever was a "Debbie," too. Some blamed Randall. Some just lamented the death of their trust.

The Internet did not create grifters—people who scam others by gaining their confidence dishonestly—they've been around as long as time. If anything, the Net has just changed the dynamics of the game. Grifters used to be out for your money. If there was a Debbie, she was grifting for something else: intimacy.

On the web, just as in real life, some people aren't really what they present themselves to be. But an emotional betrayal in a virtual place can hurt just as much as one in real life. If you take part in a virtual community, or manage one, it's important that you keep a watchful eye out for those who may be on the grift.

Symptoms to be on the lookout for include:

- **Multiple posts from the same IP address from different people in a very short time.** You can enable server session tracking to see if posts from multiple personalities are coming from the same browser, during the same session.

- **Stories that seem too amazing to be true.** If every post reads like a Lifetime movie of the week, someone may be using your site as a creative writing assignment.

- **The center of attention.** If someone always seems to do something dramatic when the spotlight begins to fade, he may be just looking for attention.

- **Strange inconsistencies.** If someone said he was a bartender on Monday and a lawyer on Tuesday, it's probably not a typo.

It's wise to remain just slightly wary. It will also help to tie the virtual to the real as much as possible (as discussed in Chapter 5) by requiring confirmed email addresses and real names to participate.

However, it's important not to lose faith in everyone as the result of a few disturbed souls. I believe that the vast majority of people I meet online are being truthful with me. And remember, every symptom listed above *could* have a perfectly reasonable explanation. The last thing you should do is get carried away in paranoia.

Obstacle 2: Computers are work

I can't tell you how many times I've heard this: "I work on computers all day," people say. "I don't want to work on one at night." This perception of computers as work is another barrier to overcome, because people aren't going to relax enough to emote if they feel like they're on the clock and the boss is around the corner.

Brenda Laurel did some groundbreaking work in this area in the mid-nineties. She founded a company called Purple Moon that made toys, games, and websites aimed at young girls. In Laurel's research, she found that young girls were taught to view technology as work from an early age. This limited their interest and involvement in computers.

Laurel concluded that there was a need to make computer games for young girls, to encourage them to become comfortable with technology. Her company, Purple Moon, launched to critical acclaim in 1996. It is now owned by Mattel.

Laurel's research is still true today, and not just for teenage girls. So many people's first interactions with computers are in the context of jobs and school, so they will always see computers as work machines first and foremost.

But as time presses forward and computers work their way into more facets of our lives, that view is quickly fading. Apple is now referring to its computers as "digital hubs," meant to connect all your home entertainment devices, like stereos and televisions, to the Internet. And as a new generation of kids grows up with this technology, the idea of computers as solitary, emotionless work machines may soon go the way of the punch card.

Until then, there are a few things we can do to help the transition along.

To begin, we must remember that this is a psychological barrier in users, so there's not a lot you can do about it as a site creator. If people see computers as work, a computer probably won't be able to convince them otherwise. But it helps to be aware of this barrier, and do what you can to minimize it.

For example, if your site is not about work, make sure to use non-work metaphors. Calling an email area the "mailroom," a user homepage "your desk," and a common area "the water cooler" only makes the users feel like they are at the office. Instead, try calling the email area something like "connections," the user homepage "your home," and the common area "the lounge." Be aware of the mental pictures your metaphors conjure up.

Pay attention to your visual metaphors, too. Avoid designing your navigation to look like Microsoft products, for example. Gray boxes and little icons that are reminiscent of programs your users may use on the job will only reinforce the idea of computers as work.

Your site's visual design and editorial tone can help differentiate your site from the workplace. All of these things should add up to communicate: "welcome home, relax, and say hello."

Obstacle 3: Bad design

Clear, elegant design can help solve both of the issues above. But bad design is a problem unto itself. Because community features often involve a lot of user-controlled functionality, and because those features have been typically coded into existence by programmers, community areas often suffer from chronically bad design.

For example, take a look at the web page navigation on the next page—can you guess what these icons do? If you have to guess, something is wrong.

The navigation of Café Utne (cafe.utne.com) is presented without explanation or helpful text (like tool tips).

If users feel lost and confused by the design of the navigation of your site, they will never relax enough to have an intimate exchange there. And while some longtime users may eventually go to the trouble of figuring out a cryptic navigation system, it's simply an unnecessary hurdle to place before new users.

Your job is to anticipate your users' needs at every point and provide a clear path forward. You want them to be thinking about the content, not the navigation.

The antidote: Clear signage

I tend to think of navigation in these spaces like freeway signage. When you're going 65mph and there's a Mack truck going 70 behind you, you don't want to have to wonder if that next exit is the right one or not—you need to know now. The same goes for community spaces. Your users need to know if the button they're looking at is going to post their comments publicly or just preview them. They need to know where their words are going to go, and who's going to see them. And they need to know it as easily as possible.

This is not to say that there isn't a place for exploratory design. On the contrary, sometimes encouraging users to explore a virtual space can be an effective way to get them to engage the site creatively. But when it comes to navigating the community functionality, don't mess around. Tell the user what to expect from each element, and be as direct as you can.

Clear navigation has another purpose, too: It communicates trust. In 1999, Cheskin Research (a strategic market research firm) and Studio Archetype (a web design shop) conducted a study of trust

A comment in preview mode in my redesign of Notes.net. Notice all the explanatory text.

> **Preview your response**
>
> I am previewing this post. Isn't that cool?
> Posted by derek m powazek on 01/18/2001 at 12:55 AM
>
> **You must click the post button below to post your response.**
>
> I am previewing this post. Isn't that cool?
>
> [preview] [post] [cancel]

online. They were looking for what makes web users trust commerce sites, but what they found can be universally applied. Research subjects listed the usual suspects when talking about whom they trust: brand identity, seals of approval, and order fulfillment, for example. But the other thing they said over and over again was that quality navigation was one of the most important factors when deciding whom to trust. The report concluded that "effective navigation is a necessary pre-condition to successfully communicating the trustworthiness of a site."

Put more simply, if users can't figure out how to get around your site, they're not going to open their pocketbooks... or their hearts.

Effective navigation is key

A 1999 study found that clear and understandable navigation was one of the most important elements in communicating trust online.

"Strong navigation can be best understood as the foundation of communicating trustworthiness," it concluded.

The entire Cheskin/Studio Archetype study, "eCommerce Trust Study," is available for download at (www.sapient.com/cheskin).

Trustworthiness is the antidote to the paranoia problem. And clear navigation, privacy statements, and non-work metaphors are some of the ways to help users trust you.

Any Hot Chicks Here?

Some of the oldest and biggest companies to realize intimate virtual communities used one simple tool: real-time chat. AOL (America Online) has become one of the most powerful companies on the Net with a simple formula of email, instant messaging, and chat. I'm convinced that AOL owes its riches to the endless scrolling lines of banter in its chat rooms.

Chat is at once the most powerful and most hated community tool available. It's hard not to write it off after taking a cursory pass through any web-based chat room. The comments whiz by like you're eavesdropping on a giant, fractured party line. People come in and out constantly, and each one seems to want to know everyone's "ASL" (age, sex, location). In researching chat rooms for this book, I got so tired of being asked to identify my age, gender, and location, I started making things up. "I'm a multi-gendered alien from the planet Zog where everyone is born at 35 and ages backwards, so I'm either 13 or 22, depending on how you count."

This is not a good way to make friends in the Britney Spears chat room.

Then, of course, there's the unrelenting search for hot chicks. "Any hot chicks here?" is probably the most commonly typed phrase in web chat. I have to wonder who all these Internet Casanovas are, and why they think this is such a good pickup line.

Chat is easy to make fun of for all these reasons and more. But, as much as it's maligned, it also stands as one of the most powerfully intimate modes of communication on the Net. All those chatters who have made AOL the largest Internet company on the planet must be getting something out of it.

Kvetch!
(www.kvetch.com)
in live chat mode,
with "Big Dude" at
the top of his
game.

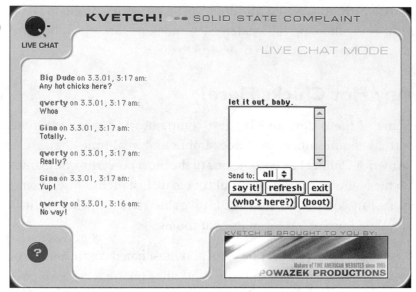

What they're getting is a real-time connection to other human beings that is hard to reproduce any other way. They're getting a powerfully intimate connection to friends and strangers all across the globe. It's no surprise that my first experience with virtual intimacy was in a simple real-time chat room. There's something powerful about knowing that the words trickling on-screen were *just typed* by someone. It's an immediacy that is lacking from other asynchronous modes of communication. And it can be intoxicating.

Why chat works

The crucial difference between chat and asynchronous communication (like web boards) is its ephemeral nature. Where web boards are typically archived for posterity, chat posts scroll away like a train of thought. And although some programs allow you to save a chat log for posterity, in most cases that log is just a local file on your computer. Usually, there is no public record of the experience.

This changes the fundamental nature of the conversation in some important ways. In the least, it avoids the whole search engine problem discussed earlier. It also creates a very temporary, ephemeral space.

The chatters know that what they say will soon scroll away never to be seen again. This can contribute to the very juvenile behavior I was complaining about (and demonstrating as the traveler from Zog). But it can also create an environment that is prone to stunning honesty. If you know everything you say will disappear, why not just tell it like it is?

The trick is to harness chat's power to create an intimate community space, without having it fall prey to its own juvenile tendencies.

How to use chat

Chat rooms are a great way to bring an existing virtual community together in real-time. Years ago, I was on a mailing list with peers all over the country. We'd discussed so much over the course of the list, I felt like I knew them. One day, while testing out a chat script, I invited the list to come help me test it. Within minutes, many of them had logged in to the chat.

Suddenly, these virtual people who had previously only existed in email were talking to each other in real-time. It shed new light on their personalities and changed the way I experienced our community.

In this way, a chat room can be a wonderful addition to an existing virtual community, especially if it was saved for special prescheduled chats with the community.

Using chat sparingly is often the best approach. If you run a website where people are connecting through asynchronous communication, changing gears to talk in real-time can be quite a thrill. Try hosting a weekly chat for the community once a week. The results may surprise you.

Another common and effective way to use scheduled chats is to bring in someone of interest to the community for a chat. It can be hard to get people all over the world to show up at one site at the same time. A rare appearance by someone the community is interested in can help draw people in.

The bottom line is, chat is a powerful way to connect your community, but it's not an intimate experience by default. It takes planning and guidance. A chat room can be sober and respectful or childish and immature. It just depends on the people involved and the presentation of the environment.

I'm ready for my close-up

Webcams can be another vital element of intimacy online. If you've never seen one, a webcam is a little camera that's usually perched atop your monitor. A program snaps photos at a user-defined interval and uploads them to a website, where viewers can watch a choppy, almost real-time view of the person behind the computer.

What real-time chat does for conversations online, webcams do for images. All the same rules apply—the immediacy, the ephemeral nature, the visceral connection. Watching a webcam can be strangely captivating.

As visceral as real-time chat can be, it's still just words appearing on a screen. But couple that with a constantly updating image of the chatter, and the experience takes on a whole new urgency. Together, they can be powerfully intimate.

No one has harnessed this power better than CitizenX (citizenx.com). There, users with webcams can have their own "Spot" up and running in minutes, including a Java-based chat room, constantly refreshing webcam, a weblog to post updates, a guest book for visitors to sign, and a profile page.

Once your spot is complete, your visitors will come streaming in. Since the site keeps track of who is online and whether they're

A "Spot" on CitizenX combines real-time chat and a webcam to create an intimate space.

broadcasting or not, as soon as a new user comes online, people will come to say hello.

I can't say I've had an intimate experience while hanging out in my Spot, but I can see how it's possible. Just knowing that the words appearing on-screen are being typed by people who can see my reaction to reading them changes the experience in some significant ways. The feeling of tele-presence is strong—you can almost feel the visitors there with you.

The idea that there are virtual communities and real ones that are separate from each other begins to fall away. In its place, we're simply left with our community, one with both virtual and real components. This is a central idea behind the site, and one that John Styn, one of the creators of CitizenX, has built his life around. We'll hear more from him at the end of this chapter.

The Magic Element

All the things we've discussed in this chapter—privacy, support, chat, cams—are all puzzle pieces. There are many ways to spread them around the table and never solve the puzzle. Whatever you do, don't think that you can put up a site with a chat room, a webcam, and a forum and expect intimacy to just happen.

In the end, intimacy online is just as fickle as it is in the real world, if not more. It takes the right group of people, in the right mood, with the right tools, to put all the pieces together and create an intimate experience.

But make no mistake, intimacy is a vital part of any virtual community, from the smallest fanzine to the biggest corporate site. It's the magic element that takes a conversation past the pleasantries and makes it truly matter. Pay attention to your community space with an eye toward making it more intimate—a little trust can go a long way.

A Conversation with John Styn

There is no one I know who has had more experience with intimacy online than John Styn. Through his personal projects (cockybastard.com, styn.net, prehensile.com) and professional endeavors (citizenx.com, therealhouse.com), he's pushed the boundaries of online self-expression to create spaces that are vital, immediate, and intensely personal. I interviewed him via email in February 2001.

John, please give us a brief introduction to who you are and what you do.

John Halcyon Styn

My name is John Halcyon Styn (or cockybastard, for short). I'm one of those people who still believe in the dream of the Internet as a revolutionary, artistic, and social tool—not just a place to buy books or auction Barbies.

I've led the community building efforts of several sites, from the intimate community that centers around my personal site to the three million member community of Collegeclub.com. My current project is CitizenX.com and its companion, TheRealHouse.com. To me, the web is a new tool in the artist's palette. Instead of brushstrokes, we create virtual spaces.

Let's talk about CitizenX. Please describe it in a nutshell for anyone who is unfamiliar with it. How did it begin? What was the intent?

CitizenX is a 90,000 member community (growing by approximately 500/day) based around webcams and streaming broadband communication.

Basically, you can see someone while you chat with them. Two years ago, I created a page on my personal site that had my refreshing webcam image and had an attached chat room. The chat room was set up so that you were automatically logged in to the chat when the page loaded. This made you instantly visible in the virtual space. You were unable to truly lurk. In this initial version of the chat/cam room, people were anonymous when they entered. But it still made you an instant participant.

Many people who were used to just watching the web suddenly found themselves in it. You are there in this virtual space. It says "Anonymous19" right there on the screen. (A screen name you can change to your own, if you choose.) I believe that was a powerful shift for many web surfers.

Very quickly a small community started hanging out in the room. Even when I wasn't there, it became evident that the combination of webcams and chat had huge community potential.

In May of last year, we launched a beta of CitizenX. The site gave anyone the ability to have an instant hub for their webcam with the goodies that I had in my initial room, plus other features. They got a personal chat room, a weblog, guest book, instant messaging, and as many of the traditional community tools as we could build. People can come to your personal hub (or "Spot") and chat with you, or chat with others who have stopped by to visit you. The Spot, with its visual aspect of the webcam, became a very real digital space. People new to online communities had no problem visualizing and feeling the presence of a Spot. "Meet me at my Spot" became a common thing to hear in the communal Lounge chat rooms. Citizens saw their Spot as a digital living room. And the interactions mimicked real life: Friends drop by to see if you're home, say hello, or leave a message on your guest book if you're away.

When I visited CitizenX, I was struck by the Andy Warhol-esque nature of the place. It was like, "your 15 minutes of fame, just add webcam!" Is fame the main idea, with community a pleasant side effect? Or was the community the goal?

Maybe we should incorporate Campbell's soup cans into the new design? Seriously, though, community was always our goal. But communities always generate "microstars"—people who develop reputations within the community and thus take on the role of minor celebrities.

When you give people a personal broadcasting avenue like a webcam, the potential for community celebrities is intensified. For example, at CitizenX, everyone knows "adigitalartist" and "Flare22." They are famous in the way that the captain of the football team was famous in high school. They are microstars and have added respect in the community.

But there is another type of fame that can happen with a webcam. It is possible to become famous instantly. You can be a star for a night. Generally, it takes a show of some sexual nature to generate a crowd in your Spot (without a prior reputation). But it is not uncommon for a broadcaster to attract a crowd of 30+ fawning citizens if they let out a little of their inner minx.

Anyone, not just people who look like strippers, can feel what it is like to be the object of desire up on a virtual stage. I'll admit that I have had a number of exciting evenings where I became intoxicated by the all-caps screaming of "TAKE IT OFF" in my chat room.

The challenge, from a community-building standpoint, is making sure that the people yelling "take it off" are only doing so to people who want that type of attention.

Because, for the majority of broadcasters, the cam is less of a performance than it is another way to share themselves to new and old friends.

How does adding a webcam to the mix change the dynamic of a community?

A webcam makes a few major impacts to traditional online interactions. It eliminates the "what-if-this-girl-I'm-chatting-with-is-actually-a-guy" element. You can't pretend to be "Thundar," a 6-foot-tall Mel Gibson look-alike if your cam shows a pimple-faced teen.

The real-time visual element truly gives the feeling of a real space, not just a virtual space. When you can see Joan and her cat in her messy computer room, it eliminates the science fiction aspect of chatting with people from a different time and place. When you can see someone in Hong Kong laughing at your clever chat room pun, it makes the space between you almost nonexistent. You truly feel like you are sitting together in a virtual space. And it is worlds more human than "LOL" will ever be.

Unfortunately, many people associate webcams with sex shows. So educating people about etiquette is a constant battle. Many cretins are quick to yell "SHOW ME YOUR TITS" behind their anonymous login name.

It's interesting that the more intimate a virtual community space becomes, the more etiquette is an issue. How do you deal with troublemakers?

The troublemaker issue is a constant battle. When your face is in front of the world via webcam, a negative comment can sting pretty badly. Since we are a free site, we have the same issue with anonymous users that many sites do. Policing can be tough since people can create as many accounts as they want.

We have a boot feature that kicks people off and doesn't let them back for 24 hours. We wanted it to be a slap on the hand, but not a hard enough hit to prompt retaliation. A 12-year-old kid with lots of time and little to lose can make a community builder's life very difficult. So we try to steer troublemakers in the right direction rather than start fights. We average about 2–3 boots a day, site-wide.

We also just rolled out personal Spot admin ability so each Spot owner can kick people out and maintain a list of citizens who don't have access. And we want to work towards giving people the ability to keep whatever kind of digital home (and company) they like.

You're blending your real life with your web life more and more these days, living in The Real House, which broadcasts your life to paying web surfers 24/7. What have you learned about people

in the process of blending your two lives (digital and non-digital)
together?

Well, I've been exploring the live interactive abilities of current
technologies.

Since I live in a webcam house and am being integrated to the CitizenX
community, people can see me, and if they have a webcam, I can see
them. We could have a theme party in the house, and someone could
"participate remotely" by dressing up in their dorm room 1,000
miles away.

They could even have a "satellite party" with the same theme. Despite
locations in different states or countries, we are attending the same
party… sharing the same vibes.

The line between real-life community and digital community becomes
blurry. I see this as one of the futures of online communities: We will
simply have "communities" with physical and digital elements.

What's the most intimate experience you've ever had online?

If you don't count the naked stuff, I think the most intimate experience
I've had online was the Virtual Grace we did using a CitizenX Lounge
last Thanksgiving.

We told everyone in the community, that if you were gonna be alone
on Thanksgiving, log in to a special chat room at a certain time, and
we would all say grace together. Is grace a religious thing? Well, it was
intended to be vaguely spiritual, I suppose.

Fifty or so people were there, 20 had webcams. The thumbnails
along the bottom of the page showed us the order that we were seated
around our virtual table. We adapted a tradition from my family
where everyone takes a turn sharing what they are thankful for. As
people began to speak in the chat room, the virtual space became
concrete. Online personas faded and people shared their hearts. You
saw laughter and tears in the 30-second-refreshing faces as people
typed about their children and families. Some were thankful that
they could be around such good friends on this special day.

It didn't matter that we were physically apart, the space was real and warm and love-filled. It felt like we were all holding hands, smelling the same pumpkin pie.

That's beautiful. What about the other side of the coin – have you ever experienced something very sad?

A year ago I was going through girl trouble. (No, not feminine troubles—my cramps were fine.) While reading an email from my (then) girlfriend, my heart broke, and I started to cry. Really cry. Huge, splattering tears. I felt so alone. So betrayed. So hopeless. On a whim, I clicked on my webcam chat room bookmark and saw that there were a handful of people there. They saw my tears and felt my pain. They offered condolences and words of comfort. The digital hugs they extended instantly eased my grief.

It was like when I was a kid and skinned my knee in the street. I was so focused on the pain and the cruel world that did this to me—until my Mom came up and swept me up into her embrace. The pain was still there, but I was surrounded by love. As I sat in the emptiness of my room, crying in front of my webcam and a chat room filled with friends, I was far from alone.

Has the CitizenX community surprised you? How?

There was one bad surprise that prompted a good surprise.

The bad surprise was the large number of people (generally men) who assumed that a site with cams (and perhaps "X" in the URL) was a place to see women put on sexual shows.

We created cam ratings (G, PG, R, X) to try to segregate the adult cams, but that only worked to a limited degree. Some broadcasters get a screen full of sexual Instant Messages despite the "G" rating of their cam and their family-oriented Spot description.

The good surprise has been the amazing support within the community to try to combat/educate/alleviate this adult cam misunderstanding. We have a team of 30 official volunteer "Ambassadors" who have limited admin ability (including the ability to boot an offending citizen for 24 hours). But what surprised me was the scores of other people who took it upon themselves to help regulate the community: spending time helping new members find their way around, setting up webcams, and avoiding inappropriate solicitations. Seeing the effectiveness and passion of the Ambassadors (both official and unofficial) has been the most rewarding part of the project.

If someone came to you and said they were thinking of adding webcams and chat to their existing community site, what would you say?

I'd say, focus on the community first. Consider the cams as merely one aspect of a member's profile. Sites like SpotLife (spotlife.com) are failing because they set up webcams as if they were programs to be watched. But cams are merely one element of a complex person… a person who wants to communicate with other people in their community. A webcam can enhance, but not replace, other communication tools.

Chapter 8

Barriers to Entry

...Making Them Work for It

"It's important to remember that just as a community includes some people, by definition it excludes others. All healthy communities have boundaries that are self-enforced through a variety of means, from informal social pressure to formal expulsion. Communities cannot function well without some means of exclusion."

– Author and interface pioneer Brenda Laurel, from "People, Communities, and Service: Shaping the Future of the Internet," a keynote speech given at GovNet '99.

There are two common assumptions about community on the web that need to be destroyed, here and now, before going any further. Don't worry, this'll only hurt for a moment.

Bad Assumption 1: Communities Are Open to All

I love the web because it's inclusive by nature. Anyone with something to say can find a place to say it online. It was this love of inclusion that led me to create sites that were community-driven and open to all.

And that's where I learned the hardest lesson of community: **All communities are exclusionary to some degree**.

This happens whether the site creator wants it or not. And, as much as it pains me to say it, exclusion is as much a part of the community recipe as inclusion.

It's true that there is, indeed, a community out there for everyone. But not all communities are available to everyone. The fine line between inclusion and exclusion can be referred to as the **barrier to entry**, and every community has one—which brings me to assumption number two.

Bad Assumption 2: Barriers Are Bad

On my first-ever homepage, I stated proudly that I was here to "specialize in intuitave [sic] interfaces." (I never was much for spelling.)

Every web designer begins with the assumption that, because the web is so often a trial to use, it's his job to make everything as easy to use as possible. He learns to smooth every transition, remove every stumbling block, and get the users to their destinations as fast as possible, no matter what.

On its face, this is still good advice. But designing community spaces is different than designing a web store or an informational utility, and the same rules don't always apply. While it may be important to give users whatever they want when you're trying to sell them a widget, in a community setting, barriers to entry are a necessary part of creating a successful community space.

In real life, communities have entry rituals—parties, hazings, blind dates, and more. And in some ways, the amount of energy you expend to join a community, the more the community means to you. The web is no different. Sometimes, you have to work for something to be meaningful.

Advice I Hate to Give

I hate to give you this advice, because it runs against the grain of everything designers want to believe, including me. And make no mistake, inclusion is still a very good thing online, and ease of use is still absolutely critical to managing a successful website, no matter the content.

But in the context of a community space online, priorities need to shift and web designers need to reexamine their assumptions.

Every community has people who are in and people who are out. A community, real or virtual, would simply lose all meaning if everybody in the world was in it, right? This line between the "in" group and "out" group is the Barrier to Entry, and every site has one.

This barrier to entry fulfills an incredibly important role. It's not that you want to keep the riff-raff out, it's that in order to create a successful community, you must focus the conversation to stay relevant to the site. As discussed in Chapter 2, it's not enough to just put up a discussion board and let people talk about everything under the sun. A well-placed barrier to entry will develop your site's identity and filter your audience to those with the most knowledge and passion for the subject. The result is a successful, on-topic, well-behaved community.

Once you've come to terms with the idea of a barrier to entry that keeps certain people out at certain times, you've taken the first step. The good news is that you have a choice about where, and how, to place the barrier. There will be times when having a low barrier can be a good thing, and times when you'll want to make it more difficult to enter your community.

What you do with that barrier will have a significant impact on the success and character of the community it guards. You just can't pretend that there isn't one.

The Three Kinds of Barriers

There are probably as many different varieties of barriers to entry as there are communities. Each community comes up with a scheme to let people in or keep people out, overtly or with subtlety. For the purposes of this chapter, I've divided them into three types, from low to high: informal, formal, and extreme.

Informal barriers to entry

Informal barriers to entry are the most common on the web. This means that there are no formalized procedures or techniques to keep people out. No logins, no passwords, no guards or gates. So where's the barrier?

Interest-level is the barrier. As discussed in Chapter 3, "Design Matters," your content itself can be used as a barrier to entry. Move the community functionality to the end of the content, bury the post button, and let the content do the filtering for you. If potential community members can't make it through your content to get to the community functionality, you probably don't want them in the community anyway. A baseline interest is a good starting place for a community.

Design can also be an effective informal barrier. Your visual design should speak to the audience you're trying to attract. For example, ShockFusion (shockfusion.com) is a web-based community for designers who work with Macromedia's Shockwave. The site is entirely created using Shockwave, and therefore requires that visitors have the Shockwave plug-in to view the site.

Ordinarily, I advise clients against requiring a plug-in on their site—it cuts out too much of the potential audience. But if your audience is going to have the plug-in anyway, why not? In fact, in

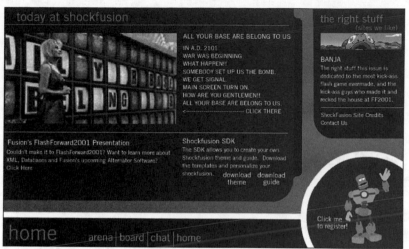

The design of ShockFusion serves as an informal barrier to entry.

this case, requiring the plug-in is a great barrier to entry. If you don't have the plug-in installed, you're probably not the audience they're after.

Other very successful community sites use the same method. ThirdAge (thirdage.com) is a site for senior citizens, one of the fastest-growing segments of the online population. There, the chats and web boards are free and open to all. But if you're looking for a lively discussion of the new Limp Bizkit album, you're out of luck. Geriatric medicine and retirement accounting advice? Come on in! The ads alone ("Where will you be when your grandson gets his first taste of the ocean? Be there. Ask your doctor about ZOCOR.") should tell you if you're in the target demographic or not.

Informal techniques like this create a low barrier to entry. You might think they wouldn't work, but they're surprisingly effective. And it's the method I use for most of my sites. From the stories at {fray} to the complaints at Kvetch!, the only thing you have to do to join the community is be interested enough to read through the content. I don't think that's too much to ask.

Cholesterol? Zocor? The ads alone convey who ThirdAge's audience is.

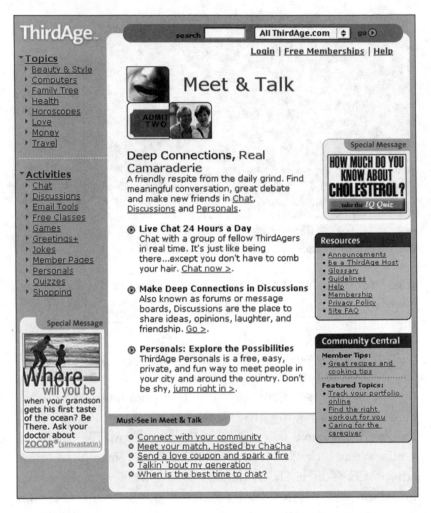

Formal barriers to entry

Formal barriers set the bar higher. While informal barriers communicate the community expectations in the content and design, formal barriers are explicit: You must be this tall to ride.

The biggest and most common application of a formal barrier to entry is the all-too-common registration requirement, where the user is forced to create an account and log in before participating in the community. This is a mixed bag—users with accounts can be a blessing. It makes troublemakers easier to spot and remove.

And, as discussed previously, when users feel strong ties from their virtual world to their real life, they're more likely to behave. At the same time, forcing a user through the registration process will severely decrease the number of people willing to participate. The annoyance factor can be high, both for the user and the owner of the site.

In the end, it all comes down to the goals of the community. If you're trying to foster prolonged conversations over time, requiring accounts is the way to go. You'll need them to promote account-ability and consistency of usernames.

If, on the other hand, you're primarily trying to foster a one-time connection, then requiring accounts is an unnecessary hassle to impose on the user, and you'll wind up turning too many people off to justify it. Imagine how you would feel if you had to create an account just to read the stories at your favorite news site. Sound crazy? The New York Times on the Web (nytimes.com) does just that.

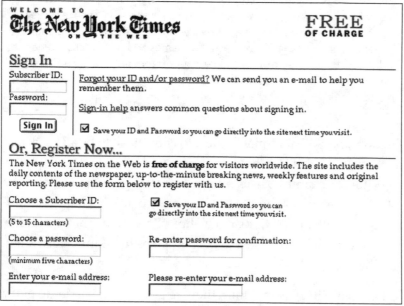

The New York Times on the Web's all-too-familiar sign-in screen (nytimes.com).

If you do decide to require your users to create accounts, you're raising the bar on the barrier to entry for your community. But you can raise it even higher still!

Once you've decided to create accounts, you have more decisions to make. Will you also require an email address? Some communities go so far as to require an email address and then send an email to that address, requiring the user to reply (or go to a custom URL) in order for the account to become active. This prevents bogus addresses from getting into the system.

Want to have an extremely high barrier to entry? Create a five-page account registration. You may not get many sign-ups, but you know the ones you get are going to be invested. I often joke that the one and only way to make sure that a virtual community is always peaceful and flame-free is to require a valid credit card number to join. Now that's a barrier to entry!

The costs of membership

Be warned: Requiring registrations has technical ramifications. Creating a database of usernames and passwords requires a very secure server to preserve community members' privacy. There's also an added support requirement, as people forget their usernames and passwords. Someone will need to answer the inevitable support emails. Be sure to factor these costs into any decision you make regarding formal account registrations.

But don't think that formal barriers to entry have to be all work and no play. It's possible to have some fun with this. The Man Show's website, for example, uses humor to both screen its visitors and establish the tone of the site (themanshow.com). It's not a community site, really. In fact, it's not a show I'd even want to endorse, unless watching two losers make bad jokes to bikini-clad women is your thing.

But even a critic has to admit, they've got a great barrier to entry on their site. The first page the user encounters is a question, designed specifically to screen their audience. The question changes with each visit, to stay surprising. The screenshot below asks: "Do you wear a fanny pack?" Other questions include: "What was the title of Michael Bolton's first album?", "Have you ever said to someone, 'Pull my finger'?", and of course, "Do you eat nachos?"

Crude? Absolutely. Which is exactly the audience they're looking for.

The Man Show's barrier to entry both screens the audience and defines the site with humor.

Choose the right answer, and you can enter the site. But choose the wrong one, and you're called a "wet-palmed, pillow-bitin', sittin'-to-pee, skirt-wearin' sally."

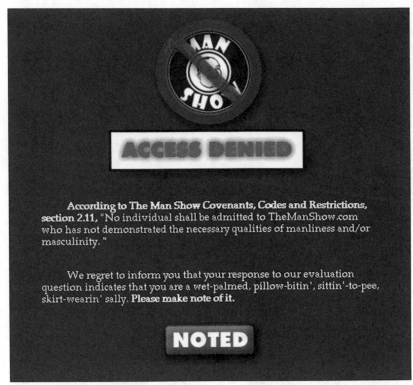

Other formal barriers include age requirements for adult content, location requirements for local communities, and experience requirements for others. The key here is to identify your audience and create a barrier to entry just low enough for them, but high enough to dissuade others.

You want to start a virtual community for your college class alumni? You'll have to create a pretty clever barrier to entry. Perhaps a series of questions only your college colleagues would know the answers to would work. Of course, you could just check names and identity information against a list, but imagine the work for a class of a thousand or even more.

One interesting example of a formalized barrier to entry was Reality Check, an experimental web community project sponsored by Web Lab, a non-profit organization devoted to innovative public interest web projects. Reality Check was only active from November 1998 to March 1999, but I haven't seen anything like it since. The site is still online in a "hibernating" state at reality-check.com.

Their thesis was simple: Web communities suffer from too many talkers and not enough listeners. So they created a structure that set caps on the number of participants and the duration of conversations. Community members could sign up for a "Dialogue Group" on a certain topic. When the group reached 15 participants, it was closed. The 15 people then had four weeks to discuss the topic at length. Their discussion was open for all to read, but only the 15 could post. After four weeks, the participants could vote to decide whether or not they wanted to continue.

This way the site was setting a defined barrier to entry—you had to be one of the 15 people to participate—but still remained inclusive, because anyone could read the conversations and register to participate in one of the open topics.

Formal barriers to entry also bring up an added requirement: People are needed to communicate and enforce the barriers to entry. These people are called "hosts," and were discussed in depth in Chapter 5.

Extreme barriers to entry

Sometimes, extreme measures are required. These are times when you have content you really need to guard, or you have an established community that is spinning out of control, growing too fast, or just generally becoming too hard to manage. Trimming the user base is one way to fix the problem. Here are two stories of communities that did just that.

Story 1: A list in hot water

Caleb Clark has a great story to illustrate this concept. Clark is the creator of NoEnd, an email-based community of geeks and wanderers out of San Francisco, started in 1997. The list was unique, and cultivated conversations that ranged from finding work to metaphysical explorations to simply talking about your week.

The list was a victim of its own success. As the membership grew, the list began to lose its cohesion. The barrier to entry was too low. Clark knew something had to be done. Then he found the hot tub.

In Berkeley, a self-described former hippie who simply goes by the nom-de-tub "Hot Tub Guy" had set up a semipublic hot tub in his backyard. When he started it in 1975, the tub was free and open to all. The Hot Tub Guy considered it a natural hot springs—there to be enjoyed respectfully by all. But as its reputation spread, the tub began to get out of control. By the mid-eighties, it was filling up when the bars let out, full of drunks being obnoxious.

Instead of shutting it down, the Hot Tub Guy set up a gate with a punch key system and distributed the seven-digit entry codes to his faithful tubbers. Now, when a crowd grew unruly, he could simply disable the codes used that night. What's more, tubbers could tell their friends about the tub, and give out their entry code. But the tubbers knew that if their friends behaved inappropriately, their code would be shut off, and they themselves would be kept out. Participants now had a vested interest in making sure the people they brought into the hot tub community behaved themselves.

It's worked that way ever since. There are now more than 800 working codes to the tub, which get logged on the Hot Tub Guy's computer as they're used.

After his visit to the Berkeley tub, Clark knew what he had to do. In his words:

> We announced that due to too many people spread
> out too far in the world, we were going to kill the list
> and start over. In 24 hours the list would cease to
> exist entirely. A new list would be started up, and the
> address given out at an in-person meeting in San

Francisco. We did just that. In a month we had 200 people on the new list, even though only 20 to 50 came to the meeting. The people far away who were long-time members got back on the list through friends who were able to come to meetings and get the address. After three months we were up to 300 and have been around 300 to 400 ever since. "Hot Tubbing" has become a known NoEnd technique, and whenever the list gets a little too active or off track we talk about it openly.

Story 2: Burning the village

Flash guru Joshua Davis never really planned on running a community. But when he started Dreamless.org on a whim to connect with his fellow graphic designers, they responded in force. Soon his humble community had exploded to more than 4,000 members. His web discussion software was starting to strain, and members were starting to bristle with each other and him. Davis decided to do something drastic.

He told his community that they were going to burn the village down. He opened up the codes that determined the look of the site and let community members "hack" it. Members turned the threads into illegible, yet beautiful, works of art. The burning lasted a weekend; then he took the site down, replacing the home-page at dreamless.org with a page that flashed the site's trademark blacks and grays behind the only text on the page: "Dreamless." The village had been destroyed.

Davis describes the process romantically:

> "It was like being in a plane that was about to crash—you scurry to say all of the things you wanted to say. Most of this took place in the board hacking. Nothing was sacred, and it produced the rawest and

Some examples of the "hacked" Dreamless pages.

most participatory global event I have ever seen. And since the members were not really sure if Dreamless was going to ever be live again, there was purity—however horrid or beautiful that could be."

But the dream was not over. Davis had actually put up Dreamless version two at a new location. After the burning was over, he told a few of the old members what the new URL was and let them spread the word to the other users they knew. He later placed a comment in the HTMLsource code of the homepage at dreamless.org. Clever participants who viewed the source of the page were treated to a surprise:

The Dreamless message in a bottle.

```
┌────────────────────── HTML: dreamless.org ──────────────────────┐
<!------------------------------------------------------------

   (c) 2001 | no one - last updated ( Friday, February 16, 2001 )

   It's not dead.
   It's just evolving.

   http://www.dreamless.org/cgi-bin/root.pl
   keep this URL to yourself.


   Its success is based on being hidden.

   dreamless@praystation.com
------------------------------------------------------------------>

<html>
<head>
<title>dreamless.org</title>
```

Visitors who went to the listed URL could re-register and participate in the continuation of the community. Davis estimates that
within two weeks, a thousand of the original community members
were back. When they returned, they found a new site with new
topic areas and a refreshed design—changes that were considered
before, but would have been too much work, were easy to make
from a clean slate.

Was it worth it? Davis is enthusiastic.

> "Does the Net always have to be open? Do you let
> someone into your house merely because they want
> to take a peek? With mass-saturation and mass-
> participation comes mass-chaos (which I secretly
> love). But it also creates a ton of user deterioration—
> so many different opinions, player haters, shock
> posters, flamers, etc. After Dreamless tightened its
> exposure, the level of communication and participa-
> tion has been top-notch."

Drastic times require drastic measures

Both of these stories illustrate extreme cases in which a near-
death experience revitalized and refocused an existing community.
Let's hope that you never find yourself in this kind of situation, but
if you do, it's good to know that a dynamic community can
survive, and even thrive, when faced with challenges like these.

Barriers Can Change Over Time

Both of these stories also illustrate another important idea—
barriers to entry do not need to be fixed in one specific place. In
fact, it can be good to adjust them over time, in response to the
changing needs of your community.

A fledgling community may require a low barrier to entry in
order to attract users and gain momentum. Once a critical mass of
users has arrived, it may make sense to raise the bar and make your

barrier to entry more difficult. Adding more required information to the sign-up process or imposing a registration, for example, would be ways to raise the bar. In many cases, after a few months of cultivating a community, you'll see how you need to filter your users. Often, the changes needed practically present themselves.

When Matthew Haughey (interviewed in Chapter 2) started MetaFilter, for example, any registered user could post to the homepage. After the site took off, it became clear that new users were making the same mistakes. Common errors included self-linking (posting a link to your own site or project) or posting inappropriate topics.

Haughey solved this problem in two ways. First, he updated the user agreement to specifically address these problems. But secondly, and more interestingly, he realized that these problems could be averted if new users simply participated in the community as readers for a while before becoming posters. So he imposed a new barrier to entry: New users were forced to do two things before posting topics to the homepage. They had to be a member for at least 24 hours (to deter people who only signed up to link to themselves), and they had to have posted at least three comments to existing threads (to encourage community participation).

The result? Membership has been increasing just as fast, if not faster, as before, but the new members come in with a much better understanding of the community.

And It Goes Both Ways

Barriers to entry can also become more lenient over time. I've personally experienced a kind of stifling in communities that erect their barriers too high, too soon.

I was once part of an email list community that formed around the common interests of a few real-world friends. Since the list was formed out of our mutual real-world friendships, it made sense to simply set the barrier to entry at the friendship level. In other words, you had to be a friend to join. Simple, right?

Unfortunately, since everyone was spread out across the globe and members of different social circles, nobody had a friend who was also friends with anyone else on the list, so the membership did not change significantly during the course of the list.

While the phrase "familiarity breeds contempt" may be cliché, in this case it rings true. After a while, we simply had less and less to say to each other, and the community waned. Had some new members been introduced, it might have reinvigorated the community with a fresh perspective and sparked a renaissance. Without that fresh perspective, the list drifted along with less and less activity. Eventually, I told my friends that I loved them and unsubscribed.

If you find that your users aren't really coalescing into a community, you may want to examine your barrier to entry—it may be too high. And remember, if you lower it and things take off, you can always raise it again. Remember, communities are always a work in progress.

Barriers Are Good

Barriers are a part of everyday life. In the olden days, when you wanted to write a letter to the editor of a newspaper, you actually had to sit down, write something on paper, stick it in an envelope, address it by hand, and put it in a mailbox.

Just because the web can make this process easier doesn't mean it should. Sometimes, the best thing you can do for your community is to make it just slightly hard to reach. And while you may not want to take it all down dramatically or hold a village burning, you should pay close attention to the barrier to entry on your site. Nudging it up or down with care may be the most important piece of design you create.

Photo by Joey Cavella

Emma Taylor

A Conversation with Emma Taylor

If I said the phrase "barriers to entry" to a guy who's unfamiliar with the web, he might think I'm talking about a first date. And while that's funny, it's not completely in jest. Getting past barriers to entry, slowly gaining trust, is a part of any relationship, real or virtual.

So it made sense to sit down and talk about barriers to entry and participation with Emma Taylor, one of the two main hosts of NerveCenter (nervecenter.com), the community arm of the alternative magazine Nerve. NerveCenter has a wide array of community functionality: chat, homepages, discussion forums, personals, and even a web-based instant messaging service. And there are different barriers to entry for each—some even use the oldest form of a barrier to entry: cold, hard cash.

For those unfamiliar, Nerve features frank talk about sex and artful nude photography, but it's no Playboy. Its motto, "think about sex," perfectly sums up the magazine, and its affiliated "community of thoughtful hedonists." Its content strikes a precarious balance between intellectualism and eroticism, but what's more amazing is that it's produced a community of people who treat this material, and each other, with seriousness and respect. Clearly, they're doing something right.

I spoke with Taylor over email in late 2000.

Emma, please give us a brief introduction to who you are and what you do.

I'm one of the co-hosts/cruise directors of NerveCenter, Nerve.com's online community (along with Lorelei Sharkey). We go by "Em & Lo" in the community, and together we host the message board and two weekly chats, write a weekly advice column (The Em & Lo Down) and weekly horoscopes, choose which message boards quotes, personal ads and member homepages to feature, and publish a daily poll. In addition, we work with designers, programmers, project managers, etc., to improve our current features and add new services.

Let's talk about NerveCenter. Please describe it in a nutshell for anyone who's unfamiliar. How did it begin? What was the intent?

We call NerveCenter "The Community of Thoughtful Hedonists." It's Nerve.com's online community, where readers can meet like-minded people. It includes lively message boards on everything from the ethics of polyamory to how to take care of your sex toys; regular chats with Nerve-friendly experts and celebrities (e.g., director John Waters, author Jerry Stahl, anal sex expert Dr. Jack Morin); Nerve Personals; The Em & Lo Down (weekly advice column by near-experts); the Instant Gratifier (so members can send notes to other members online right now); plus member-created homepages, free email accounts, e-cards with Nerve photography and more.

NerveCenter launched in November 1999 (Nerve.com launched in June 1997). We have a total of 200,000 members, 20,000 personal ads. We get about 1,000 new members a day, and couple of hundred new personal ads are posted each day. Nerve.com has a million unique readers a month.

How do you let your users get directly involved in the site?

There is a feedback button at the bottom of every article and photography gallery, so readers can immediately post their feedback to the site and browse what others have said. More in-depth conversations take place in the message boards. NerveCenter also includes chat (open 24/7), a daily poll, personal ads, personal homepages, and the above-mentioned Instant Gratifier.

What are the barriers to entry for your community tools?

The message boards are open to all members, though you have to log in to read or post to them. The only areas where members pay are in the Personals and the Instant Gratifier. In Personals, it's free to build and browse ads; you only pay if you want to respond to someone's ad (and once someone has responded to your ad, it's free for you to reply to their response). Also, we offer a "Collect Call" feature in the Personals, where you can send a canned response to someone, and if they really like your ad, they can pay to reply to your Collect Call.

The Instant Gratifier is also a "pay to initiate" kind of service. You pay two or three Nerve credits for a 30- or 60-minute session, and during that time you can send IG notes to any other member who is online. If someone sends me an IG, I can respond to them for free, even if I'm not in an IG session myself.

Nerve's tagline is "think about sex" and the material ranges from intellectually smutty to graphically intense. How does that influence your community features?

Many other community sites ban certain images, language, and behavior. For example, nudity on homepages, cybersex in chat rooms, personal ads by people who are just looking for a sex partner to experiment with. It would be hypocritical for us to ban this behavior in NerveCenter, seeing as we publish nude photography and explicit writing every day! But, we don't want to be a dumping ground for every porn redistributor on the web, all those people who got kicked off Geocities or Lycos for building homepages solely consisting of images stolen from seventies *Penthouses*! For this reason, we haven't focused so much on our homepages feature—that's there as sort of a bonus for members, but our energies have really gone into message boards, chat, and personal ads. It's easier in these areas to encourage members to act "within the spirit of the NerveCenter community," as we like to say. (More on that below.)

For NerveCenter, the boards were a natural fit—we were receiving an incredible amount of very intelligent feedback about the site and the subjects it raised, and it made sense to allow these smart readers to say these things to each other, and respond to what each other was saying. But message boards aren't for everybody—some people prefer the immediacy and flirtatiousness of chat, and others prefer the one-on-one nature of the personal ads. Some people want to meet and discuss Nerve articles, but the majority are merely interested in meeting like-minded people. It doesn't mean that every NerveCenter member will get on with every other member, but it's a good base to start from. Hence the popularity of our personals, for example. Many people who have used the Nerve personals (myself included!) would never have posted a personal in their local newspaper, for example—but if you just happen to be reading Nerve and notice them there, it's an easy step over to the section and to creating an ad. Rather than feeling like they're joining a community of losers who need a date (their words, not mine!), they think of it as joining Nerve's community and hey, they might get a date, too.

Let's talk policy. What's not allowed in NerveCenter? How do you enforce the rules?

On the homepages, pretty much anything that's legal is okay. If it's very explicit (e.g., penetration shots, etc.) we will probably ask the member to make it password protected (our homepage builder offers this functionality), but only if the homepage is brought to our attention. The homepage is a self-policing area for members to express themselves however they feel!

On personal ads and member profiles, we allow some nudity, but not sexually explicit conduct (penetration, oral sex, etc.) and no genitalia. And, in some cases, if we feel the nudity is offensive to the spirit of the Nerve community (e.g., a spread-eagle shot of a woman that was clearly stolen from a porn site), we will write to the member and ask them to reconsider. Oh, and for reasons of privacy and safety, we don't allow users to post their email addresses or any other contact information in personal ads or member profiles.

In chat, anything goes! We have created various rooms, from the Bar to the Bedroom. We encourage users to create private rooms for cybersex, though we don't monitor the chat rooms and only intervene if we receive complaints from members. No one has ever complained about walking in on a cybersex session! We generally encourage members to deal with troublemakers themselves, or simply ignore them, and only intervene if a member is being so abusive that he/she is driving regulars and new members away.

Oh, and the exception to this is during the two weekly chats that Lo and I host when there are two rules that apply only while we are there: 1. No emoting (we can't stand it!) and 2. Be nice to the hosts. On the boards, we tend to be slightly more heavy-handed. Or, at least we were in the beginning—now it generally takes care of itself. We seeded the boards with a hand-selected group of about a hundred users (regular readers who had written to us, plus friends and acquaintances) and opened the site to them back in April of '99. They helped us create a forum for intelligent, witty, open-minded conversation about sex, gender, and culture. There aren't really any rules—it's more like a fun party where you figure it out as you go along. And just as some people will walk into a party and immediately become the life and soul of the event, so others may hover on the edges for a while before they feel comfortable jumping into a conversation.

Has the NerveCenter community surprised you? How?

I think the thing that has surprised me the most is how little we've had to worry about enforcing rules and etiquette. There aren't many places on the Web where women can talk openly about sex without being ambushed by idiot guys typing, "any ladies wanna cyber?" In fact, on the boards, Lo and I are constantly trying to shake things up and get them to disagree more—they all get on so well together and agree about so much that sometimes it turns into a bit of a love fest! I can't remember a single flame war on the boards, and without us doing anything, they have arranged face-to-face gatherings across the country of their own volition.

Basically, we weren't sure how easy it would be to create and sustain a community that had the Nerve vibe—i.e., a smart magazine about sex that's not porn and not erotica. But the members created it themselves! We've had to remove a handful of ads in Personals that were for adult services and boot one member from chat for harassing other members. And that's it. No doubt these numbers will rise as the community grows, but it's already a fairly self-regulating place—we can go away for a week and leave boards or chat alone and not worry that we're going to return to anarchy. After some of the flame wars I've witnessed online—amongst ostensibly rational, intelligent people—this was certainly a surprise!

You could leave for a week and not worry? That's amazing. To what do you attribute this peacefulness in the community? (Could it be that people are paying for membership?)

Well, the message boards used to be paid, but since November of last year they've been free, and the members have been just as well behaved!

One of the things I attribute this to is that Lorelei and I have always been a very visible presence in the boards (and on NerveCenter in general). We're not just some faceless censor from on high, but rather, friendly hosts with photographs, personalities, etc. We post in the message boards frequently and since the beginning have encouraged friendly debate and discouraged harassment and flaming.

Also, we have provided different areas of NerveCenter for different forms of communication and community. If you only have one forum for interaction and try to cram everything into it, there's bound to be more conflict. Chat, for example, lets people be silly and flirty, and the boards are for more in-depth discussions. And we don't allow anonymous posting anywhere on NerveCenter.

Mostly, though, it's that the members have a real sense of ownership over, and pride in, the community. They don't want it to get out of hand—it's their home, and they're very careful to keep it a respectful place. If someone posts a potentially inflammatory remark, they'll put that person in their place and then continue the debate without letting that person send them off on a tangent.

And we've made sure, within boards, to provide a wide range of discussions so that everyone can find a home for the kind of post they want to read or write. For example, there were three male posters who dubbed themselves the three musketeers of NerveCenter. They were becoming rather dominating on the boards, and it could have been intimidating or annoying to new members (or even to regulars). But, they clearly felt the need to express their deep bond to all the other members! So we created a "Clique Here" discussion for them and anyone else who was interested. Members who wanted to avoid their declarations of loyalty and friendship could simply "unbook-mark" that discussion. And then there's a "Silly Putty" discussion for members who want to make jokes and wordplay about runner beans or Pod Racers (both have happened!)—this way the members who are discussing Bush's latest misstep or whether American pharmaceutical companies should slash their AIDS drug prices for Africa aren't fighting for space with the Pod Racers.

In your time leading the community at NerveCenter, what have you learned about virtual community? Any tips for other aspiring virtual community leaders?

Listen to your members! Reward the loyal members with privileges (hosting privileges, etc). To create a scalable community, give the members as much control as possible while still maintaining the kind of voice you want. Don't try to launch something with 10 services at once—start small and grow the services you offer as your member-ship grows. Anonymous posting rarely adds anything to a community, in my experience. Focus more on bringing the best elements of your community to the surface, rather than on keeping the bad elements down. Make sure that when someone first arrives at your community, they see examples of discussions/community that you want them to see. This will do more to keep the community the way you want it than a hundred little censorship monkeys ever could!

Our members jokingly (well, kind of jokingly) call me and Lo the benevolent dictators of NerveCenter, but it's not a bad idea. They know that we're friendly and that we listen to them and do take them up on much of their feedback, and care as much as them about making the community work. But they also know that we're not pushovers. You don't want to be so accommodating that a bad apple feels like they can come in and spoil the whole thing. But mostly, listen to your users. As long as they feel like they have a stake in the community, and as long as they feel like it offers them something that no other place does, most of them will do everything they can to make it last and to make it better.

Chapter 9

Email Keeps the Conversation Alive

...Community That Comes to You

When it comes to the Internet, there's one activity people do more than any other, and it's not stealing mp3s. It's email.

And it's little wonder. Email connects people in an immediate, personal way. So it's not surprising that some of the most powerful community experiences can be found in your inbox.

Email lists are a key part of community on the web, whether they're the main conduit of the community, or just one part of a larger digital world.

Email has a wonderful ephemeralness that is lacking in other community tools. Where message boards are archived for all eternity, email comes and goes, scattered throughout the globe. And while the text in chat rooms flies by at the speed of light, email can be slow and considered.

But the biggest difference between email and other community tools is the most obvious: Email comes to you. And that single difference can create an entirely different community vibe.

Tools of the Trade

There are many tools and websites you can use to create email-based communities, aka mailing lists. Majordomo is the most widely used server-side software for maintaining mailing lists.

Major who?

According to David Barr, the author of the Majordomo FAQ, before it became synonymous with email lists, the definition of "Majordomo" was: a person who speaks, makes arrangements, or takes charge for another. From Latin "major domus"—"master of the house."

The entire Majordomo FAQ can be read at greatcircle.com/majo domo/FAQ.html.

Majordomo is a clever program because it can receive commands via email itself. So subscribing to and unsubscribing from a list can be easily done by sending an email command to the program.

```
To: majordomo@designforcommunity.com
From: derek@designforcommunity.com
subscribe dfclist
```

This email would subscribe derek@designforcommunity.com to a list called "dfclist."

Majordomo gets a whole lot more sophisticated, too. Lists can be configured to require passwords or approvals. And you can send all sorts of commands to the program as well. Member lists, archives, and reports can all be had by sending a short command in email.

Of course, to use Majordomo on your server requires that you, or someone in your organization, be technically minded enough to install and service a Perl program. If that's out of your league, don't fret. Several websites have stepped in with some elegant, web-based solutions.

First, there was OneList, then there was eGroups, now it's Yahoo Groups. This company has changed hands more times than a playing card in Las Vegas, but the core idea has stayed the same: web-based control of mailing lists.

At Yahoo Groups (groups.yahoo.com) it's frighteningly easy to set up and maintain a list. And what's even better, it provides a nice, simple way to use a web interface for your users. So I could subscribe to your list, but opt to view it in a web browser instead of having it mailed to me. Very nice.

The trade-off is ads, of course. If you run a mailing list with Yahoo Groups, it will put text ads at the bottom of every message that goes out to your users. Plus, if your users do opt to view their mail online, they'll be doing it at Yahoo, not your site. If you need to integrate email functionality with your own site, this may not be the solution for you.

Then there's NotifyList (notifylist.com), an independent web tool brought to you by the talented Andrew Smales. This site is only designed for one-way lists (more on that later), but the tools are great and the site even gives you the code to put the sign-up form on your own site, so you don't have to send your users away to create a subscription.

Notify List includes no ads as of this writing, save one line at the bottom of any email you send out that says:

```
Get your own free notify list at
http://Notifylist.com!
```

NotifyList takes care of all the subscribing and unsubscribing tools, so it seems like a fair trade for the service (which is free).

But before you get too lost in tools, let's talk about the different kinds of lists.

Two Kinds of Lists

There are two categories that email lists can fall into: one-way and two-way. And, yes, they do exactly what you think they do.

You talk I listen

One-way lists, aka announcement lists, only go one way. If I run the list, I can send email to all the people on it, but they can't send email to each other—they can only send email back to me.

While this kind of list isn't a great community-raising tool in and of itself, it can be a valuable part of a web-based community. One of the smartest things I ever did was start an announcement list for {fray} when I started the site. My reasoning was simple: I wasn't going to be updating the site on any sort of regular schedule. And, since I couldn't expect my visitors to just keep reloading the site until new content showed up, I decided I owed it to them to tell them when it updated.

The {fray} mailing list sign-up/off form (fray.com/is/mail).

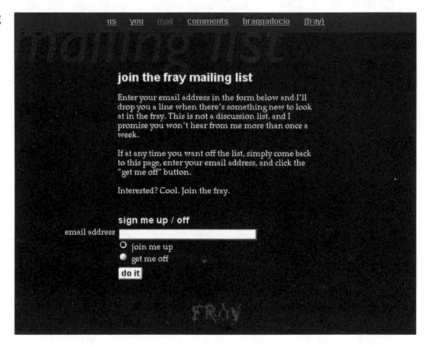

Shortly after the site launched, I put up an unassuming form that just asked people to sign up for the announcement list. This form also included a sign-off button, too, so people always knew that they could come back and remove themselves. People who had a good experience at the site could sign up to be the first to know when there was an update.

The list has grown steadily over the years and now hovers at around 5,000 people. And I can really tell that it works—when I send out a note to the list about a new story in {fray}, the traffic on the server quadruples the next day.

I strongly encourage community sites with irregularly updated content to start one-way lists. Like mortar between bricks of a house, it strengthens your community by connecting people together in between the core, web-based, community functionality.

Another great use for the one-way list is to enable temporary, interest-based groups. For example, when Amazon has to take its site offline temporarily to work on its immense database, it puts up the infamous "be right back" screen. Is it annoying to have to wait to buy that book you were after? Sure. But at least the company emails you when it is back open and ready for business.

This technique is great for "coming soon" pages, too. A coming soon page is what you put in place at your URL while you complete your site. Any place where you have to turn away interested users for some reason, ask them to voluntarily leave their email address before they go. If they're interested in what you're up to, they'll sign up and come back around when you're ready.

The Amazon "be right back" screen.

amazon.com.

We'll be right back!

We're sorry, but our store is closed temporarily. We expect to be back soon.
If you would like to be notified when we reopen, please leave your e-mail address below
and we will be happy to let you know.

Per our Site Availability Policy, if this closure lasts longer than 30 minutes, but less than or
equal to 2 hours, all auctions scheduled to end during the closure period will be extended
by at least twice the amount of the time closed. If the closure lasts longer than 2 hours,
all auctions scheduled to end during the closure period will be extended by 24 hours.

Again, we apologize for the inconvenience, and thank you for your patience.

Your friends at Amazon.com

Please enter your e-mail address: [   ] [Submit]

Going both ways

Two-way lists, aka discussion lists, go both ways. In this case there is one email address that acts like a big alias for a list of email addresses. *Anyone* on the list can send a message to *everyone* on the list.

These lists can be entirely open, so that anyone can subscribe, or closed, so that new members must be approved before being able to send mail to the list. Sometimes, two-way lists also have digest versions, a one-way announcement list where a moderator sums up what's happening on the two-way list on a regular basis. This is good for people who are interested in the material but don't want their inbox flooded with daily mail.

And flood they can. Two-way lists can be wild. I was once on a two-way list called "yadda," where the entire point was to have long, funny, nonsensical threads that went on forever, with each response being just a line or two. I only lasted on the list for a few hundred messages, which all came in less than an hour.

Two-way lists are where the really interesting stuff happens. When I talk about email-based communities, two-way lists are what I'm talking about. And email-based communities are very different creatures than their web-based siblings.

Community That Comes to You

Caleb Clark has more experience than almost anyone as a host of web-based *and* email-based communities. His full interview is in Chapter 5, but he said one thing that didn't make it in that I really liked. When asked what makes email communities different from web-based ones, this is what he had to say:

> The most important difference I've found is that you have to *go* to the web, but email *comes* to you. Thus, web communities are based more on what will motivate folks to click an address, log in, and check

threads. Email flows right to people, which makes it easier, but also easier to get flooded with and blown off.

This may seem commonsensical at first, but it underscores an important point: ownership. The email in users' inboxes belongs to them. They feel like they own it because it's sitting there on their hard drive. But when they're participating in a web-based community, while they will feel a connection, it's always clear that they're a guest in someone else's house. Their sense of ownership is reduced.

In fact, this is a design issue. Users can control the look and feel of their email. Email programs allow users to change the fonts and colors, move messages where they belong, and delete messages they don't want to see again.

But participants in web-based communities can do none of those things. Design plays a much larger role in the web-based world.

Designing Email

Of course, nothing is without design, even email.

And while it is possible to use HTML and even images in email, I recommend against it in most cases. That HTML email message may look great in an email client that reads HTML, but it's going to look like gibberish to someone with a plain-text email client.

Just like you shouldn't require a plug-in to view your website (unless it's absolutely integral to the goal of the site—like showing videos on a movie site or playing audio clips for your band's site), you shouldn't require an HTML-enabled email client just so your users can keep in touch with your site.

If you absolutely must use HTML in your email, offer your users a choice between HTML and plain-text, and make sure plain-text is the default. This choice can be presented on the sign-up/off page itself, and users should be reminded of the choice in list messages.

When it comes time to send that text-based email, don't forget about design. Your control is limited, of course. You can't choose the color or font, the leading or spacing. But don't think that means you can just slop any text together. Especially when sending out announcements in a one-way list, your email is a text-based representation of your site. You want to make sure it looks good.

What you can control is the content and the information design of your email. Consider the way people use email—they scan it quickly for anything that seems important. So present the information in order of importance and divide it up into scannable bits. And format it so that it flows well—vertical spacing is the only thing you can control in text-based email, so use it wisely. Put lots of vertical white space in between separate bits.

Here's a common formula for a one-way announcement email. Let's say it's for a nonprofit organization:

```
Nonprofit Newsletter: http://nonprofiturl.com

Reminder: You're subscribed to the Nonprofit
Newsletter. If you'd like to unsubscribe,
please visit: http://nonprofiturl.com/unsub/

In this issue:
    1. Hot news!
    2. New content.
    3. Meeting Minutes.

1. Hot News!

    (Here's the text of the hot news.)

2. Important Reminder.

    (Here's the text of the new content.)

3. Meeting Minutes.

    (Here's the text of the meeting minutes.)

That's all for this installment. Thanks for
Subscribing to the Nonprofit Newsletter.
See you next time!

-- Personal signature.

To unsubscribe, just visit:
http://nonprofiturl.com/unsub/
```

There are a few important things going on here. Beginning with the name of the newsletter and a reminder of the URL, the mail is associated with reminders to the readers of what they're reading. Placing the subscription information next will save you from a lot of angry email, and allow users to manage their own subscriptions. Placing a mini table of contents at the beginning gives readers the chance to get a glimpse of what they're about to read (and decide if they're interested at all). This is a great way to make sure that the issues at the bottom of the email get seen, too.

Then present the issues you outlined in order. Note that I've put two hard returns (one blank line) after each heading and three hard returns (two blank lines) at the conclusion of each point. Don't be afraid to use white space this way! It communicates important information (in this case, that a point has concluded and a new one is beginning). Blank lines are the only spacing we have control over in text-only email—use them wisely.

The email concludes with some appreciation—if the user has read all the way to the bottom, you should be thankful—and a personal signature. If the email is being sent out by a company, don't be afraid to let one person be the voice of the company. A personal voice can make a bland newsletter feel more friendly.

The email ends with unsubscription information. Don't worry about including this information—if users unsubscribe from your list, it's not a personal comment. They may have just decided to visit your site every day instead.

The Good and Bad of Ownership

The thing about running an email community is that it's never really yours. There is no value in a Majordomo list with no one on it. It's your users who create the value.

Accordingly, they will feel a strong sense of ownership in a two-way list that they take part in, and rightfully so. That means that you'll need to exercise caution in asserting your authority. Members may begin to feel entitled to say whatever they want—after all, it's their list.

It's more important than ever to be a good host in an email community. (See Chapter 6 for a refresher course on hosting.) Just be prepared for that sense of ownership your users will feel—it's only natural. And, actually, it means your community is working.

The great thing about email lists is that same sense of owner-ship. Because the email is coming to them, your users will feel like they're in a safe, private place. This can become an amazing conduit for intimacy (see Chapter 7). Some of the closest friendships I've ever developed in virtual communities have been through two-way email lists.

Email and Web: The Two Great Tastes That Go Great Together

Some of the most interesting things in a virtual community can come in the interaction between email- and web-based communities. Because the two tools can bring out different sides of a person, it makes sense to mix them together in a community setting.

Good communities have both homes and parks, or, put another way, private spaces and public spaces. Email feels like a private place, a bedroom or living room. The web, on the other hand, is much more like a public park: outside in the sun, available to everyone.

What happens when you mix the two up? For a good example, let's look at Evolt (evolt.org), where community members communicate all over the web/email spectrum.

Evolt is a community of web designers and developers from all over the world. They discuss everything from interface issues to coding problems. According to the site, Evolt combines the best of evolution and revolution, "with a bit of voltage thrown in for good measure."

Evolt started in March of 1999 as a mailing list with an associated website. It grew fast, and by June it had relaunched with the system it has in place today.

What's wonderful about Evolt is that it manages to use the web and email in concert, each for what they're good for. Email is good for direct, user-to-user, nearly real-time communication. So the lifeblood of the community takes place in email, with small messages and little conversations sprouting up every day.

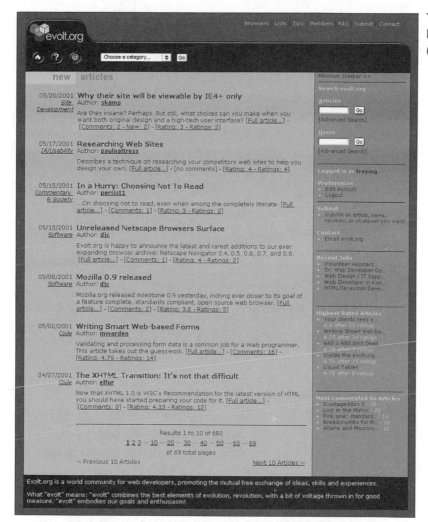

The Evolt homepage (evolt.org).

At the same time, members of the list can post stories to the website in categories such as code, news, and design. This is high-quality editorial content that any developer site would be happy to have. At the end of every story, members can rate the story and post their comments.

The beauty of this is that the members' email addresses and usernames are the same on the web and in email, and one registration takes care of them both. This cohesion is important to establish reliable identities, while, at the same time, using each medium for

The tools attached to the bottom of every Evolt story include ratings and comments.

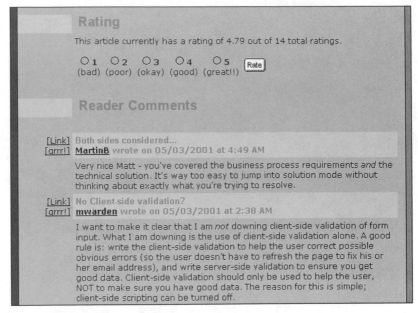

what it's good at: email for discussion and web for static, archived, content.

Evolt has other smart interactions between email and the web, too. There's a digest version of the email list, if you can't stand all the traffic and just want to hear the good bits on a weekly basis. And there's a web-based archive of list mail that's searchable by members. But my favorite thing is the Tip Harvester.

The bane of every email list is off-topic posts. It's hard to keep a list on target when anyone can say anything, and topic drift is always a problem. Evolt came up with an innovative solution to this problem that kills two birds with one stone.

Off-topic posts are allowed, but discouraged. If you want to post something that is off-topic (not about web development), you must preface the subject line with "OT:" so that people who don't want to see off-topic email can ignore it. But even better, you have to include a <tip> in any off-topic email.

A <tip> is your "payment" for going off topic. It should be a short blip about web development: a trick in Photoshop, a good book, a coding tip—anything so long as it's on topic and will be of interest to your fellow developers.

There's even a special way to format your <tips> in email. It is:

```
<tip type="META Tags" author="Your Name">
Include META tags in all of your pages for
better search engine placement.
</tip>
```

Then, once a week, the Tip Harvester runs through that week's email archives and creates a web-based list of that week's <tip>s. Over time, the <tip> archive has grown to become an amazing repository of wisdom for web developers.

This integration between web and email is inspirational to anyone who's ever struggled to sync up a web community with an email one. It can be a difficult task, and Evolt has done it with flying colors.

The Dark Side

Like all good things, email lists have their price. Don't step your toe into these waters without being aware of a few things.

Spam

If you've had an email account for any length of time, you already know how annoying **spam** is. Unsolicited commercial email advertisements clog inboxes and mail servers all over, making usually mild-mannered list managers extremely grumpy.

What you may not know is that, as the proprietor of an email list, you may be accused of spamming. Remember that {fray} list I mentioned? Every once in a while, someone subscribes to the list and then promptly forgets about it. Then, a couple weeks later when I send an email to the list, I receive an angry response.

That's why you have to be very clear in the email you send out about what it is, why users are getting it, and how they can get off the list if they choose to. In some cases, I've preceded the entire mail with an explanation and removal information. For example:

```
Hi! You're getting the fray.org newsletter
because you signed up for it. Don't want it
anymore? No problem! Just go to
http://fray.org/mail, enter your email
address, and click "remove me." You will be
removed lickety-split.
```

Another option you should consider if you're using a web-based form to add people to an email list is requiring a confirmation. Majordomo (and other server-side email packages) can be configured to send an email to a new list member. That member is then required to reply to the message before he is officially added to the list. No response, no subscription. Easy.

This is helpful because it keeps bogus addresses from getting on your lists, as well as people maliciously signing other people up without their approval. In the end, this will keep accusations of spam to a minimum, as well as minimize bounces.

Bounces

The great thing about email lists is that direct, user-to-user connection. But when you run a list with thousands of addresses on it, there will be quite a few that will **bounce** at any given time.

An email that is sent to an address that is no longer valid will be bounced back to the sender by the server that received it. This could be because the account has been deleted, it's full and has run out of space, or was mistyped to begin with. It's up to the list administrator to remove these bouncing addresses. If you don't, they'll only increase over time.

Don't discount what a hassle this can be. When you send out mail to 5,000 people, you can get buried in bounces if you're not careful. And while some mail server packages (Listserv and Mailman, for example) can be configured to automatically remove most of the bouncing email addresses, Majordomo does not, so it's up to you.

Bounces become an even bigger hassle in two-way discussion lists, because an address that bounces back to the list address may wind up being broadcast to everyone on the list. And if there's an address on the list that's bouncing, this can cause an endless loop. This is the kind of thing that keeps system administrators awake at night.

So whatever you do, keep an eye on your list and look out for bounces.

Mailing list software

In the market for a mailing list backend? Here are a few URLs to get you started.

Majordomo	www.greatcircle.com/majordomo
Listserv	www.lsoft.com/products
Mailman	www.list.org

Managing subscriptions

With most email lists, there's one address for commands to the program, and one to send email to the list. For example, to subscribe to WebDesign-L, a famous web design list moderated by Steve Champeon (interviewed at the end of this chapter), you have to send mail that reads "subscribe list" to "majordomo@webdesign-l.com." Once you're on the list, if you want to send out a message to the other members, you have to send an email to "list@webdesign-l.com."

Seems easy, right? But as anyone who's ever spent some time on a high-traffic email list can tell you, eventually someone will send an email to the list itself that says "unsubscribe list," after which he will be relentlessly taunted.

It's such a chronic problem, in fact, that the number one item on the WebDesign-L policy list is: "Do *not* send administrative messages (*e.g.*, "unsubscribe me") to the list itself" (webdesign-l.com/policies.html).

Creating Connection

In spite of the difficulties, email lists flourish online. You can find a list for anything your heart desires, from keeping up with your favorite band, to finding a date on Saturday night. It's the nearly real-time, personal connection that makes email so powerful, and a welcome addition to the web community cannon.

A Conversation with Steve Champeon

Photo by Derek M. Powazek

Steve Champeon

There's no one I know with more experience running email lists than Steve Champeon. As part of his job as CTO of hesketh.com/inc, a North Carolina-based web development shop, he spends countless hours a day being "list mom" to WebDesign-L, an email-based community of webheads. Steve is thoughtful and patient, the very things needed to survive running a high-traffic, two-way list, and it shows in his answers to my questions. We spoke in early 2001 about email communities and how they can work with the web.

Steve, please give us a brief introduction to who you are and what you do, specifically your work in community and the web.

I'm the CTO and co-owner of hesketh.com/inc., a small but vital Raleigh, NC-based web design and development shop now entering its sixth fiscal year. I've been with the company since 1997, and before that I was the founder and technical manager of a twelve-person web services department for a defunct, midsized imaging and work-flow software company called imonics, where we built and maintained a large intranet. I've been on the Net since 1991, when I used it to keep in touch with Heather, my partner (and the "Hesketh" in hesketh.com) while I was attending school at Syracuse University.

I mention imonics because my primary interest in online community came about as a result of massive layoffs there back in 1996. We found ourselves cast adrift after years of work with a company to which many of us were fiercely loyal, with the resultant insular society, and after a few attempts at forming local user group-style communities, realized that we might be better off looking online instead. So I started haunting various mailing lists, mostly about web design or the web industry, some private and others public, such as the NY-based WWWAC list, Bill Weinman's webmonster list, and SF-based NoEnd.

Let's talk about WebDesign-L (webdesign-l.com), the email community you created for web designers. How long has it been around? How many members does it have? What's the goal of the list?

I founded WebDesign-L (aka [wd]) back in April 1997, to address the need for a more integrated approach to the web—I have a fondness for multi-disciplinary approaches, and saw that most of the existing communities were focusing on one aspect of web design or development to the exclusion of the others. In my experience, web people tend to be multi-faceted—for example, I write, do markup and some design, systems administration, programming, security, and more—and I think that we all benefit from knowing more about the other aspects of the web. So that's the basic mission: to cross-pollinate ideas that would otherwise be trapped in specialized subcommunities or subcultures.

We've had some growth in January due to my having relaxed the guideline that the list members not popularize the list in what I call "uncontrolled" forums. I'd rather you told your smartest, most experienced friends than shout out to a wildly noisy list that [wd] is better. The reason it's got such a high signal-to-noise ratio is because we try not to invite the gate-crashers. I think of it as a party—you don't invite every fraternity on campus if you want a nice, quiet conversational tone at your dinner party. Currently, we're at around 1,700 people, slightly more on the digest than the list, but still pretty evenly split.

At any rate, whatever we're doing seems to work—we've somehow managed to grow ten-fold in four years and keep the respectful tone, the helpful and informative posting style, and a sense of ourselves that I think is unique among such communities.

When it comes to fostering community, what is The Right Way to use email?

Heh. I've acquired a bit of a reputation as a curmudgeon for refusing to allow HTML email on the list. I use several such technical barriers to entry (refusing HTML, attachments, and posts that contain the entire message to which they are replying, for example) to keep the noise down. I believe in plain text as a simple and powerful way to express ideas, despite its obvious shortcomings in other respects. I figure if you can't take the time to configure your mail client not to send attachments (like V-Cards) or HTML email, or take a few seconds to trim all but the most relevant portions of a message, your answer is likely to be similarly careless. It's not always true, but I've found that overall the benefits outweigh the hazards—simply forcing someone to think for a minute about *how* they are going to present an idea often influences the *content* of that expression. And, of course, stripping even ten careless or low-content messages a day helps keep the list volume down to a manageable level.

As for the best way to manage a list, though, in my opinion it changes over time. Back when the list first got started, I was posting about half of the messages myself, trying to get threads going, or answering every question so as to ensure that no question went unanswered. It took an unbelievable amount of time, though, and I found that later I had to give some posts a day or so before answering them, because people who otherwise would have shared their knowledge just figured I'd get it before they did and didn't post. So once you reach a certain critical mass, you need to step back as a list mom and let the list take over. List members need to acquire a sense of belonging, a sense of ownership in the community, and the best way for them to do that is for them to participate.

One other thing I found is that the speed of distribution matters a lot. I was the first member of the list, and my address was always first to get list mail. So I had a longer and longer lead over everyone else as the list got bigger and took longer to distribute. I've rectified the speed issues a bit through various sysadmin tactics, cutting the distribution time down from a couple hours or even a day in some cases to a few minutes. And that helped immensely—people now jump right in and answer questions because they know they've got an equal chance to be the one to give the best answer. And that act of helping someone publicly can make an enormous difference in one's confidence and feeling of having made a real contribution to the community—plus it increases your chance of getting a similarly informative answer when *you* need help.

What's a typical day as the "list mom" of WebDesign-L like?

I usually get up in the morning and check email while I'm caffeinating, and there's usually several posts that came across the list during the night (it's a worldwide list, and so the Australians tend to post their morning messages while the rest of us sleep). I try my best to read every one and answer those where I feel I can add something to the thread that hasn't already been said. When I'm done with that, I'll hop over to the server that handles the list and check for bounced messages, subscription requests, and other administrivia. I'll approve some subscriptions, notify anyone whose mail bounced for some reason (maybe it ran afoul of the filters, or they posted from another account that the list doesn't know about, etc.) and unsubscribe anyone whose mail is bouncing with any regularity. I've learned how to determine when mail is bouncing for a reason and when it's just transitory, for the most part. Running a list for four years will do that to you. Mostly, this part is just drudgery, but it doesn't take that long on most days. I check in on things during the day, and basically repeat the process.

The fun part is starting threads that go outside the realm of desperate cries for help, such as asking more philosophical questions about best practices, choice of tools, project management approaches, and so on. There's such a wealth and variety of knowledge and experience there that it is always interesting to hear people's perspectives and rationales for why they do what they do.

The not-so-fun part is having to deal with people who are being rude or intentionally disruptive. Usually, they are just having a really bad day, and some offlist email can set them straight, but sometimes you get a really bad egg, someone who simply won't leave well enough alone, and I have to gauge whether they should be unsubscribed, and if so, how to explain it to the community. Sometimes, I get some resistance, especially if I don't do a good job of explaining my rationale, but for the most part there's a consensus and I feel confident in removing the troublemaker. In four years, I've only had to remove a few people, one of whom mail bombed me afterwards by subscribing me to a few hundred mailing lists! (Fortunately, most of them required confirmation for subscriptions, so the effect was minimal, if really annoying. The lesson there is that if you are responsible for a mailing list, make sure you require confirmation via email before subscribing someone. You'll save everyone a lot of grief that way.)

The other not-so-fun thing is dealing with people who can't figure out how to unsubscribe or who don't bother to try. That always makes me question whether I should even bother to host the list. It's really depressing to me. I mean, is it really that hard to read and follow some simple instructions? I always come away wondering how they drive a car, or open cans of food. But usually someone will send me mail offlist thanking me for all my efforts, and that restores the faith.

Can you give us an example of an email that took your breath away?

I remember one post, from a list member named Joey Siggens, in reply to a message I sent asking everyone how they found out about the list:

> It's basically company policy to be on this list. The first
> thing I was instructed to do on my first day at this job was
> to join this list. I thought that it was kind of silly at the time,
> as I had never belonged to such a thing before. I never
> really saw the point. I think I see the point now, as I con-
> sider this list to be an invaluable tool in my workday. At
> work, and at home. Thanks for providing me with knowl-
> edge that I never asked for.

That one still sits in the back of my head and works its magic.

I've found there's a real Zen about email communities. Knowing when to respond and when not to, for example. Can you give email list members some tips from your experience?

The most important thing is to be aware of and respect the culture. Some lists are extremely tolerant of newbies, and others see them as a needless source of noise and stupid questions. I try to walk the line and make sure that anyone feels free to ask any question, but that they should provide enough detail and evidence of their earlier failed efforts to find answers on their own.

There's more than just an elitist principle at work here: It's much easier to ignore a question phrased like "I can't make my webpage work—can anyone help!?!?!?!" than one like "I'm having trouble with the contents of a DIV on this platform in this browser—my page is valid, and I've consulted the O'Reilly book, but I think it may be a problem with my CSS properties," especially if you've had a similar problem and want to save someone the heartache. Often, you learn as much by sorting through your thoughts on the matter and even highlight things you missed during the crunch. I used to be a teacher (peer teaching assistant, actually), and I've found that often the best way to learn something is to teach it to someone else.

Another important thing to understand is that list communities work on the principles of the gift economy. Nobody is being paid to take time to help you—except in terms of an increased status in the community, or the enhanced understanding of a problem that comes from sitting down and thinking about it more. Once you understand that the *answers* are coming out of a sense of personal gain, only spread out over the whole community, you begin to understand how to ask *questions* that tend to encourage the sort of response that the respondent can be proud of or find useful. And those are the most helpful and valuable by far.

Another thing I've learned is that you can't rest on your laurels—you have to keep contributing, in one form or another, or you lose credibility, because the community evolves. You can't easily jump into a community with cred established outside, either, though it may help if the members already know you from outside. But it is a thin shield against the demands everyone faces—participate and contribute or lose social capital. I may have a goodly store of social capital in the eyes of the first thousand members, but I have to start all over again with the latest to join. And that constant pressure keeps me on my toes.

So, depending on how much social approbation you can stand, and how much you can assume about the community based on its scope, you can either jump right in and start posting, or sit back and see what kinds of posts are acceptable and which are met with resistance or simply ignored. I always recommend that people wait a week or so before posting, just to get a feel for the tone and style of a list. It's a lot harder to win back credibility after causing a major flare-up and irritating the list moderator and possibly hundreds of others than it is to just wait a while and post confidently.

Nobody likes a flame war, but sometimes they're unavoidable. What do you do, as a moderator, when you see list members getting hot?

Oddly enough, we've been lucky not to have had many real knock-down drag-outs on [wd]. People there tend to be fairly respectful of one another, and most can tell the difference between what I call a "strongly worded statement of opinion" and a troll. But when someone crosses the line, most of the longtime members know they can email the person and Cc: me, or just email me alone, and discuss the matter without bothering the rest of the list with it. Most times, that is enough. On those rare occasions when a thread approaches flame war status, I can usually jump in onlist and try to restate the matter at hand (so the other list members know I'm aware of the problem, and so I can try to get other, saner, heads to participate and bring the overall level of discussion back up to a professional level).

I actually encourage lots of strongly worded statements of opinion, rather than discouraging them, because I had my argumentative skills tempered by hanging out with beer-happy philosophy grad students in college, and because I think that it is important that people learn to speak their minds without fear of reprisal. Any subculture, whether it's the alt. hierarchy on Usenet or a cat-lovers chat on AOL, has its rules and conventions and tolerance levels. I've been on lists where such an intense level of disagreement has made other folks uncomfortable, and I personally feel like that's something we all need to learn how to deal with. I understand that it's generally bad to make people too uncomfortable, but I also resent the idea that two people, who are capable of maintaining a strict distance between an exchange of ideas and whatever personal feelings might come into play, should have to tone down their statements just to please those who can't tell the difference.

I find it interesting how email and websites can create communities with very different vibes. Why do you think that is? What can we learn from this?

The biggest difference between the two is that on a mailing list, the ebb and flow of conversation are more natural, in my opinion. Posts keep coming and older posts are forgotten; all that remains is the reputation you formed with those posts, or the knowledge or perspective you imparted. Of course, with a site like MetaFilter or Slashdot, you have a similar dynamic (all the top-level posts rotate off the home page eventually) but the threaded discussions can stick around and get passed around in other ways, such as on—go figure—mailing lists.

The other thing about web-based discussions is that the focus of the individual discussions isn't in the forefront, as it is with mailing lists. It doesn't matter if a thread is weeks, months, or even years old, I can reply to it and everyone on the list gets the reply at the same time; you can revive old topics that way and revisit them in light of recent events or new information. With a web forum thread, though, odds are that the mad first day rush of readers and posters has long passed it by.

On the other hand, archives (whether they be of list traffic or discussion board threads) can also serve as a collective history for the community. With the right sort of search engine, this history can be as relevant for newcomers as for anyone else. And I'm interested in that aspect of things, too. Just think of what Deja.com (a now-defunct website that maintained an extensive archive of Usenet newsgroups [which is now owned by Google]) did to the Usenet community: In one sense, it helped speed its demise, as any joker could come along and do a search and then post to the group where the discussion took place, breaking down the walls between the groups and effectively ruining the community's sense of self-identity, that had previously flour-ished in splendid isolation. In another, though, the simple fact of the archive's existence gave the larger Internet community a sense of itself as worthy of its own detailed history. Identity arises through self-reference.

The choice of technology (mailing list, moderated chat, web-based BBS, etc.) can make all the difference in the world. But I think many of the so-called differences in vibes between the various technologies all come down less to any characteristics inherent in the medium and more to the specific implementations. It's perfectly possible to allow gating of discussion board posts to mailing lists, for example, just as it is to archive list discussions on a website and allow subsequent follow-up postings to the threads that originally took place on the list. The big question is whether you want to allow random web surfers to post to a list via a web forum interface, without any knowledge of the community's tone and character, or vice versa: whether you want to allow old discussions from a list to continue without the knowledge of the list as a whole. There are many of these decisions that must be made, and just as the media shape the nature of the message, so do changes to the media.

I'm keenly interested in that crossroads between email and web. How do you mix the two with WebDesign-L?

Right now, due to lack of time and various other factors, the [wd] site is only a few pages detailing the history, policies, and administrivia surrounding the list. However, we're about halfway done with an effort to put the archives online. It will be a members-only access site, to protect the members from spammers and other undesirables, and each member will have the ability to provide and maintain a profile. We're hoping to have a bunch of other features that test the waters a bit with respect to the merging of web and email, such as a home page with industry news and articles written by list members.

One exciting feature is the ability to save a post for later reference and add comments to it so that we will be able to gauge which members are most respected for posting good content. We're still deciding whether to allow users to share their comments, or whether that will be a private feature, mostly due to the concern I have over letting threads continue offlist. I'd rather someone posted to the list with the URL of the post they're referring to, so everyone benefits. Maybe if we get up to a few hundred posts a day, and I want to offset some of that traffic, I'll add annotation capabilities to the site. But that's the game you have to play—tweaking knobs and making sure that you get the intended result. Communities, especially virtual communities, are little ecosystems. You can't just throw in some kudzu and hope it doesn't swallow the landscape.

Probably the most exciting thing we're doing is "skins," which allows anyone to provide a template and stylesheet set for displaying pages on the site. We have a design-heavy membership, as you might imagine, and this gives them the ability to experiment with branding and layout in ways that they might not be able to on client sites, as well as a way for them to show off their design skills, but on a well-known site frequented by their peers. As an extra incentive, they can use a specially formatted URL that sets the skin for the site and then redirects the viewer to the post or page in question, which will then be displayed in the format intended by the designer. So, I'd say that the extra presentation capabilities of the web are a big plus, especially in this case as a way to draw the site and the list closer together.

Any final words for people who are considering using email to foster community?

Yeah. If you want to start a community because you think you're pretty cool, and you want legions of devoted followers, think again. If you want to spend hours every day performing minor maintenance, playing mom, stoking good threads and throwing water on bad ones, reading posts and contributing what you know, learning about what you don't know, making friends (and sometimes, enemies), and being constantly surprised both by some people's willingness to share what they know and by other people's stubborn refusal to follow simple instructions, all for free, then by all means, start a list.

First, though, be sure you know your audience, their expectations and their capabilities. Find the core values around which your community will revolve. Defend them like you would your home or family. In time, they may well become your home and family.

Chapter 10

Commerce Communities

...How to Keep Money from Screwing Everything Up

The web has created an unprecedented opportunity for consumers to openly discuss the products that fill their lives. From email to web sites to Usenet, there are millions of conversations on anything and everything you can buy, rent, or do. If you want to know what people have to say about that DVD player you're considering, or what movie to see this Friday night, or even where to get the best burrito in your home town, you can find it. Fast.

No wonder companies are scared.

Informed customers are picky customers. They're hip. They won't be fooled by last year's model in a new package—a website already warned them. Slick advertising can no longer make up for shoddy products or service.

Some companies have embraced the wild world of the web, and, in doing so, have created amazing communities. Informed consumers may be picky, but they can also be devoted customers, and sometimes all it takes is owning a product to bring a community together.

A Commercial Web Begets Commercial Communities

The notion of a community formed around commerce is heresy to community purists. Some believe that introducing commercialism into a community setting is like putting bleach in a tide pool. And, for some communities, they're right. A community founded around personal stories or intimate exchanges won't take kindly to an ad for your lemonade stand.

But what if your lemonade stand spawns a group of people who love your lemonade? Isn't it possible that they might have other things in common, too? And, if they're given the opportunity to communicate, your users may create a community themselves. In the end, it's not you who creates a community, it's your users.

Like it or not, the days of the anti-commercial web ended long ago. The web is now a part of everything, and communities form around people with like interests. Sometimes, those communities form around local organizations (like a church). Sometimes, they form around an interest (say, golf) or a demographic (parents, teenagers, elderly). And, sometimes, they form around a product.

Early Adopter: Saturn

In 1995, a new car company called Saturn added a section to its website where Saturn owners could list themselves as part of the "Saturn Extended Family." The members could upload their name, email address, hometown, occupation, and even their favorite book and movie. And, of course, the year, model, and color of their Saturn.

The company also created a way to search the database, so you could find other people in your town with the same car, or other sedan owners who liked *Star Wars*. Once you found someone, you

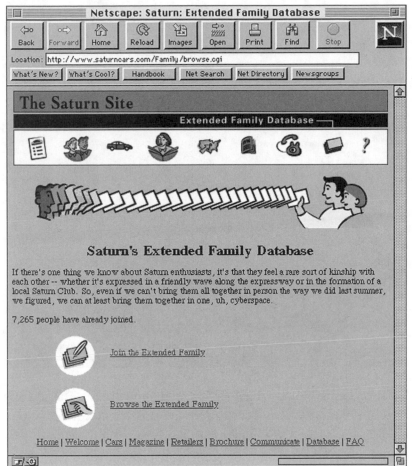

The Saturn Extended Family, circa 1995. Ancient browser chrome left in for dramatic effect.

could send him an email via the included address.

I must admit, I was skeptical of this as a community feature. But as I clicked through pages and pages of people gladly listing themselves with their cars, the truth sank in. These people loved their cars, and, by extension, loved meeting each other.

Now, six years later, Doris Mitsch remembers the website fondly. Mitsch was the Creative Director of online projects at Saturn's advertising agency, Hal Riney & Partners, and the creative force behind the Saturn Extended Family. "The idea came from the realization that the web was good at bringing people together in new ways and that Saturn owners, as a group, were particularly

A sample entry page in the Saturn Extended Family. Dig those square Netscape buttons.

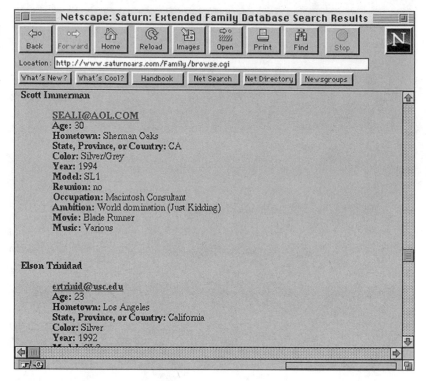

keen on being brought together," Mitsch remembers. "The site was created in late 1994, and the database feature was added as soon as HTML progressed to the point where you could pull information from a database onto a page. This was in the early days of the web as we know it—it still wasn't possible to use tables for layouts or to change the background color of a page, as I recall."

Saturn proved that commerce communities were a real and powerful thing, even before the table tag. Way back in 1995, it proved that not only could you create a virtual community around a product, you *should*.

Harnessing Customer Loyalty

Where Saturn got it immediately, other companies took a little longer to catch on to the power of community on the web. Lucasfilm, the creators of the wildly popular *Star Wars* movies, initially cracked down on *Star Wars* fan sites. While they were legally justified (that image of Han Solo you scanned out of a magazine is a copyright violation, after all), the result was just a lot of pissed-off fans. And when you anger your customers, you only wind up with fewer customers. It's not rocket science to understand how this can apply to your bottom line.

Copywhat?

If you're doing design on the web, you'd better know about copyright. In a nutshell, if you create an original work of art (be it a website or a sketch on a napkin or an epic novel), you own the copyright on it. You can register this copyright with the U.S. Copyright Office, but that's just for bookkeeping—you own the copyright either way.

Owning the copyright means you have the **right** to **copy** it and no one else does (with the exception of comment and critique or parody, which are fair use). You also have the right to make derivative works from the original artwork, but others do not (unless you specifically give them permission). In the least, that means grabbing an image from one site and putting it on another is a strict no-no. And if you run a community site, you'd better make sure your users know that.

For more on U.S. Copyright laws, visit the U.S. Copyright Office (loc.gov/copyright).

Lucasfilm learned its lesson. When it relaunched its site in early 2000, it added a section where users could create their own fan sites, right there on the *Star Wars* website. Since all the images stayed on the starwars.com server and were used with permission, there were no more copyright problems. Now users could create fan sites to their heart's content, and they had every image of Han Solo they could ever want to pick from.

Other companies have long understood the power of letting their customers help each other out. Software maker Adobe, maker of Photoshop, the most widely used image software anywhere, has hosted a discussion system on its site for ages. There, users help other users through the complexities of the software. Just don't call it a community—the system is called "support" on the Adobe site.

The "Star Wars"
Fan Site section
(starwars.com/co
mmunity/fansites).

Two example Han
Solo fan sites,
hosted at
fan.starwars.com.

But, in a way, it *is* a community. It's a group of people with something in common and the tools to communicate with each other.
It's a support community, and it's not rare. Many savvy computer
and software makers do the same thing.

For example, Apple Computer (apple.com) has a discussion forum
as part of its support area that also features a huge "knowledge
base" of Apple information. Software maker Macromedia (macro-
media.com) has a support forum for users, as well as a community
area where users can sign up for beta tests of new software and join
user groups. These companies have clearly learned that their
users want to help each other.

Successful Companies Encourage Community

When companies encourage communities to form around their
product or service, amazing things can happen. Blogger
(blogger.com) is a web-based application that enables people to
easily update their website. When the service slowed down in early

2001, the company asked its users for help. They set up a donation drive to help raise the $6,000 they needed for a new server to speed up the service. In a week, they earned more than $10,000.

Of course, when companies discourage community, amazing things happen, too. Amazingly bad things.

I can think of no company that inspires more rage than Pacific Bell, my local phone behemoth. Almost all of my friends have a horror story about the company, and every story is the same. It begins with "I'm going to get DSL" and ends with "I loathe Pacific Bell." Usually, the cycle takes about three months, only most of which is spent on hold, waiting to ask why it's not working, being forced to listen to some kind of evil easy listening.

Pacific Bell isn't alone—big companies making big promises and not following through is the unfortunate norm in the high speed-Internet access business. And it's safe to say that none of these companies are encouraging their customers to talk with each other, either.

Fortunately, we have the web. One look through a website like DSL Reports (dslreports.com) tells the sad tale. The site is full of horror stories (and even the occasional endorsement) of DSL companies. There's information on every provider in every city, and enough tales of woe to make anyone consider sticking with his trusty 56K.

The lesson here is that if you discourage your customers from forming communities, it won't stop them. They'll just find some-place else to meet. And, chances are, you won't like what they have to say when they do.

The TiVo Success Story

Not all companies make this mistake. In mid-1999 a new company called TiVo appeared. It makes a product called TiVo, which is a Personal Video Recorder, or PVR. A PVR is like a VCR that records on a hard drive instead of videotape. But even better, TiVo will record your favorite programs automatically, even preemptively. For anyone who's owned one (myself included), it can be quite a watershed experience. Suddenly, TV is interesting again.

David Bott followed the advent of PVRs with interest. Bott is the administrator of AVS Forum (avsforum.com), a discussion site full of discussions about home theater equipment. He started a section for discussions about PVRs. Soon, the TiVo discussions were growing too fast to control, so he gave TiVo its own forum. It grew like a weed.

About that time, Richard Bullwinkle, the webmaster for tivo.com, began taking part in the AVS Forums. It seemed natural, since people were discussing TiVo there. As the discussions grew, Bullwinkle and his superiors at TiVo reached a crossroads. TiVo could have called in the lawyers. Threatening letters could have been sent. Fans could have been spurned.

Instead, Bullwinkle and Bott worked together. They spun the TiVo forum out into its own site at tivocommunity.com. There, TiVo users gabbed about the product they loved, exchanged tips and tricks, and even formed something called the "TiVo Underground," where hackers exchanged advice on how to do things TiVo probably didn't want you to know. For example, if you wanted to

Inside the TiVo Underground— notice the official TiVo branding above some very non-official content.

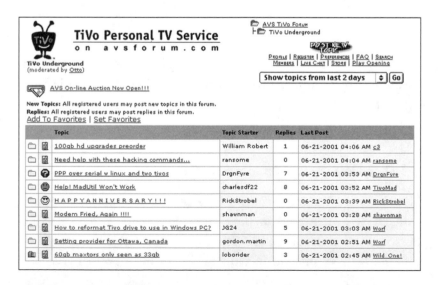

find out how to add another hard drive to your TiVo to increase its recording time, or fix the remote so that the buttons skipped commercials, all the information was there to be found.

TiVo fully embraced the community, even going so far as to sponsor the forums, giving them a source of revenue to pay for the servers. (AVS Forums is a labor of love for Bott.) And instead of worrying about copyright issues, the company asked Bott specifically to change the colors of the site to more closely match the design of tivo.com and add the TiVo logo and branding to the site. TiVo even linked to the site from its own support page.

Does TiVo like everything that goes on at tivocommunity.com? Of course not. "Every now and then some executive says what is *this*?" says Bullwinkle. "My response is, what part of the Internet don't you understand?"

Bullwinkle talks about the importance of good rules and moderators, but says that, in the end, "not censoring is key."

"Customers won't go unless they can get their point across," he says.

The users know the rules, too. They're not to flame each other or TiVo's competitors. Criticism of TiVo is allowed—even encouraged, so long as it's constructive—but no discussion of how to steal the service is allowed. These rules are communicated on a rules pages, reiterated by the regular contributors, and enforced by Bott.

In the end, the fact that the board is not owned and maintained by TiVo has worked to its advantage. This way, when Bullwinkle posts, he can always be the good guy. And when someone has to step in to be the authority, it's not Bullwinkle. It's Bott, who is not a TiVo employee.

By encouraging the community, TiVo is showing its customers that it cares about them and avoiding a consumer backlash. Not to mention the fact that it can keep close tabs on the community. TiVo now has its finger on the pulse of its customers. It's first to know about the problems customers are having, the new features they're dreaming of, and even the hacks that have leaked out.

And by aligning itself with the creators of the forum, it created a team that looks out for each other with mutual goodwill. Bott told me that representatives from TiVo have, at times, asked for certain threads to be removed. But in every case, they're threads that would have been removed anyway, because they were in violation of the posted rules.

Bott told me that most users play by the rules almost all the time. In the five years he's been running the AVS Forums (of which the TiVo forums are a part), he's only had to remove six people. Not bad for a site with about 18,000 active members.

And things worked out well for Bullwinkle, too. After the forums took off, his bosses asked him to attend a meeting with the top brass in the company. He was afraid he was going to lose his job, and, actually, he did. Bullwinkle is no longer the webmaster for tivo.com—he's now the Chief Evangelist for TiVo, or as his username is in the forums, "TiVolutionary."

Community members make great customers

If you're a company considering adding community features to your website, know this: People who participate in online communities spend more money online than those who do not. And that's not just my opinion. In a study published by community consulting company Participate.com in April 2001, it found that: "85 percent of e-Marketplace users that reported above-average transactions are community users, 51 percent of e-Marketplace participants use online community programs to source a product, and community users buy and sell five times more than non-users in terms of total transaction value" (source: http://www.participate.com/post/releases/986324417.html).

Of course, the company that produced this study is in the business of creating communities for companies, so it's safe to say that it is not without bias. Still, it's conceivable that people who participate in online communities are more likely to buy from the same site.

TiVo now employs people to answer questions on the AVS Forums website. And when the TiVo programmers make an appearance in the boards, they're treated like royalty. When one programmer asked for beta testers for the next version of the TiVo operating system, he was buried in volunteers.

The benefits to TiVo are clear. It has a community full of passionate, devoted, and best of all, *informed* customers. These people feel a bond with TiVo that won't easily be replaced. And that's more important than ever right now. Microsoft's competing PVR, Ultimate TV, came to market in late 2001.

And the benefits to the customers are clear, too. They get inside advice from the programmers themselves, access to news and information, and a community of like-minded enthusiasts to talk with. Clearly, everybody wins.

If you run a business, take a lesson from TiVo. Giving your users a quality product or service and the tools to discuss it, along with plenty of involvement from you, is a recipe for success—both in customer appreciation and your bottom line. Reject your own community at your peril.

Follow the Leader

Perhaps the biggest leader in the area of commerce communities is Amazon. Amazon (amazon.com), which has included community features since it started selling books online in 1995. Over the years, as it has added more things to buy, it has added even more ways for users to communicate with each other. Amazon is the undisputed leader in e-commerce now, and part of its success can be attributed to its community features.

Amazon started with the obvious: book reviews. If you can buy the book, why not let people review it, too? The response was amazing—people wrote thoughtful, interesting reviews, and far more than expected.

In watching this, Amazon learned a valuable lesson: People want to express themselves, and they'll do that in the context of products. In fact, it's sometimes easier for people to discuss products than themselves. In writing a review of a book, the user is being personal. He is telling the world: this is who I am, this is what I think. People communicate their identities in their reviews.

There's a thread of that theme of self-expression in everything Amazon does now. Creating a wishlist on Amazon not only encourages people to buy gifts, but it allows users to tell the world who they are by what they like. Amazon's "Listmania" allows users to create lists of products they like. "My top ten books about web design," for example. Does this help Amazon move product? Absolutely. But does that commercial bent disqualify these lists from being a form of self-expression? I say no.

But the community feature I find most interesting at Amazon is the "Friends and Favorites" section (amazon.com/ community). Amazon has learned some very important lessons about the way people buy and relate online, one of which is deceptively simple: I care what my friends think much more than I care what some random reviewer thinks.

So, in the Friends and Favorites section, I can tell Amazon.com who my friends are. Once I've listed a few, the Friends and Favorites section begins to act like my own private small town newspaper. When a friend of mine writes a review of a product somewhere on Amazon, it shows up at the top of the Friends and Favorites page. If a friend of mine has a birthday coming up and has created a wishlist, I'm reminded to visit it. If several of my friends have all bought a particular item, that item is recommended to me.

When I get "product recommendations" in my email, it's called spam, but here it's called community, because here I actually care what my friends think. Amazon is just the middleman.

ck
ck St.
:O 80126

Description	Format	Our Price	Total
Derek M. Powazek	Paperback	$21.00	$21.00

Subtotal		$21.00
Shipping & Handling		$3.99
Order Total		$24.99
Paid via Visa		$24.99
Balance Due		$0.00

Return Label – Please cut along dashed line.

Lexington, KY 40511-1013

Items that are returned more than 30 days after delivery, are in unsellable condition, or are missing parts will be charged a re-stocking fee at our discretion.

* If you are returning an item for one of the following reasons, please contact us at returns-problems@amazon.com:

☐ The item is missing parts/accessories.

☐ The product became defective/damaged after it arrived.

☐ You are returning an item that was delivered by a specialty shipper (e.g. Eagle or NationStreet).

Note: To return a gas-powered item, please contact the manufacturer directly.

For other questions or issues with your order, please visit our site first and click the Your Account button. In Your Account, you can access many account maintenance features, such as viewing the status of your orders, canceling unshipped orders, or changing your e-mail address or password. If you need additional assistance, please contact us at orders@amazon.com.

Thanks for shopping at Amazon.com!

Returns are easy!

http://www.amazon.com/returns.

No need to contact us—most returns can be handled by visiting our Returns Center at the above Web address. * You'll be able to print a return label from there; our step-by-step instructions will guide you through the process. Here are a few details:

- Within 30 days of receiving this shipment, you may return any book in its original condition (or that we recommended and you didn't enjoy), any unopened media (CD, DVD, software, video game, etc.), or any other item in new condition with original packaging and accessories for a full refund of the cost of the item(s). We'll even refund the shipping cost if the return is the result of our error.

- You can expect a refund in the same form of payment originally used for purchase within 7 to 14 business days of our receiving your return. If you are returning a gift, you will receive a gift certificate for the value of your return, which may be used at any time toward purchases at Amazon.com. Please note that we cannot exchange items (unless they are defective or damaged).

If you cannot access the Returns Center on our Web site, please fill out the form to the right, include this entire packing slip with your return, wrap the package securely, and send it to the address below. For your

Did you receive this order as a gift?

☐Yes   ☐ No

If so, please know that we will not send the gift giver confirmation of the return, and you will receive a credit for your return in the form of an Amazon.com gift certificate to be used toward any future purchases.

Please choose the reason for your return:

☐ Product was defective/damaged when it arrived (please indicate below if you want a replacement).

☐ Product performance/quality is not up to my expectations.

☐ I ordered the wrong item.

☐ Item took too long to arrive; I don't want it any more.

☐ No reason, I just don't want the product any more.

☐ Product is not fully compatible with my existing system.

☐ Amazon.com sent me the wrong item (please indicate below if you want a replacement).

☐ I found better prices elsewhere.

If so, where? _____

http://www.amazon.com
orders@amazon.com

Amazon.com
Coffeyville Ind. Park
2654 N. Highway 169
Coffeyville, KS 67337
USA

Lou
9261 S
Highland

Your order of September 3, 2001 (Order ID 104–8626953–1350312)

Qty	Item
	In This Shipment
1	Design for Community : The Art of Connecting Real People in Virtual Places (P–1–B224E1)

This shipment completes your order.

You can track the status of this order, and all your recent orders, online by v
"Your Account" page at http://www.amazon.com/your–account.

Thanks for shopping at Amazon.com, and please come again!

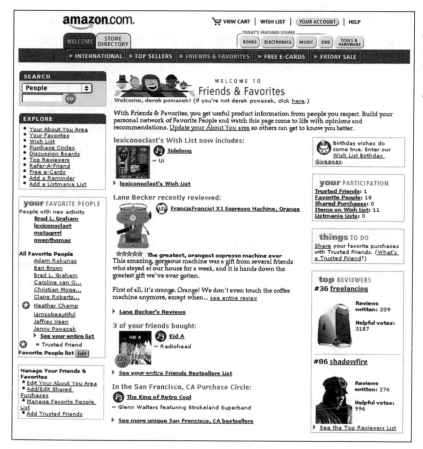

My custom view of Amazon's Friends and Favorites section (amazon.com/community).

There's a second level of trust to this system, too. I can "upgrade" any of my friends to "trusted friend." Everyone on Amazon has access to my product reviews and wishlist, because those things are public by default. What I buy, however, is not public information. That's where trusted friends come in.

My trusted friends have access to extra information about me, namely what I buy. If I upgrade someone to trusted friend status, he is alerted via email. Then, the next time he visits the Friends and Favorites section, he'll be able to view my purchase history. Amazon uses this information to make purchase recommendations on the Friends and Favorites page.

Trusted friend or just plain friend, it was surprising to me how quickly this page became one of my most frequently visited bookmarks.

No one is confused about Amazon's motives here. The company wants you to buy things. But it has been smart enough to realize that, when you give your customers the ability to express themselves within the bounds of your catalog, they will do so with vigor. And that self-expression creates its own value over time.

Your Turn

If you're considering adding community features to your commercial site, you have to be especially careful. Don't let the success stories above fool you; community features in commercial settings can go terribly wrong. Here are some tips for avoiding the big mistakes.

Tip 1: Be honest

If your site is about selling widgets, don't pretend to be anything else. One of the reasons Amazon is successful is that it's not pretending to be something it's not. Even the naming is important here. Calling the section "Friends and Favorites" is a great idea—everyone has friends and favorites. But not everyone wants to join "The Great Amazon Community!" Get the difference?

This honesty is important in other areas, too. When users complained about certain aspects of the TiVo operating system in the AVS Forums, the TiVo programmers agreed and said, "We're going to fix that in the next update." This makes the users feel like they're on the inside, positively contributing to the product, and valuable to the process.

The fact of the matter is, commerce communities have to be extra careful. Users know that your bottom line is about making money, so they may greet community features with suspicion. Honesty is the best way to disarm a suspicious person.

Tip 2: Be prepared

Let's face it, we're not all TiVo. If you open up your site to user contributions, you have to be prepared to face what might not be total adulation. In fact, you may get some pretty harsh criticism.

The way you handle this criticism will define your relationship with your customers. It's imperative that you are prepared with well-informed, well-mannered hosts to respond to questions and comments.

The value you create in your community space is equal to the amount of energy you put into it. Don't think that just because you have customers they will automatically want to help you out. You need to be there for them, before they'll be there for you.

And remember, when you send representatives of your site into the community areas, you have to make sure that they look like they are affiliated with the site. One of the problems with Amazon's community implementation is that when an Amazon representative posts on its message boards, the post looks the same as every other post. This makes it hard for community members to recognize the voice of authority, as well as making it possible for anyone to come in and say, "Hi! I work here at Amazon!" (Remember my "KVETCH CONTROL" story in Chapter 4?)

Tip 3: Be clear

It's important in these settings to be clear about the rules. The AVS Forum accomplishes this with a detailed rules page. At Amazon, the user-generated reviews pass through a human before going live on the site to make sure they're appropriate. Those solutions may or may not work for you. Just remember to set rules and communicate them clearly, and you'll avoid most pitfalls.

You also have to be clear with the design. It's scary enough to some users to post some words on a site. But in the context of a commerce community, the stakes are even higher. As the site owner, you're asking users to give you their credit card, tell you what they think, and maybe even who their friends are. This is going to take a lot of visual hand-holding. If users feel lost and confused, they're not going to get involved.

Up with People!

Like it or not, it's a commercial web. And the commercial web has created commerce communities. While some may lament this as the death of the pure community ideal, I applaud it for the same reason.

Commerce communities create better informed customers, and everyone benefits from that. If one customer had a bad experience with a certain product, she can save another from the same fate. And if companies encourage communities to form around their product or service, they'll be more informed about their users' needs, and, in time, more responsive.

Everybody wins, except maybe lazy companies making bad products. But not even a community site could save one of those.

The web makes this new breed of informed customer possible, and commerce communities allow them to get to know each other. Community ideal or not, it's happening now, and we all may be better off for it.

A Conversation with Matt Williams

Matt Williams

To get a better feel for how the biggest e-commerce company in the world thinks about community, I went to Amazon's Director of Community. Matt Williams was gracious enough to answer my questions in mid-2001. After all my discussions with Internet dreamers and scrappy idealists, it was sobering to sit down and discuss "customers" and "buying decisions." No matter what you think of Amazon or the idea of commerce communities, it is the undisputed leader in this space. Personally, I find the idea of a cross-site community platform very intriguing, and it's only the beginning.

Matt, please give us a brief introduction to who you are and what you do, specifically your work in community and the web.

I am Director of Community at Amazon.com. Our community group includes such features as:

- Customer Reviews (a feature that touches just about every product throughout our site—it provides an opportunity for our customers to share their opinions and recommendations about a product to help others make informed buying decisions)

- Wishlists/Shopping Lists/Gift Registries (enables customers to shop with and for others more easily)

- Listmania! (a feature displayed on Search Results throughout the site as well as a number of other places—allows customers to contribute their favorite lists of products, i.e., "Top 10 gadgets for gadget lovers")

- Purchase Circles (sharing purchase history of the collective customer base by affinity and geography)

- Discussion Boards (offering customers the opportunity to have more in-depth discussions on products and other related topics)

- Friends & Favorites (providing customers with an opportunity to share information with "trusted friends," as well as track favorite reviews, reviewers, and other information)

That's an amazing number of community features. How do you pick which ones to use on the site?

A community is only as strong as the members supporting it. We allow our customers to participate in community features throughout the Amazon.com site. We do not limit the capacity of our "community" by having it exist solely on a destination page—the software supporting our community is a platform used across the website, a few examples include having customer reviews on detail pages and offering Listmania on search results.

Customer reviews represent a shining example of how community can shape the entirety of the Amazon.com site. [Amazon CEO] Jeff Bezos made a very customer-focused decision when, from day one, he made a point of incorporating customer reviews. The customers loved it, and quickly sanctioned it as not only a core part of the "Amazon.com Community" but also a core part of the Amazon.com overall experience. Now, in 2001, we have accumulated millions of reviews, something that gives our customers invaluable information at the time of purchase across a wide variety of products. Our breadth and depth of customer reviews has helped drive Amazon to be the destination of choice for consumers who seek product research before they buy.

In selecting new community features, we always gauge how much a given feature can help or positively impact the customer experience. Amazon.com's mantra is to be the place where you can find and discover anything you might want to buy online. Therefore, the more that we can help our customers locate a product and make better shopping decisions, the better for the customer and for Amazon.com.

I often meet people who scoff at the idea of web community. How do you, at Amazon.com, define the word "community"?

We define community as "customers helping customers"—usually in the context of helping customers make better buying decisions.

What about self-expression? It seems to me that many of the Amazon community features are about letting users express themselves, albeit in the context of the Amazon.com catalog. "These are the books I like." "This is the stuff I want." "Here's what I thought of this CD." All of these things, put together, paint a pretty interesting picture of a person. Is this the point or just a side effect?

In building a vibrant community, the real challenge is allowing many different personalities, opinions, and perspectives to all co-exist in the most organized and engaging manner possible. Freedom of expression is a key ingredient. What that means is that we absolutely want members of the Amazon.com community to express themselves—it is not just a side effect. At Amazon, stating whether a product was simply good or bad is only part of the story. We enable people to discuss their experience of the product in the context of their own lives, because these expanded comments are interesting, entertaining, and more helpful to other customers.

I'm especially enamored with the Amazon Friends and Favorites section. How did that come about? How will it grow in the future?

Our Friends and Favorites area is a combination of many features and services that help the customer 1) make more informed buying decisions, 2) connect more often with friends, and 3) browse and participate in shopping by affinity interests. Friends and Favorites came about through listening to our customers and reacting with features that created the most value. During Amazon.com's rapid growth over the past five years (now having over 30 million customers), we realized that we could offer some truly revolutionary things that were never possible in the physical retail world. Namely, to share buying preferences across our aggregate customer base in real-time (known as Purchase Circles), and to enable customers to share product reviews, wishlists, and purchase histories with their friends, family, and community. Reaching the scale that we have contributed greatly to the success of these features by having many customers sharing across similar interests. We expect our Friends and Favorites area to expand a great deal. As the Amazon.com customer base continues to grow, we expect that our Friends and Favorites area will grow organically due to more friends finding one another and sharing information.

In my experience, things can get dodgy when you introduce commerce into a community setting. In the least, it could cause some to question the use of the word "community." Do you feel a tension between commerce and community? And, if so, how do you attempt to resolve it?

I think that in any community—or even more broadly, in any interaction with customers—you gain trust when you are upfront about contributions made and benefits received. Amazon.com has established itself as a very trustworthy company and brand. Given that Amazon.com is synonymous with e-commerce, and that we have made the customer experience our number-one priority, we have not seen any issues with introducing community into a commerce environment. Additionally, bricks and mortar retail has been introducing community into commerce for years. For instance, bookstores sponsor book clubs, author readings and signings; hardware stores offer "how to" seminars, etc.

Absolutely, but I'm sure there are those who are suspicious of community features in the context of a web store, where the goal is to move product. How do you make paranoid users feel comfortable participating?

Our goal is to offer a convenient way to purchase anything a customer might be looking to buy online, and hand-in-hand with that to help customers make better buying decisions. Most customers feel comfortable that we are doing both—specifically, our customers frequently visit our website to read other customers' product reviews. Amazon.com does something that almost no other retailer does in the world, which is to provide honest and open feedback from its customers right on the shelf where the product sits (or in our case, on the product detail page of the website). Our customers have come to respect and trust Amazon.com because of this and other features like it where customer feedback helps each customer make better buying decisions. Additionally, Amazon.com has always taken the high road when it comes to protecting customer privacy, enabling our customers to quickly opt in or opt out of features/mailings, and for being clear and straightforward with all communications between Amazon and the customer.

Of course, community features have their limits. Book reviews, for example, are screened by editors before appearing on the site. How do you keep people from abusing the community systems?

A community in the simplest terms is a system of people interacting with one another. As I mentioned previously, self-expression is an important component of a vibrant community. At the same time, you also need to provide a reasonable amount of organization and structure. We accomplish this through a combination of efforts, some automated and others more manual. First, we rely heavily upon our community to self-police—for instance, through voting on whether a given review was helpful or not. Second, we employ many automated means for purging, filtering, sorting, and displaying reviews to the customer. Third, we manually screen a small cross-section of reviews prior to publishing them on the website. Underlying those three methods, we do have a set of policies and procedures, publicly published to our customers, which outline the expected behavior/language of members when participating in writing reviews. As the above methods indicate, preventing abuse is not always a simple matter; however, it is something that can be reasonably accomplished through setting rules/guidelines/policies and then enforcing them quickly when violations occur.

Has the Amazon community ever surprised you?

The Amazon.com community is always surprising us. As an example, we launched a feature in late 2000 called "Listmania!" Listmania is a service for our customers to create lists of their favorite products, such as "Things I Liked when I was a Kid," "Books I'd Like Oprah to Pick," or "The Best Party CDs." What was surprising is that our customers were immediately drawn to the feature because it allowed self-expression of each customer's individual interests. A few short months after its launch, our community had added tens of thousands of lists. Our customers love having a voice, especially when their voice can help others make better buying decisions. Since launching this feature, we have placed it in several areas throughout the site, including the main product-search page. The high visibility of the feature has certainly helped increase participation, but Listmania was popular from the outset because it empowers customers to express their preferences and ideas.

There have also been many, many other surprises that have come from our customer community—a customer who randomly bought products off a stranger's Wishlist, old friends finding each other through reviews and other community features, an author who wanted to buy a copy of his book for each person who had that book on his/her wishlist.

What kind of new community features can we expect to see from Amazon in the future?

We will look to change the website anywhere we can improve the customer experience by allowing our community to have a voice. This could be as simple as taking the technology for voting and customer reviews and expanding it beyond the products we carry, or by growing our wishlist product to include other types of list making and registry needs customers have, or perhaps by expanding the community to include members from other websites and/or communities. In addition to specific website improvements or new features, we certainly will look for more opportunities to connect community members with one another—one key example of this will be in the area of birthday reminders. Imagine having one place that both helps you keep track of your family and friends' birthdays, but also provides recommendations on the types of presents you could buy for them.

Any advice for other commerce sites that are considering adding community features, based on your experience?

I think the answer varies depending on the type of e-commerce site and its size (customer/member base). A community is only as strong as the members supporting it.

You gain a lot by allowing the community to have a voice, regardless of whether you have an e-commerce or any other type of site. Corral interest around a common theme, event, affinity, item, or just about anything specific... and some benefit will likely result. Set up the community to be self-policing while enabling individual personalities to shine through, and you will create a space that is both educational and interesting. That combination—where education gets interesting, and where information has personality—should, in my opinion, be the ultimate goal of any online community.

Chapter 11

Killing Your Community

...Nothing Gold Can Stay

> Nature's first green is gold,
> Her hardest hue to hold.
> Her early leaf's a flower;
> But only so an hour.
> Then leaf subsides to leaf.
> So Eden sank to grief,
> So dawn comes down to day.
> Nothing gold can stay.
>
> *– Robert Frost*

In the year 2001, there was an endless parade of dot-coms going belly-up. One after another, websites with high hopes and tenuous business plans went down, leaving a trail of disappointed users and 404 pages.

But what happens when the site going offline isn't just a pet store or a clothing catalog? What happens when the site is a community of users, who have contributed to the site and invested themselves emotionally?

All good things must come to an end. But when you ask your users to form relationships with the site and each other in a community setting, endings are more complicated than just turning off the servers and selling off the Aeron chairs. You owe your users something more.

This is the dirty secret of online communities: They end. But like the ending of any relationship, it can happen with anger and betrayal or respect and understanding—the choice is up to you.

This chapter examines some of the reasons why community sites end and how to best handle the process. You'll hear two stories of endings from different perspectives: a personal site and a corporate one. It concludes with an emotional conversation with Noah Grey, who ended a support community site after three years of hard work. In each case there were different reasons to end and different outcomes from the closure. But they all have one lesson in common: Ending community sites is hard, hard work.

All Good Things Must Come to an End

You can't just end a community, but you can end a community site. It ends for different reasons. In the business world, companies go out of business, go through a merger, or shift priorities. In the personal realm, people can burn out, get too busy, or just lose interest.

In March of 1998, Netscape proudly announced the creation of Professional Connections, a community center for Internet professionals to meet and talk. (I worked with Netscape as a contractor on the design of the forums.) The forums were a success, and drew thousands.

Less than a year later, Netscape was bought by AOL. By April of 1999, Professional Connections was dead. One day the site was just gone, without warning or explanation. Even the paid hosts didn't know until the last moment. The community members were left with no home and no way to contact each other.

What happened? No one really knows, because AOL never issued any official statement. But the skeptics had a good theory: The

Netscape forums were seen as a competitor to AOL's own community offerings. After the merger happened, it was a simple business decision—why compete with yourself?

But for the thousands of people who had formed intimate relationships with each other in the forums, this was like going to their favorite coffee house to find it demolished. They'd lost a vital part of their social lives.

Caleb Clark was a prominent host in the Netscape forums at the time of the closure. He now sees the problem systematically:

> In corporate sponsored online communities, leaders usually do not have control over the community they put their heart and soul into. One wrong spread sheet number, one merger with a company that has different ideas, and your community can vanish at the hands of hurried people who don't see the people behind the servers and telephone lines.
>
> Netscape ended badly due to no time and respect being put into its end. Now, I'm not saying they should have kept it going, but a few hundred dollars would have paid for a person to at least tell the community what was happening. Instead, they heard about it from the press, and the PR coming from the company was insultingly transparent to what was really happening. This resulted in some very mad members, hosts, and administration personnel.

Time to Pull the Plug?

Before getting into how to end a community, you should first determine how you make that decision. How do you decide when to end a community site? Assuming that you have some control over the process (the repo man didn't walk off with the servers or

anything), you should take a lot of time to consider several important questions.

First, go back to the goals you wrote down in Chapter 1. Is the site
meeting the goals you outlined in the beginning?

If the answer is no, can you think of anything that would change
this? Consider adjusting the barrier to entry (see Chapter 8) or clar-
ifying the rules (Chapter 5). Sometimes tweaking the environment can bring a community back from the brink. Try bringing in
new hosts, adjusting the barrier to entry, or getting more specific
with the rules and the sample content.

If you can think of anything to try, try it and give the site a little
more time. If you can't, consider taking a break. Pass the reins to
someone else for a while. Get a fresh perspective.

Fish Rapped

When I was in college, I was the editor of a small alternative newspaper
called *The Fish Rap Live*. We had a tradition there—when the senior
editor's year was up, they passed the torch to a new editor and a new staff.
As a result, the newspaper is still going strong today, years after my
graduation.

So if you're really considering calling it quits, consider passing the torch
on to a new leader and bowing out. It's a safe bet that someone in your
community has the interest and talent to do the job (or, at least, is willing
to give it a try), and someone has a server to offer. Remember that just
because you're done with the community doesn't mean they're done, too.

But, in the end, if it's time to go, it's time to go.

Good Reasons to End

It's clear that there can be some good reasons to end a community.
Here are a few:

1. **The site is not meeting your personal needs.** Communities
   are always in flux. Many times, the idea you start out with

evolves as more people get involved. If the main idea of the site has changed beyond your comfort or interest level, it may be time to end. (Here's where passing the torch to a new leader may be the right choice.)

2. **The site is not meeting the community's needs.** Perhaps you're still happy with the site's direction, but it just hasn't attracted the audience you hoped for. Again, there are avenues open to you here. Perhaps you need more attractive content. Or your audience is out there, but they just haven't found your site yet. Or your tools are too complicated, so they're discouraging participation. If you've tried to solve these problems with no success, you may be out of luck. (A community site for people who don't use computers will never find its audience, for example.)

3. **You're just not interested anymore and no one else is, either.** If you get the feeling that you could take down the site tomorrow and no one would care, that may be an excellent reason to do so. But remember to ask your community first! They say that fish don't know they're wet—you may be too close to it to see its value. Remember to get some outside advice before you pull the plug.

4. **Money.** A popular site can get expensive. Good servers and fat pipes don't come cheap. If you don't have the financial resources to keep your site up, ask your users for help. Many communities have pitched in to buy new servers in times of need. But this can be a temporary fix. If the money runs out, you may have to close up shop.

5. **No one says communities have to last forever.** Community sites can be built around specific events. A web community devoted to discussing a hot new movie will wane when the next hot new movie comes along. There's nothing wrong with letting the site die gracefully, as the need for it fades.

If you've tried everything and realize it's time for your site's final exit, tread carefully. Many great movies have been ruined by a lousy ending. It's up to you to make your final curtain call with grace.

Community Kevorkian

Once you've made an internal decision to end your site, you have to begin the process of communicating that decision externally. Treat this with kid gloves—even the smallest community site will have dedicated members for whom this news will be hard to take. Here are some good do's and don'ts to remember in your ending process.

DO be honest. Communicate your reasons for shutting down the site. If there exists the possibility to change this decision, communicate what that is. If you need help, ask for it. But if the decision is final, and the reasons unchangeable, communicate that, too.

DON'T take it lightly. The worst thing you could do is treat this moment like you don't care. That would only make your members feel stupid for investing themselves in your community and provoke a very angry, very personal response. People may be mad either way, but you can count on an angry backlash if you minimize the importance of this event to the people who care.

DO provide ample warning. Remember that even your most devoted members may not check the site every day. So set a closure date a month or so in advance and let the community know when it's coming.

DON'T just shut off the servers! In the Netscape example, they pretty much did everything wrong, especially this. If you just turn everything off without warning, it may save you from the possibility of community members flaming you in your own forum, but it's extremely cruel to anyone who's become invested in the site. That's no way to reward the people who put their time and energy into your project.

DO enable alternatives. Your members will want to continue the virtual relationships they've established. And though it can be extremely difficult to move a community from one setting to another and still retain the established vibe, providing a life jacket to someone on a sinking ship will earn you a friend for life. In your announcement to the community, recommend other sites where the community could take root. There are plenty of free sites to do the job (groups.yahoo.com and communityzero.com, for example). A member of the community may come forward to offer up a lifeboat. Encourage conversation about this—it shows your users that you care about the relationships they've formed and want them to continue.

DON'T blame your users. You may be angry about the end of the site, too. Though it may be tempting to scream "you won't have me to kick around anymore" and take off in a helicopter, don't. That will only kick-start a firestorm that will surely follow you around for years to come.

DO encourage closure. Anybody who's ever gone to a funeral knows that endings often catalyze emotional reflections. Start conversations on your site *about* the site. Ask for users' most favorite and least favorite moments and funny stories from the site's life. This is the barroom conversation after the funeral where everyone sits around and tells stories about the recently departed— it can be a wonderfully healing experience.

To Archive or Not to Archive?

It's important to remember that while you were working so hard to create a good environment for conversation, it was your users who were doing the talking. That means they feel a strong ownership of the space.

If your community was based in chat or email, archiving isn't much of an issue because of the temporary nature of those mediums. But if your community was based around web discussions, you'll face a choice about whether or not to archive that content.

While you may want to rip it all down and start fresh, your users have contributed this material, so they deserve a say in the decision. In the least, giving your users ample warning of the closure allows them to weed through the forums and save their contributions to their home computers.

Assuming that the server isn't going offline altogether, you may want to consider leaving the community forums online in an archived state. You can turn off new posts and include an archive statement ("Conversations on this site began in July 1999 and ended in May 2001.") so that community members' contributions are preserved. Just make sure you communicate visually that the site is only online as an archive. Add a graphic element to each page, or a black frame across the top of each page, that says "archive"—anything to ensure that no one mistakes it for an active site.

In the end, the archive question depends on the nature of the site (if it was public or private to begin with), the circumstances of its departure (if the servers are still on at all), and the will of the community (if they want their contributions to linger). The best thing you can do is weigh the options and allow your community to have their say.

Story: The Glassdog Club

Glassdog (glassdog.com) has been Lance Arthur's digital playground since 1996. It's a personal labor of love for Arthur, in spite of the site's ironic corporate voice and references to "global world domination." Fans of Arthur's design and writing had been gathering there for years when Arthur decided to give them a community setting to talk back.

In 1999, Arthur launched the Glassdog Club. He started with a free Yahoo! Clubs site, finally migrating to glassdog.org, where Arthur had installed the frustratingly popular Ultimate Bulletin Board (infopop.com), a low-cost server-side community tool. (See Chapter 4 for more on community tools.)

Arthur started the club for the same reason he's done everything at Glassdog—for kicks. It was a personal site community, built for an audience that was already invested in Arthur's personal stories and design tips. Initially, the site exploded with posts, some of which even stunned Arthur. For example:

> There was one eye-opening discussion I remember. A member posted a fairly simple but loaded question: If you are homophobic, why are you? He could not remember meeting anyone who was truly homophobic, was neither gay nor homophobic himself, and wasn't looking for a fight. He was genuinely curious about that particular human trait. What makes a person homophobic?

This is the kind of discussion that raises a red flag for any community moderator, but for Arthur it was especially personal. What the community didn't know was that its host was gay. He took a back seat in the discussion and waited to see what would happen.

"The responses were, for the most part, fair and non-judgmental," Arthur said. "But a few members admitted that they had negative feelings to one degree or another concerning homosexuality, from a woman who feared for her children if they were gay because the world would be so difficult for them, to a man who genuinely resented and detested gay men, calling them selfish and sexually overactive perverts."

Arthur said he was blown away by both the content and the largely civil tone of the discussion. "I just had no idea that those impressions and opinions were out there from people who visited my site, in some cases expressed by people I would call my friends."

In time, though, the conversations waned. "Slowly but surely, the forums devoted to open discussion of news and opinion started to die out. The ones that stayed active were a Q&A forum devoted to site building and another where people who'd built sites wanted opinions about them. Everything else degenerated into either incendiary flame wars that burned out very quickly, or deadly dull me-too-isms nobody cared about."

When Arthur decided to pull the plug, the community had been alive for just under a year and had more than 1,200 registered members. He announced his decision prominently, well in advance, and encouraged conversation about it. He was candid about his missteps as well as the shortcomings of the community. Many in the community agreed with what he had to say, and organized their own lifeboat. A member of the community stepped forward and volunteered to host the community on his site, so many transitioned there. The new site had a higher barrier to entry, to solve some of the perceived problems with the Glassdog Club.

Today, when you visit glassdog.org, you're greeted with a simple closing statement that thanks the communities for their participation and suggests other sites to join or create a community.

In this case, Arthur did almost everything right. He was upfront about his decisions, honest about his reasons, gave plenty of notice, and supported the community in organizing lifeboats to a new server.

Could he have made other decisions early on to avoid this outcome? Probably. Setting up clearer guidelines, having helpful hosts, and taking a stronger leadership role might have kept the community on track.

But, in the end, it was a personal site, and Arthur was the person. It was his call, and by and large, the community supported his right to make this decision. The ending was handled with mutual respect and a minimum of flames. We should all be so lucky when our time comes.

> **1 July 2000**
>
> **glassdog.CLUB is officially closed and will not be reopening. We would like to thank our membership for their participation over the past year and apologize if you were not aware of this action. If you are looking for another venue for online conversation, may we humbly suggest the following sites:**
>
> - **<u>dreamless.org</u> which provides discussion forums concerning Web design and designers**
> - **<u>Astounding Web</u> for the sharing and critique of Web sites**
> - **<u>Yahoo! Clubs</u> which gave birth to the original "I Hate Glassdog" forum that inspired glassdog.CLUB and allows anyone to start their very own online discussion group**
>
> <u>glassdog.com</u>

The Glassdog Club's fond farewell (glassdog.org).

Design Considerations

The most important design consideration in this process is the initial announcement. The design should communicate its importance. Don't just post a small comment at the bottom of a long forgotten thread. This is probably the most important post you'll ever make—it should look like it.

So, when making your announcement, make sure it floats to the top and stays there. You may also want to make it a separate page, outside the community framework, but linked prominently from the forums. This communicates its importance.

Then, from the bottom of the announcement, it's imperative that you link to the discussions about it. Consider starting the conversations yourself on topics such as initial reactions, fond memories, organizing alternatives, and saying goodbye. Keep the page up-to-date on the latest developments, especially on how community members can stay in touch with each other.

All of this shows your community members that this is not an off-the-cuff decision. It's for real, and you're taking it seriously. If you show them that, they'll take it seriously, too.

Saying Goodbye

Death is a natural part of life, as any nature documentary will tell you. And knowing how online communities end, good and bad, can help you end yours with grace when the time comes. It may even help you avoid it altogether.

Unlike in life, online we can plan our deaths. May yours be a good one.

A Conversation with Noah Grey

Photo by Noah Grey

Noah Grey

Sometimes, the most sensitive people make the best community moderators, because they are so empathetic to their members' emotional needs. In that case, Noah Grey may be the best moderator in the world. I've never met someone capable of so much empathy over email. In the end, though, that very quality may make running a community impossible to continue forever.

Grey ran a very personal, very private online community for three years, devoted to letting male sexual abuse survivors reach out to each other for support. And he started the forum for the best reason of all—because he needed it himself.

He describes ending the community as one of the hardest things he's ever done, and it's easy to see why—it's not every day you get death threats online. His story is a strong reminder of how personal a virtual community can be, for both the members and the moderator. Grey and I talked via email in early 2001.

Noah, please give us a brief introduction to who you are and what you do, specifically your work in community and the web.

Noah Grey, 26. For about three and a half years (1997–2000), I ran the Male Abuse Survivors Support Forum (MASSF), the first and largest community and resource network on the Net for male survivors of sexual abuse. The MASSF had around 700 members altogether throughout its lifespan.

Why did you start the forum?

In 1997, I had a very severe and traumatic flashback—an experience common to many rape survivors in which sights, sounds, and feelings from the event come back with sudden, overpowering force. I felt fundamentally misunderstood and alone. I started searching the Net for a place I could talk about it and find some kind of understanding, but all the groups I found were female-oriented, and I didn't feel comfortable enough to take part in them. Other than a handful of dry psychiatric pages, I found almost nothing that fully, specifically addressed the sexual abuse of males at all.

It was clear to me there was a great need here that nobody was meeting. So, as a kind of desperate lark, I threw together a very basic bulletin board for the most selfish of reasons: to gain support for myself, and to see if I could help myself by helping others. (At the time, I was already running another bulletin board on my site which had become quite successful in its own right and I had run countless bulletin boards and chat rooms going all the way back to my late-eighties BBS days, so setting up yet another board was a fairly natural process for me.) I did so very quietly and hesitantly—I was no expert, after all. I had no professional training and had never offered counseling to survivors before—all I had to offer was the fact that I was another survivor. And that's what I wanted it to be: by survivors, for survivors.

What was it like to run the site?

It was both the most profoundly rewarding and most profoundly demanding experience of my life. Demanding because the subject matter was so obviously intense and personal, and something that I had to engage myself in with all these other people on a near-daily basis. Rewarding because I got to see how much of a positive, healing difference it made to so many. Men from 11 to 70 have told me I've saved their lives, but I didn't, I just made a place where together they could learn to find their own strength and save their own lives. I never felt right claiming credit for that, any more than an instrument maker can take credit for a great concert or performance. But in the moments I could truly let myself feel that I had some real part of it, that I'd been a part of this beautiful, healing thing which so many needed—that was the greatest feeling in the world.

Most of the moments and exchanges that remain most vivid to me couldn't be explained without talking specifically about matters relating to the people involved, which (for obvious reasons) I don't want to do—but I think the defining moment for me was the first time that someone told his story and the ways he dealt with facing it, overcoming it. The MASSF had been going for several months by then, but hadn't truly found its footing, and I think that was the turning point. Afterwards, other men (including myself) slowly came forward to tell their stories on the site, and that was when the MASSF became something more than a bulletin board, a real community. The stories soon became the MASSF's main focus, and indeed for most of us it was a watershed event when we were finally able to put it down in words, to say "This is what happened to me," and to let the world know it—for many of us, that was when our healing truly began.

Why did you decide to end the site?

In large measure, I think it was a victim of its own success. When it was smaller, it felt like much more of a tight, close-knit group of fellow survivors and friends; but as the membership grew, so did the tensions. The point inevitably came when I wasn't able to personally be there for everyone like I once was—and, feeling the strain, I appointed a co-administrator and several moderators to essentially run the show (or, at least, that was the intent; I still ended up taking more of a hands-on role than I think was good for either them or me to have by that point). I stopped reading most of the stories and responding to almost all the posts. I knew (or at least feared) it would cause friction and resentment if I gave support and feedback to some and not to others, and I just didn't have the strength or energy to keep up with it all anymore—so I largely restricted my involvement to private support, and to technical upkeep (of which, by that point, there was much to take care of—especially since I had written its chat room program, and essentially rewritten the board software).

So part of it was, I think, that it simply grew too large and was torn apart by internal tensions; too many people needed the MASSF to be one thing, too many others needed it to be something else, and after a point it simply wasn't able to be everything that everyone needed it to be. It lost focus.

Finally, it simply reached the point where either it was going to go or I was.

When you made the decision to end the site, what did you do?

First, I think I should emphasize that we (and most other abuse-survivor groups) differed from most web communities in a very fundamental respect: Most of us were, at least as compared to the norm, quite needy and often very hypersensitive. And I don't mean that as a criticism, I was one of the neediest and most sensitive guys there—on a site like this, it comes with the territory, almost by definition: You're there because you need to talk about what happened to you, and you need to be told you're all right and that you're not alone.

This is all in contrast to a site like Slashdot or MetaFilter, which focus on intellectual discourse, and where issues of a personal nature don't fit in unless offered objectively in the context of the issues being discussed. We had plenty of relatively objective discussions about abuse-related issues, but predominately we were there to talk about ourselves. I tried to provide a place where survivors (including myself most of all) could feel safe to be as nakedly emotional and vulnerable as necessary, and a site like that is really a world apart from something like MetaFilter, Slashdot or most web communities. It's also an inverse from them in that a survivor-community moderator doesn't fundamentally want there to be a need for his/her site; to have a high new-member sign-up rate, to be "successful," was more bitter than sweet—and nothing was better than seeing a member leave when he felt secure enough within himself to not need us anymore. Thus, in a sense, you want to "fail" because you don't want there to be a reason for you to continue being in business.

So, with all that said, I chewed on the decision for several months before making it final. When you have hundreds of people all gathered together talking about the most sensitive possible subjects, tensions and conflicts are bound to develop, and by that point they were tearing us all apart. More and more people started saying the site just wasn't helping them anymore—I kept telling myself that it served its purpose as long as it was still helping someone, but that slowly became more outweighed by the tension, the dissatisfaction, the sheer weariness. Eventually all that kept me from closing it was a fear of change, a fear of throwing away my crutch—a fear that this immense thing which had been a part of my life for three years would leave a hole that would never heal.

Towards the end, there was a central conflict involving me and several other longtime members who had also been longtime friends, and as that came to a head, I finally caved in and said, fine, I don't have the strength to keep it up anymore, I need my life back—the site comes down in a couple of weeks. A few loyal and understanding friends supported me, but the general reaction was anywhere between unspoken resentment and virulent hostility, even including one death threat. (And the day I got the death threat, I moved the closing date up a week.) Because so many had invested so much of themselves personally into the site, people took its closing very personally. I just didn't realize until then how many people felt they had a claim on it, felt like they owned it. Instead of seeing it as a gift that I had given them for three years, they treated me as if I were the worst kind of thief, someone who'd broken into their homes and stolen some irreplaceable, invaluable memento. Of the 700+ members the MASSF had altogether, I can count on one hand the number of them I still keep in touch with—and we never talk about it anymore.

Any tips for people considering ending their community site?

First, don't be hasty. Allow yourself a waiting period, to see if you feel the same way in a week or a month as you do now. Give yourself as much time as you can to make sure that it's something you really want to do—which applies as much to starting a community site as to ending one. Also, it might not be a bad idea to talk with at least one friend on the outside, to get the perspective of someone who isn't directly connected or involved with the goings-on (but who, ideally, cares about you regardless).

Just think about it, really ask yourself if your site is still doing what you need it to do—and if not, what could you do to change it, and would it be worth the time and effort to do so. Sometimes, a change of policy or direction may be the best medicine, for you as much as the site. But in the end, don't be afraid to put yourself first; as cliche as it is to say, listen to your heart, because whatever it is in your heart that led you to start it—and whatever it is inside you that made your site a good and beautiful thing in the first place—that spirit won't steer you wrong at the end, either. If it's no longer what you want or need it to be, then it's probably no longer what it needs to be for anyone else.

Now that it's in the past, is there anything you would have done differently?

I hate to say it, but you couldn't pay me enough to go through that again. But hypothetically, I'd start by laying down the clearest and most unambiguous ground rules possible and have them in place from day one; having no rules (as I did at first) may help you establish a more relaxed atmosphere in the beginning, but in the end, the lack of them does much more harm than good. And I'd probably aim for a certain goal/limit of members and institute a member cap, and have only so many people active at one time. On a site like ours, more voices present means more need, the less personal it feels when personal is what it most needs to be—it just doesn't work to have so many people "competing" for each other's attention and validation with such an intensely intimate subject. But really, to run a site like this needs a resilience, maturity, and fortitude that I just didn't have (and am still too far from having achieved).

The bigger the community you plan to run, the thicker your skin needs to be, and the more patience you need to have. Granted, an abuse-survivor community is much more sensitive and demanding than what most people who want to set up a web community will have to deal with, but still, most human beings are emotional creatures—the more time you can spend deciding in advance how you're going to handle emotional conflicts, the better. And with all this said, I really don't want to discourage anyone (however I may sound to the contrary!); I just want to advise caution and encourage people to be as prepared as they possibly can. Running a good community can be a great and rewarding experience like no other. I met some wonderful people, learned some incredible things, and had some of the most fulfilling experiences of my life, through my site, and I still wouldn't give that up for anything. Be prepared for the worst to happen, because sooner or later it probably will—but be prepared for the best, too.

Chapter 12

What's Next?

...Back to the Future

I'm a lousy futurist. I sat through the late nineties without making a dime in the stock market. I probably would have bought a Betamax if I'd been buying electronics in the eighties. I can barely keep track of my own schedule a few weeks out.

So I'm not going to make any bets about the future and commit them to print where they can embarrass me later. Instead, I'm going to talk about right now. When it comes to virtual community, there's all sorts of incredible stuff percolating in the web's nooks and crannies, just around the corner from going big.

This is about taking the usual formula of threads, posts, and chat, and turning them on their head. This is the stuff that keeps me up at night, excited about the future.

Digital Diaspora

The year 2000 saw the rebirth of a very old web idea, repackaged in some new technology, and unleashed as the weblog (or "blog" for short). The recipe for a weblog is simple: Make a web page, a single page, and put microcontent (short blurbs and blips) on it. Then update it again and again, all day, every day, with the newest stuff always at the top.

I designed the Blogger site in March 2000. Note the "recently updated" list on the homepage (blogger.com).

The content of these updates can be anything. The weblog started as a kind of personalized link list, literally a *log* of the author's travels on the *web*. Tools sprouted up all over the web to make these updates easier, including Blogger (blogger.com), Pitas (pitas.com), Manilasites (manilasites.com), and GrokSoup (groksoup.com). (Full disclosure: I designed Blogger's web presence and later worked as the company's creative director in late 2000.) Each of these tools came with its own quirks (some required that you host your site on their server, some updated remote servers), but all of them did one thing: Let you update your weblog quickly, easily, and from anywhere.

Getting personal

Of course, human beings being personal creatures, the content of weblogs rapidly expanded from being a simple list of an author's web travels to encompassing any and every kind of niche interest. There are now weblogs on everything from show tunes (mermaniac.com) to interface design (37signals.com/svn). I even kept a weblog during the course of writing this book (design forcommunity.com) to keep interested readers up-to-date on how it was going.

But mostly weblogs became the new homepages. Give people a tool to update a web page quickly and easily, and you wind up with a lot of people talking about what they had for lunch. And while that may not be everyone's cup of tea, to the people doing it, it fills an important need for self-expression.

The cheese sandwich connection

My friend and fellow New Riders' author Jeffrey Zeldman once summed up the power of the weblog in a way I'll never forget. He said, on the web, you can post, "Today I had a cheese sandwich," and within an hour you'd get email that said, "I, too, had a cheese sandwich." It's a trivial example, but it perfectly exemplifies the power of microcontent to promote connection on the web.

Think back to Caleb Clark's recipe for good conversations in community spaces (in the interview at the end of Chapter 5). There was one called "How was your week?" Weblogs are a little bit like that thread, exploded into thousands of separate sites.

But that, alone, does not make it a community. What was needed, was a way to connect all these disparate sites and give their users a way to talk back.

Tools of the trade

Enter websites such as Weblogs (weblogs.com) and Linkwatcher (linkwatcher.com), where weblogs can create a membership and automatically get listed when they update. The result is that everyone can see when webloggers update their sites. Weblogs.com also has an ad service, where people can upload an ad for their site that may get included in any other weblogger's site. And Blogger automatically lists updated sites on their homepage by the minute. And, of course, the webloggers themselves often link to each other, based on like interests and similar styles. All of these things create the connections between sites that can foster community.

So now we have all these people talking about their lives and interests on their sites, and we have a web of connections between them. The last piece of the puzzle to achieve a real community feel is to let the readers of each site talk back. Enter Dotcomments (foreword.com/dotcomments.php), which is designed to work with Blogger, and allows weblog readers to talk back by posting comments to each individual post.

But is it a community? It's certainly not the usual kind of community. Every example I've used so far in this book has been one site with many participants. Here there are many sites, each with (usually) just one author and a handful of participants. But they do have all the pieces of a virtual community: They have users who have the tools to use their voice in a public and immediate way, forming intimate relationships over time. Nowhere in my definition of virtual community does it say "on the same site."

A further evolution of this idea is group weblogs, where multiple authors are brought together to post on the same site, unified by a common interest. Previously discussed sites such as Slashdot and MetaFilter fall into this category. In this way, they can be seen as both a weblog and a community site.

Weblog as community

I don't believe that there is one cohesive weblog community. Instead, there are many communities, groups, cliques, and clubs in the weblog space. Any weblog with comments can quickly turn into a community of one, attracting a small group of people who are interested enough to follow along and participate. And if each of those readers then starts a weblog of his own, with comments that the others take part in, you wind up with a giant, interconnected, ever-evolving community. Or, better, a hazy cloud of overlapping communities, each with its own feel, and sharing a few members.

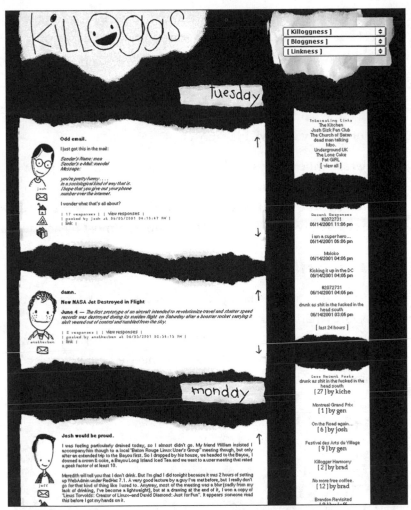

Killoggs (killoggs.com) is a multi-person weblog. Note the illustration of each author next to his post.

Where this model diverges from the usual community site is in its multitude of separate sites. And yet it's this multitude that gives the weblog community model its strength. Because a person has control over his own piece of the community landscape, he feels a powerful ownership of his space that's lacking in traditional community sites. In this way, it's the same as a real-life neighborhood—each participant has his own space, his home, where he can feel safe, yet he is also a part of a larger community, the neighborhood.

Weblogs have been around long enough to prove their longevity, and yet when journalists and academics consider them critically, they always come up short. Most of the journalistic profiles of the phenomenon focus on the intimacy and voyeurism of the idea. It's an easy journalistic peg ("They post intimate details of their lives!"), but it's missing the big idea entirely—it'd be like judging Slashdot by only Rob Malda's posts.

Weblogs are inherently social creatures, just like the people who create them. If you can step back and view them from afar—a dozen or two of interlinked sites at a time—you can see why they're so effective. They form communities, almost by accident.

One step further

The apex of this trend is best encapsulated by Noah Grey's labor of love, Greymatter. You may remember Grey from Chapter 11, where he talked about shutting down a support forum that was very close to his heart. When he did, he needed a new project to keep him busy. That project became Greymatter.

The Greymatter homepage (greymatter.com).

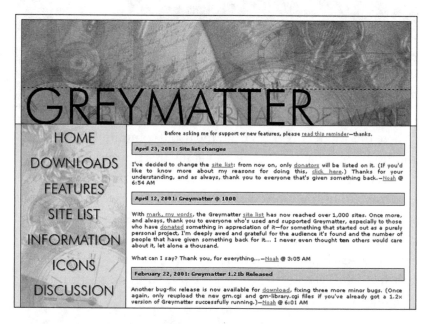

What started as a "super guestbook" script has become the ultimate weblog/journal tool of the moment. Once installed on a server and configured, Greymatter allows the administrator to easily update the site. The content of that site could be anything—a personal journal, a movie review site, a webzine with multiple authors—the tool is content agnostic.

But what is really powerful about Greymatter, from a community perspective, is that anything the administrator posts comes with comments enabled by default, so your users have a way to talk back. Almost any Greymatter-powered site immediately becomes a fertile environment for growing a small, personal community.

Greymatter comes with plenty of other niceties, too: Archives, searching, and user-configurable templates are all included. The catch? There is none. The software is free to download and use (noahgrey.com/greysoft).

The blog beyond

And what's most exciting is that all of these tools (Greymatter, Blogger, et al.) are all in their infancy. All of them could be improved in obvious ways. Greymatter could stand to add some more advanced user management tools (like account creation). Blogger and Weblogs could be a whole lot more reliable when it comes to service uptime. We still have not really seen the ultimate offspring of a weblog and a threaded conversation.

But these tools are exciting because they point to the future of online community—a future where everyone has a home of his own, a place where he has control, a private space in an ever-more-complicated virtual community sphere.

Plus, you get to find out what people had for lunch.

Personification

If the key element of the weblog community meme is user-controlled homes, the creators of traditional, large, multi-user community sites may feel like they have nothing to learn here. After all, you don't want to be in the business of creating and hosting a multitude of sites, right?

But it would be a mistake to ignore the key elements of this lesson entirely, because there are things large site owners can do to create these user-controlled homes within the boundaries of their own site. The key is to allow your users to personify a small corner of your site—saying "this is me."

Many sites do this in incredibly rudimentary ways. Most community software packages create profile pages for users that list their name, rank, and serial number. But these pages don't feel representative of a person—they feel more like one card in a giant card catalog.

Sony ImageStation's member profile could be greatly expanded.

I was lucky to work with Sony on its photo sharing community site, ImageStation (imagestation.com), in mid-2001. In my review of the site, I spent a great deal of time talking about the importance of user home pages. Its current member pages had the bare minimum information and felt very antiseptic. One nice feature was that members could select one of their previously uploaded photos as their member photo. While this was a nice starting point, I suggested that Sony dramatically expand the role of the member pages.

For example, the pages could include a sampling of the user's photos, links to recent albums, and a guestbook where other members could leave comments. Other ideas included adding weblog functionality, so that members could talk about their lives, and private messaging so that users could send each other private intra-site messages.

The basic theme is clear—give users the power to use their voices on their homepages, and make it as easy as possible for them to do so.

For a better approach, again we turn to Amazon (see Chapter 10 for a refresher on Amazon). Because its community features are so diverse and spread throughout the site, it became obvious that each user needed a home base to bring them all together. So Amazon automatically creates an "About You" page for each user. Write a review, create a wish list, and it'll show up here. Even better,

My Amazon "About You" page.

your name will link to this page from wherever it appears in Amazon, reinforcing the idea that this is your personal space. This page is your digital stand-in.

You can even choose to make some or all of your purchases public on this page, and the page will automatically link to other Amazon customers you list as your friends. It also comes with the ability for you to upload a photo and say a few words about yourself.

The page has a way to go before it becomes the ideal tool for personification. I'd love to see Amazon give users more control over both how the page looks for them, as well as how it appears to others. And, like much at Amazon, it takes some digging to even find it in the first place. But it's there, and it's a great start toward the ideal of web community personification.

Diversification

It's time for us, all of us, to move beyond thinking about virtual communities in terms of chat, web-based discussions, and email. These three little worlds are becoming less distinct every day as they commingle with newer technologies such as instant messaging, peer-to-peer file sharing programs, and video conferencing.

If virtual community is about connecting real people together, then it's those real people and the interconnecting relationships between them that are at the core. The "virtual" part of "virtual community" is the digital connections between those real people, but what form those connections take is becoming less and less important.

In fact, I believe that all these tools are important in creating a community-rich environment online—each should be used for what it's good at, and blended with the rest. The way that Evolt (see Chapter 9) exists in email and on the web simultaneously is a good example of this diversification. The Evolt members have the same names and email addresses in both worlds, forming a consistency regardless of the medium.

Just as the Amazon "About You" page takes diverse community functionality from all over the site and brings it together on one page, so should you allow your users to express themselves in many ways, with many tools, brought together.

A healthy community will have times when an intellectual web-based discussion is in order. Then there will be times when a heady chat room giggle is appropriate. Email will keep the community together when they're offsite and alert them to events when they happen. Instant messaging will give community members a private place to talk back and forth in real time. And it doesn't end there.

Even if you only consider web-based community tools, there's so much more than simple discussion to the community equation.

Community site alt.sense (altsense.net) does a good job of diversification. In addition to the usual web boards, and a multi-user weblog, members can join the Birthday Project (altsense.net/happy) and list their birthday with the site. When the day comes, they'll be featured on the home page of the site, along with their email address and a built-in way for the community to send them happy birthday wishes.

There are plenty of other ways to interact at alt.sense, too. There are polls that members can vote in (or email submissions for new polls), as well as the Photo Album project, where members can create albums full of photos and any other artwork. All the albums are viewable by the public, and in addition to the users creating their own albums, there are also group albums that anyone can contribute to.

Each of these projects contains the minimum requirements to create a community, but put together they form a rich tapestry of community interaction. At alt.sense I can talk with people in the forums, send them well wishes on their birthdays, and even see their artwork in an album. This layering of projects and features makes the site more powerful as a community.

The alt.sense open photo album (altsense.net/ projects/albums/ open_album).

And even better, the beautiful look of alt.sense is carried through each project with grace and style. While the interactions change (voting, uploading, talking), the look and feel are remarkably consistent. This creates a fantastic community vibe.

The key is to take community sites beyond the convenient realms and comfortable spaces we've settled into, and to use as many of the mediums as make sense. Soon it won't be enough to just toss a discussion package and a chat room at a site and call it a day (if it ever was). Your users deserve a toolset as diverse and personal as they are.

Visual Sophistication

The web is a text-based medium, and (probably) always will be. But that doesn't mean there aren't a few treats in store for the visually inclined.

Checking into the
Habbo Hotel
(habbo.com).

When I see things like the Habbo Hotel, it feels at once futuristic and nostalgic. Futuristic because of the silky smooth visual interface. Nostalgic because we've been here before.

In 1997, The Palace appeared on the Internet. Less a place than a program, The Palace was an application that each user had to download and run, and site administrators had to install custom server software to use. But once all that was done, users could chat in a visual medium.

But the application was so buggy and the "visual medium" so hackneyed, I'm convinced it set the idea of avatars (digital stand-ins for real people) back a decade. For me, interacting in The Palace was a little bit like dragging icons around my desktop, with little speech bubbles popping up randomly.

At the time I was working at Electric Minds, a start-up company founded by virtual pioneer Howard Rheingold. As part of the Electric Minds site, we had a custom Palace that we experimented with, going so far as to have authors do readings and conduct inter-

The Electric Minds Palace in 1997, during an interview with Robert Hass, U.S. Poet Laureate.

views. With Minds Palace's cartoony look and flat icon characters blipping in and out, the results were mixed at best.

Compare that with the visual sophistication and fluid movement of today's Shockwave or Flash-based communities, and you might feel like you were around for the Model-T. At the Habbo Hotel (habbo.com), I can design my own avatar, move and interact in virtual rooms, and even create my own private room and furnish it to my liking.

Habbo Hotel was launched in early 2001, and is powered by a powerful Java backend technology developed by Sulake, a company based in Helsinki, Finland. The frontend is created entirely in Macromedia's Shockwave, which means that users must have this plug-in installed, but it's well worth it.

Chat still pops up like thought balloons over the characters' heads like it did in The Palace, but here they float up over time like traditional text chat to show context. And even better, you only see the comments spoken by people *near* you. If you want to talk to someone, you have to move your avatar over to them. This solves the long-standing "everyone talking at once" problem of chat (discussed in Chapter 7) and creates a real feeling of being there.

The avatars are clearly little pixelated people, but they're eerily expressive. They can sit on chairs, lie down on beds, and open cabinets. They can even pick up a drink and carry it around, sipping on it occasionally. But my favorite part? The avatars' eyes blink. Sure, it's just a looping flash animation, but it has an amazing subliminal effect. It makes the avatars more believably real.

There's plenty to do in addition to just wandering around and chatting, too. Habbo is stocked with game rooms, where users can challenge each other. Or you can go to the dance floor and dance all night without breaking a sweat. You can even create your own custom room and furnish it to your liking, but be prepared to pay. While the rest of the site is free, the items in the virtual catalog cost real money.

The site does little to reinforce the fact that these virtual avatars have real people behind them. Participants are listed under user names, not real names, for example. But in this case it works because the playfulness of the place is its own reward. And there's still a strict code of conduct. The rooms automatically censor certain words, and they ask users to respect "The Habbo Way," which is broken into a few simple rules (habbo.com/terms.html):

Don't

- Swear or use sexually graphic names or insults

- Pester people who don't want to talk to you

- Give personal information to people you don't know

- Break the law in the hotel or talk others into breaking it

Do

- Hang out with your friends, without traveling to meet them

- Respect other people's views and beliefs

- Be whoever you want to be—there's no need to be shy in the hotel

And the site ties the virtual to the real in other ways. If you list your email address with the site, it becomes tied to your profile. Then when you make a friend in the hotel (other users must send you an intra-site request to become a friend—you are free to agree or disagree), those users have the ability to send you an email from within the hotel. Your email address is protected, but the ability is there.

Because the site originates in the United Kingdom, where the use of SMS (Short Message Service) is much more prevalent, the site can also send short text messages to your cell phone from within the hotel. So, while the Habbo Hotel revels in its "virtualness," it ties the virtual hotel to the real world in some interesting ways. Imagine getting a message on your cell phone from a tiny pixel person you just met online!

Inside the Habbo Hotel (habbo.com).

Will visual community tools like these supplant traditional text-based forms of virtual community? I wouldn't bet on it. Text is still the fastest, most direct way to communicate online. But I think virtual communities could learn a thing or two from places like Habbo Hotel.

I was tripping around the hotel the other day and met a woman from Spain in the form of a black-haired pixel person in a red shirt. I asked her if she ever chatted online in places without graphics like this.

"Yes," she said. "But this is more fun."

Shall We Play a Game?

In *WarGames*, the 1983 movie that was perhaps the first-ever hacker flick, a computerized voice ominously asks young Matthew Broderick, "Shall we play a game?" The movie ends with crafty humans outsmarting a military computer at a game of tic-tac-toe to avoid a nuclear war.

Humans playing games against computers seemed like a pretty futuristic idea in the eighties. Yet, when it comes to online community today, it's more likely that the future will be more about humans using computers to play games against each other.

The Virtual Gaming Room

Take the Habbo Hotel above, for example. There you can wander into the "Cunning Fox Gameall," where users can challenge each other to games of Battleship, chess, and poker. Just sit down at a table and wait for someone to join you. And, of course, you can chat while you play.

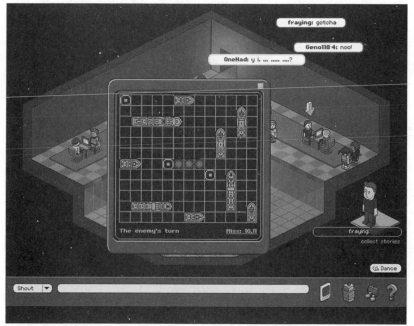

Playing Battleship in the Habbo Hotel.

It almost goes without saying that almost all video games are networked to some extent now. Even console games (that you hook up to your TV) are getting packed with modems and ethernet cards. And any PC game will have online features. In Quake, a popular first-person shooter, you can add insult to injury by mocking the people you just blew away. A primitive messaging application is built right into the game.

While few would call Quake a community-building application, some online games hold community interaction close to their heart. And what's more surprising is the complex social hierarchies these games can create.

Role-Playing in a Virtual World

Games such as Ultima Online and Everquest are role-playing games that create entire virtual worlds. Unlike other games, when you leave the game, it goes on without you. When you come back, time has passed, and your character is still there where you left it. The plot of these games will be familiar to anyone who will admit to playing Dungeons and Dragons in high school (you know, go on a quest, find a sword, fight a dragon, that kind of thing). The end result is a world with a sense of purpose, a shared history, and complex social interactions.

So complex, in fact, that sometimes the virtual world and the real one become indistinct. These games have seen weddings (both real and virtual), friendships gained and lost, and even a number of scandals that spilled over into the real world. Recently, when a member of the Everquest community reportedly committed suicide, the virtual community started placing calls in the real world, only to discover that the suicide and the person were faked. While this may be the extreme, even the average user must log hundreds of hours in the game to progress to the highest levels. All the while, these people are forming relationships, making allegiances, joining communities.

Grade School All Over Again

Another favorite is SiSSYFight 2000 (sissyfight.com), a Shockwave-based game created by the gone but not forgotten *Word* magazine. Imagine yourself in grade school again, out on the playground during recess, in the shifting winds of a pre-adolescent's social world. What's important is being popular, and you accomplish that by picking on someone else.

On the battlefield playground of SiSSYFiGHT 2000 (sissyfight.com).

So groups of up to five girls (boys play as girls, too) gather in each game. Each participant has 60 seconds to decide her move. It can be something defensive (cowering, tattling) or offensive (grabbing, scratching, teasing). And, of course, everyone has a chat window to taunt the other girls as they decide, and to try to motivate the others to gang up on the weakest girl. When everybody's decided on her move, each combination has its own result. For example, if you chose to tattle and I chose to scratch, I'd get in trouble, losing a heart or two. Each player has ten hearts, and when they're all gone, you're out of the game.

This is all hysterically funny or horrifyingly traumatic, depending on your point of view and your experience in grade school. But it's developed an insanely dedicated community that plays for hours at a time and posts in the attached message boards.

What Is It About Games?

There's something about the combination of a strategy game (even one as thin as hair-pulling or fighting dragons) and a communications medium that is an undeniably powerful way to bring a community together. I think the power comes, for some, in creating a virtual world with rules to follow and an understood course of action.

An open community discussion site can be a daunting prospect for some, because it's not always clear what the expected course of action is. There's too much freedom. A common newbie statement is that the person doesn't feel he "writes well enough" to participate in online discourse. But put him in a game of blackjack and watch the conversation fly.

There's an important lesson in this for anyone building communities online. Different users will feel comfortable in different spaces. Some may need the structure and immersive qualities that a gaming environment creates. Others may just like playing poker a lot. If you're running a large community space, consider adding a game and seeing what happens.

One thing's clear: The futures of virtual community and online gaming are inexorably intertwined.

Community Controlled Editorial

What happens if you like running a community site but don't like being in charge? If you're a programmer like Rusty Foster, you just create a site that lets the community be their own editors.

Foster is the creator and moderator of Kuro5hun (kuro5hun.org), a community site about the intersection of technology and culture. At first glance, Kuro5hun (pronounced "corrosion") looks like yet another Slashdot-style weblog community. But if you dig a little deeper, the site has some fundamental differences that create a much different vibe.

At Slashdot, when a user submits a story, it's put into a queue until it's read, edited, and, if deemed appropriate, posted to the site. This creates an unavoidable lag time, and can sometimes result in hurt feelings on the part of the submitters, who might feel like they're sending their valuable material off into a black hole.

But at Kuro5hun, everything submitted to the site becomes immediately viewable. When a story is first submitted, it appears on a submissions page that's viewable by the community (logged-in members). Then the community has a chance to review the story, make editorial comments, and vote on its inclusion. If a story receives negative votes, it's dropped off the page. If it receives positive votes, it gets promoted to a section page. If it receives a significant number of positive votes, it appears on the site's front page.

This gives the community itself the power to decide what content appears on the site. It's an incredibly powerful idea, because it's really giving the users ownership of the site. According to Foster, future versions of the backend will allow a story submitter to make edits to the story while it's in the public queue, which actually allows the community to work together, trading roles as editors and writers.

This idea is spreading, too. At Plastic, a site based on the Slashdot engine, when users reach a high karma level, they're invited to help rate the submission queue. This is not as much direct control as Kuro5hun allows, but it's the same idea: Let the community help choose the content of the site.

I think this is an idea we're just beginning to truly utilize. As communities evolve, I hope for more innovative solutions that give community members more control of the space they inhabit. If you'd like to try it on your site, the Kuro5hun engine is called Scoop, and it's available online (scoop.kuro5hin.org).

Getting Real

The last future trend I'd like to mention is going to seem familiar, because it's where we came from in the first place: Real Life.

The future of online communities is reality. In fact, I look forward to a time when terms like "virtual community" won't be needed anymore. We'll just have communities, with real and virtual elements.

For example, on the {fray}'s second birthday, I took a chance and invited the community to a real-life gathering in San Francisco. There, we held a real-life version of the same interaction {fray} was built to create—an intimate storytelling open microphone, where anyone could get up and tell his story.

We attracted about 75 people that year. For the site's third birthday, we did it again, and this time drew about 150. When members of the {fray} community began to complain that they'd love to participate in the event but were too far away from San Francisco, I invited them to throw their own events. Fray Day was born (fray.org).

Fray Day 5,
September 8, 2001
(fray.org/5).

And this year, when the {fray} turns five, Fray Day will come to at least 10 cities across the globe, from Australia to England to the U.S., all run by active members of the community.

So, in the end, community comes full circle. From real to virtual and back again.

Back to the Future

The things mentioned in this chapter are all interesting ideas and technologies that are currently tickling the edges of community on the Net. They point the way toward an exciting, unknown future.

But, in all likelihood, something will come out of the woodwork and take all the pundits by surprise. Something that no one saw coming. Something that will change the way we relate online forever. Just like the web did in 1995.

I look forward to the time when Habbo looks as quaint as The Palace does now, and beyond that.

Howard Rheingold

A Conversation with Howard Rheingold

Very few people have been at this virtual community business as long as Howard Rheingold. He wrote the seminal book on the subject called *The Virtual Community*, and, though it was published in 1993, he started it in 1988. That's *way* before the web, even in real years.

Rheingold was an active member of The Well in the heady days before the web. In 1995 he helped launch HotWired and was in charge of Threads, HotWired's web-based discussion service (one of the first on the web). He left HotWired and founded Electric Minds in 1996, a start-up company with a groundbreaking community of its own. And though the business side didn't last, the community itself left a high water mark for years to come.

In a way, I've been following Rheingold around for the last few years. His book was an inspiration to me in college. I worked at HotWired after college, though it was after his departure. In 1997, I joined the team at Electric Minds as a producer. There, I got to work with him directly, and that experience has shaped much of my vision of community on the web. I didn't always agree with Rheingold, but I've never worked for someone more passionate about what he does.

What many members of the web generation don't know is that virtual community existed way before the web, and will likely exist long after it. For an inside perspective on the history of virtual communities and a glimpse at the future, there's no one better to talk with than Rheingold. We spoke on the phone in mid-2001.

Let's start with the past. How did virtual community start?

Most people are unaware that virtual communities really go back to the very beginning of the Arpanet (a precursor to the Internet) and before with the PLATO project, so they're at least 30 years old.

Before the Arpanet, there was a group of people in the Minneapolis area using computers to build an educational resource, and it included a conferencing component and had a lively community. Not a lot of people know about this, but all of the people who designed things like Picospan (the systems that ran The Well) and Novell knew about PLATO. I think it's important to acknowledge that.

And of course, the Arpanet was built by a community. There were about a thousand researchers that were scattered all over the U.S. They met face-to-face at government expense a couple of times a year. And contrary to the usual myth, the Arpanet was not created as a nuclear bomb-proof communications system. It was created to connect to this community and enable them to share data from one computer to another and connect different research efforts.

Almost from the beginning, they started doing unauthorized communications. Unauthorized in the sense that it wasn't part of their mandate. Suddenly, they were talking about their favorite science fiction books.

The first email lists started when the first Arpanet nodes were up. So virtual community in the sense of many-to-many, person-to-person communications goes back to the very beginning of computer networks and has driven the growth of it ever since. I think that's probably the most important piece of history.

It's a very rich history that goes back quite a ways. Now, for most of that time up until the mid-1990s, it was sort of a subculture of enthusiasts. It was worldwide and it included tens of thousands if not hundreds of thousands of people. But it was not the mass phenomenon the Internet later became.

What do you think that those days have to teach us now?

I think there has been a partial breakdown of the cooperative ethic that started things. Back then there was a certain amount of understanding of basic netiquette and an expectation of a cooperative behavior. That was the norm from the very beginning and that has made the Internet valuable. Those norms are not located in any handbook, although you can find some basic documents on netiquette. They've mostly been taught to newcomers by the people who were already there.

What used to happen was, every September, a bunch of new freshmen would join universities and get their first Internet accounts and would start flooding Usenet, asking questions that were already answered in the FAQ and doing other things that were breaches of basic netiquette. They would then be educated by the old-timers, sometimes rather rudely, sometimes more patiently. But the old-timers took the time, even if they were flaming, to pass on the norms.

Then the growth of the Internet began exploding. There was a time that America Online dumped 3 million people on the Internet with absolutely no preparation, no explanation of the existing culture and of its norms. And that became known as the September That Never Ended. The old-timers became overwhelmed and that norm became overwhelmed, although there are still people teaching newcomers about netiquette.

There are more newcomers than old-timers who have time to do it, so it's a classic tragedy. The Internet and virtual communities are valuable to the degree that people put in more than they take out. If they start abusing that resource, then it becomes less valuable to everyone. Spam is an obvious example of that. But what's happened with Usenet and many public communities is that people who just want to use a medium to vent their emotional frustrations, abuse other people, or get on their soap box about their one particular issue have somewhat diminished the utility of a great many public forums.

I don't even go to Usenet anymore.

Yeah, a lot of people withdrew from the commons. That's what happens when it's ruined. These people haven't disappeared—they've created more private communities. You have to be invited to come in, or you get thrown out if you don't follow the rules.

Similar to what you've done on your site (rheingold.com/community.html).

Exactly. I think it's fine and important and healthy that we continue to have forums like Usenet and IRC channels that are open to anyone who wants to join. But I think that because of this problem, it's also important that we have places that raise the bar somewhat.

Let's move on to the present. I think the birth and the popularity of the web have changed the virtual community formula. What worked in Usenet doesn't work exactly the same way on the web. With your experience before the web, and then of course with Electric Minds, what have you learned about how this formula works on the web?

You know, I think it's important to know that we're still in the earliest days. Electric Minds, in terms of Internet history, was a long time ago.

When we started HotWired in late 1994, the question was, could you build a communication forum in a medium that does not have persistent connections? Brian Behlendorf assured me that that was easily done. I think Time Warner's Pathfinder beat us by about two weeks, but HotWired and Pathfinder had the first web-based bulletin board forums in late 1994. And it worked okay. It didn't have sophisticated user interface and features that you see today.

So, we started a community called Threads. One of many reasons I left HotWired, but probably the most important one, was that Louis (Rossetto, Wired's founder) did not want to put any resources into the community. I felt we needed at least one full-time person whose job was to maintain and develop the online community, but I was not given a budget. Despite that, a community did develop there.

The important point here being that the importance of asynchronous communication can be joined with the advantages of the web. The advantages of the web are that it's accessible anywhere with a web browser and it has a graphical user interface to the Internet. You don't have to go through the kind of arcane commands you had to go through to post to Usenet or to participate in The Well or BBSs. For most people, that's too techie, so it made it possible for the web to become a social medium.

When we started talking about Electric Minds in 1996, the phrase that I used a lot was "the social web." We're looking to the inevitable emergence of social communication on the web, which previously had been only a publication medium. And then, of course, it became a medium for commerce. But the point is that when you added this availability (more people able to access the web than the old command line Internet) with what we know as attractive about virtual communities, it can be a place where people who share an affinity can come together. Asynchronous conversations enable people in different times and places to have continuing dialog. Structured conversations enable you to find the subjects that interest you very quickly. All of those meant that the conditions were right for the emergence of the web as a social medium, which in fact we have seen.

There were a few years in which you had to be a hacker or you had to have access to expensive software in order to run a sophisticated message board or chat. But now, it's pretty easy. Message boards and chats are available pretty easily for people who want them. Five years is a long time in Internet years, but we've actually seen quite an evolution of the tools that are available to people.

Now, the other thing I want to say about the present is one of the things I said in my book, which is that if I had known about social network analysis in 1993, I might have talked about online social networks. Virtual communities are a subset of online social networks.

That's a great phrase.

There is something called "social network analysis" that sociologists have been doing for quite some time and have discovered that a lot of our folk notions of community are rather skewed. In fact, what community "is" has been defined and redefined for a long time and has co-evolved with changes in communication media.

The printing press, for example. It used to be that when you got news, it was a community event. It meant you were in some little village in

Europe and somebody came down the road from somewhere else. Everybody gathered in the town square to hear what the news was. Well, the printing press came along and pretty soon there were a significant number of people who could read and they had broadsides that had information, so getting the news became a private act. So a community activity was eroded by a new communication medium. At the same time, people who didn't speak the same language or live in the same country began identifying with this idea of virtual community that they heard about through print known as the Protestant Reformation, so we saw the formation of a community that did not exist before, at the time we saw erosions of communities that had existed before.

Interesting. Wouldn't it be ironic, then, that the next giant shift in communication, the web, actually has the side effect of delivering news and also reintroducing a new kind of community?

Well, one of the things that's interesting about community on the web is that most software affords the use of links in conversation. So no longer do you have to have: "There are more Chinese in California than there are Latinos." You can have, "Well I think there are more Latinos than Chinese in California and, if you check this link, the U.S. Census Department agrees with me." So suddenly you have all of the collective knowledge of the web available for discourse.

Exactly. Okay, let's move on to the future. What's coming next?

I think there are several things to say about the future and the first and probably most important thing is the question of whether a literacy about the effective use of online communication media will spread or whether that will become a thing of the past. At the crudest level, you can already see that most businesses are choking in email. People go into their offices and spend the first two hours of their day dealing with email. People send email with no subject line. People cc hundreds of people on a stupid simple email. I mean, we're talking about basic stuff. If you're talking about literacy, this is about knowing the alphabet.

I had to teach my father that he could use the return key when he was sending email. He was sending me email that read like a telegram. "Derek. STOP. Doing fine. STOP. When are you coming home? STOP. Dad."

Well, you don't get an education about this now, so the question is will there be? That's a very fundamental problem. Then there are more sophisticated things such as the fact that irony and sarcasm don't convey well online. It is easy for people to misunderstand all of the basics of netiquette that people who are sophisticated in these virtual communities know. Those are things that you don't necessarily know when you're starting out. So the value of virtual community in the aggregate will depend upon how many people are literate in this and how many people are just going to flame and start useless, redundant topics—all of the things that newcomers who don't understand the norms of netiquette will do.

And if there's more noise in the channel than there is information, then people will abandon it. It will be less useful. You know, television was once regarded as the great educational medium of the future, and the early years showed a great deal of promise, and then, you know, it gradually became crap. Will that happen here, too? There will always be groups who are strongly motivated to use a medium. But will it be a mass medium such as print in which there is a widespread literacy? I think that's the most important question about the future.

Do you think that technology can aid in that learning process? Can websites make themselves easier to use, more prone to netiquette?

I think that there is only so far that user interface and other technical means can bring you. If you go back to the earliest visions of Doug Engelbart in 1963, in his paper on augmented human intellect, he was talking about a system that used humans using methodology, language, artifact, and training. Human interface is only part of the artifact part of this. There's the language and methodology and the training. You don't go out and buy that when you buy a box. How is that going to be delivered? How is that going to be disseminated? I think that's a big problem that I don't think is going to get solved by making an easier user interface. Human communication is, by its nature, somewhat complex.

We're all pretty good at it. I mean, you know not to say things to people on the street that are going to cause them to punch you in the face. Amazingly, people don't know that online. That's just because people aren't going to punch you in the face.

Right. One of the repeating refrains in my book is that this is about connecting real people and having real relationships in virtual places. So, everything about this is real except for the conduit. That's the only part that's virtual.

Right. So there is part of your answer: a group of people who care enough—whether it's fray, brainstorms, or a support group for people who are caregivers for parents with Alzheimer's. These are people who have a common affinity who care about each other's participation in these forums strongly enough to educate each other about netiquette and be helpful and contribute. And I think we will always find that. The question is are those going to be enclaves or are those going to be the dominant discourse?

And what's your sense?

I want to be an optimist, but realistically, you know, we've seen what's happened with Usenet, and you just see that there are a lot of people who are vandals online. I don't see any kind of massive education campaign happening, so I want to be optimistic but I don't want to be naively utopian. I think that we face some very difficult challenges in terms of education if the medium is to remain useful. Even five years ago, if we had been shown what our daily lives would be like in terms of all of this spam, and now you just accept it. It's part of life. You accept that there are people who abuse this medium in a massive way. And that's a sign that the medium is not invulnerable to abuse.

What are your other thoughts about the future of virtual community?

We're seeing the beginning of a very disruptive era in which the Internet is going global. More people will access the Internet through mobile devices than through PCs in just a couple of years. That's going to create a lot of changes. No longer is your connection to the Internet one and the same as you are sitting at your desk in front of a PC. We're already beginning to see some mobile communities emerge. People whose interaction with their community isn't limited to their PC. So I think, in some ways, it's going to have more of a connection with people's lives whether they are in their automobile, walking down the street, or sitting in the subway.

Do you think that this will reinforce the idea that virtual community is real and not some sort of make-believe community?

Oh, definitely. I mean you don't have to convince young people of that because that's what they've grown up with. You know, is it real to get into this metal thing and travel along at 60 miles an hour to this city of inhuman scale and get into a building with tens of thousands of other people? I mean, we already accept a certain level of unreality and that's sort of the human condition. We are very adaptable to our artifacts.

How do you think the birth and expansion of online mobile devices will shape the future virtual communities?

Well, that's part of my next book. For one thing, people use it to coordinate their activities in the physical world, particularly young people, teenagers, use SMS.

Do your kids use it?

Oh totally! Yeah. But the U.S. is way behind.

If you look at Scandinavia or Japan or Philippines or Singapore or the UK, people are using SMS all the time. Something like 50 billion SMS messages per month are being sent now.

There's only so much you can do with a little device, but one thing you can do is stay in touch and coordinate your physical world. And to get very futuristic, you can also communicate with devices in the environment.

For example, you can go to a bar and your friends were there half an hour ago and they moved to another bar and have left a message for you in the air. And you've already seen it—they call it swarming—teenagers all show up at the same place at the same time to view SMS messages.

So what's the connecting thread? The connecting thread is people who have an affinity or a goal in common who can coordinate their communications and activities with others online or on the street.

There's a project at the Media Lab by Rick Borovoy called "Folk Computing" in which they created devices people could use to make little animations and exchange them by beaming them to each other. They showed how those things circulate. I think we'll see a lot of that. It's like people passing jokes and hoaxes around online.

Any other future trends you see coming?

I think we will begin to see people aggregating numbers of people to do things. You know that book *Net Gain* really exaggerated what the potential commercial aspect of it was, and we've seen that price-line.com is facing some problems with business. But in the long run, the ability of groups to get together and make mass purchases and do other things in the aggregate is going to be advantageous to them, so we will see virtual communities that begin to confer benefits upon people.

I think we've already seen that with medical knowledge. If you have a certain disease, I'm talking about thousands of diseases, finding the right online support group is essential. Once you find that online support group, you've got a powerful source of information and support that people never had before.

Any last thoughts?

Well, of course the exciting thing about it is that it is up to us. It's not like everything else, from news to entertainment to buying a package. I think that what continues to be exciting about it is that people have the power to do it themselves.

I mean, you know, storytelling has always been something people do with each other. It's only been recently that you have to go to Disney or ABC to get your stories.

One of the other important things about democracy is not just about voting for your leaders, it's about intelligent conversation among citizens. And we've lost a lot of that communication in mass media. So a corollary to the question, will we see an emergence of a literacy of netiquette is: will we see intelligent political discourse continue online and will that have an effect?

I hope so.

I hope so too. I think it's important. It's the most important question to me. If I'm going to end on any note, that's what I would want to end on.

Postscript

Where Do We Go from Here?

I began writing this book in August 2000. I quit a job as creative director of a small Internet company to do it, knowing for certain that there'd be another job like it waiting for me when I was done.

These were the days before the fall, when *Business 2.0* and *Wired* were still publishing magazines as thick as catalogs and every day was a record day for the stock market. In the 10 months I've been working on this book, things have changed.

The bubble burst, as the market-watchers, say. The market dropped, companies went chapter 11 left and right, and even the promising start-up I left had to lay off all its employees. One by one, over the course of writing this book, almost all of my friends and colleagues wound up out of work. It seems like the salad days of the Internet revolution are over.

And slowly, after the days of bad news turned into months, and all the prognosticators of the Internet joined in a rousing chorus of "the sky is falling!" one question began reverberating in my mind louder and louder.

"Who needs this book now?"

Surely, if the bloom is off the rose, no one will be willing to spend the time and money to build community features. Now that companies are laying off their employees and the venture capitalists are running away from any business plan that ends in dot-com, no one is going to want to build a community, right?

Wrong.

The web is still new, and we're still figuring out how to use it well. Just because our collective giddy enthusiasm for this new medium propelled us into an unsustainable business environment, that doesn't mean some of the discoveries we've made about the Internet along the way aren't as valuable as gold.

As Howard Rheingold said in our interview, the Internet began as a community. Sending and receiving email is still the number one activity online, with chat running a close second. Add in the recent ascension of instant messaging and peer-to-peer file sharing, and you should have a good picture of what people do online: They communicate with each other.

In fact, I'd take it a step further and say this: **Any Internet technology that does not allow for its users to communicate directly with each other is doomed to failure.** This is the first, and most important, lesson the Internet has taught us.

Now, more than ever, with the ruins of the late nineties dot-com failures at our feet, it's time for us to make new creations that deliver on the promise of the original goal of the Internet: to create community.

It's the Internet's native use, and it's time for us to build it.

Who's with me?

Join the continuing conversation at **designforcommunity.com.**

Index